ATOMIC PILGRIM

Advance praise for *Atomic Pilgrim*

"*Atomic Pilgrim* is an inspiring memoir about courageous actions taken for peace and a world free of nuclear weapons. While Thomas's intense internal battles rocket from hope to despair, both parts of the book reflect his faith in God and belief in the basic goodness of human beings."
~Kristine Morris, *Foreword Reviews*

"*Atomic Pilgrim* is both a journey of public witness but also one of examination of the soul. As Jim chronicles the details and daily experiences of this phenomenal leap of faith . . . he also lays bare the internal crises of faith he encounters that rocks his very soul in the process. In addition, *Atomic Pilgrim* recounts the real-life experiences of downwinders whose faith in the United States was shaken as their lives were devastated . . . by the toxification of their hometown by political silence and corporate greed. Inspiring - Informative – Impactful."
~Charlene Howard, Executive Director, Pax Christi USA

"*Atomic Pilgrim* is a riveting account by James Patrick Thomas of the 6,700-mile pilgrimage for peace. Father George Zabelka led the arduous journey across the USA and nine other countries to Bethlehem. For Thomas, the experience was transformative. Returning to the USA, he sought the truth about radioactive contamination released from Hanford and other nuclear weapons sites. *Atomic Pilgrim* is an inspiring memoir that raises important questions for today about the human costs of nuclear weapons."
~Cynthia C. Kelly, President of the Atomic Heritage Foundation

"*Atomic Pilgrim* is a remarkable and deeply personal account of perseverance and self-discovery. . . . Thomas's messages on the importance of faith, reflection, persistence, and acceptance, and his vivid description of the struggles and rewards of fighting for truth and justice will inspire readers, and hopefully encourage at least some to live a life of service and walk a similar path for peace."
~Stephen I. Schwartz, editor and co-author of *Atomic Audit: The Costs and Consequences of U.S. Nuclear Weapons Since 1940*

"A passionate memoir by an anti-nuclear activist and committed patriot."
~Gregg Herken, author of *Brotherhood of the Bomb: The Tangled Lives and Loyalties of Robert Oppenheimer, Ernest Lawrence, and Edward Teller*

"Spanning thousands of miles and decades of research and advocacy, Jim Thomas's message is at once hopeful and haunting: Peace is more than a dream. It is a necessity."
~Shannon Cram, PhD, author of *Unmaking the Bomb: Environmental Cleanup and the Politics of Impossibility*

"Jim Thomas is a peacemaking miracle. He walks a way of peace that can turn humanity from extinction to life. Read him and believe in miracles for us all."
~James Douglass, author of *JFK and the Unspeakable*

"*Atomic Pilgrim* is an inspiring reminder of the many paths opened by courageous people of faith leading to a more peaceful world. Now with a renewed nuclear arms race, *Atomic Pilgrim* challenges us all to be prophets testifying to the truth."
~Massimo Faggioli, Professor of Historical Theology,
Villanova University

"This is a wonderful hope-inspiring book! A tonic for sagging spirits in these dark days."
~Shelley Douglass, co-founder of the Ground Zero Center
for Nonviolent Action

"*Atomic Pilgrim* relates the journey of a person deeply committed to a world without nuclear weapons. Uniquely, the book provides both scientifically solid information, personal sharing of faith in God, and rich stories of friendships with a variety of people in different parts of the world."
~Mercedarian Missionaries of Berriz Sister Shizue "Filo" Hirota,
consultant for the Catholic Council for Justice and Peace
of the Bishops' Conference of Japan

"This book, for me, is about quiet heroism. Tenderly written from the perspective of a young man who found himself walking from Seattle to Bethlehem in the name of peace, this trip served to inform Thomas's entire life's work. During these chaotic times, when we so desperately need to identify our heroes, this book will give you new and important perspectives."
~Teri Hein, author of *Atomic Farmgirl: Growing Up Right
in the Wrong Place*

"*Atomic Pilgrim* is a deeply moving narrative of personal struggle in the face of an existential threat that we ignore at our peril, and an indictment of government secrets that jeopardize human health and survival. It is a ray of hope for citizens who want to hold government accountable."
~Steve Colecchi, Former Director, Office of International Justice and
Peace, United States Conference of Catholic Bishops

"Author Jim Thomas tells an inspiring story of ordinary people on a courageous journey to stop the world's unstoppable nuclear arms race. *Atomic Pilgrim* is about courage, transformation, and community. It reveals a way of being and a level of commitment desperately needed today. Expect to be challenged!"
~Marie Dennis, Former Co-President of Pax Christi International (2007-2019) and Director of Pax Christi's Catholic Institute for Nonviolence

ATOMIC PILGRIM

HOW WALKING THOUSANDS OF MILES FOR
PEACE LED TO UNCOVERING SOME OF
AMERICA'S DARKEST NUCLEAR SECRETS

A MEMOIR

JAMES PATRICK THOMAS

Contents

Trail One – Searching for Peace from Bangor to Bethlehem

1 – Becoming Fully Alive	1
2 – Growing Up in Fear	19
3 – Waiting for My Turn	31
4 – Walking at Last—Through a Field of Missile Silos	45
5 – Surrender to Carrying My Cross	61
6 – Grand Irish Welcome	75
7 – A Week in a War Zone	85
8 – Scotland & England: More Nuclear Subs, More Rain, and a Princess	91
9 – France & Switzerland: Approaching Burn Out	99
10 – Italy: The Fateful Decision, Papal Snub, and a Wedding	117
11 – Yugoslavia: Communism and Isolation	131
12 – Greece and a Heartbreaking Farewell	145
13 – Setting Foot in the Holy Land	155

Trail Two – Pursuing the Truth about Hanford

14 – The Plutonium Factory in My Backyard	173
15 – Documents Reveal Citizens Exposed to Invisible Radiation	187
16 – Dismantling Hanford's Iron Curtain of Secrecy	203
17 – The Case of the Two Autopsies	213
18 – Cold War Ends and Family Tragedy Strikes	221
19 – First Visit to Hiroshima and Nagasaki	231
20 – The Pervasiveness of Atomic Deception	237
21 – Emotional Return to Hiroshima and Nagasaki	245
Epilogue	251
Appendices	255

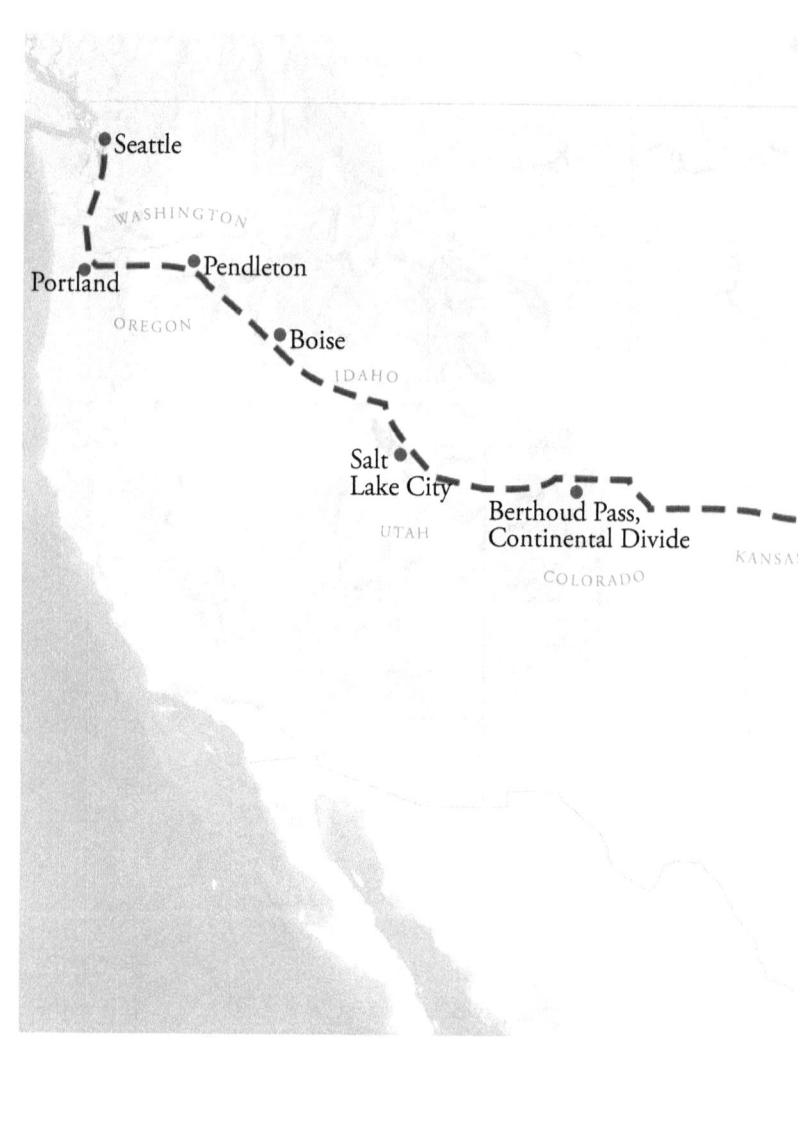

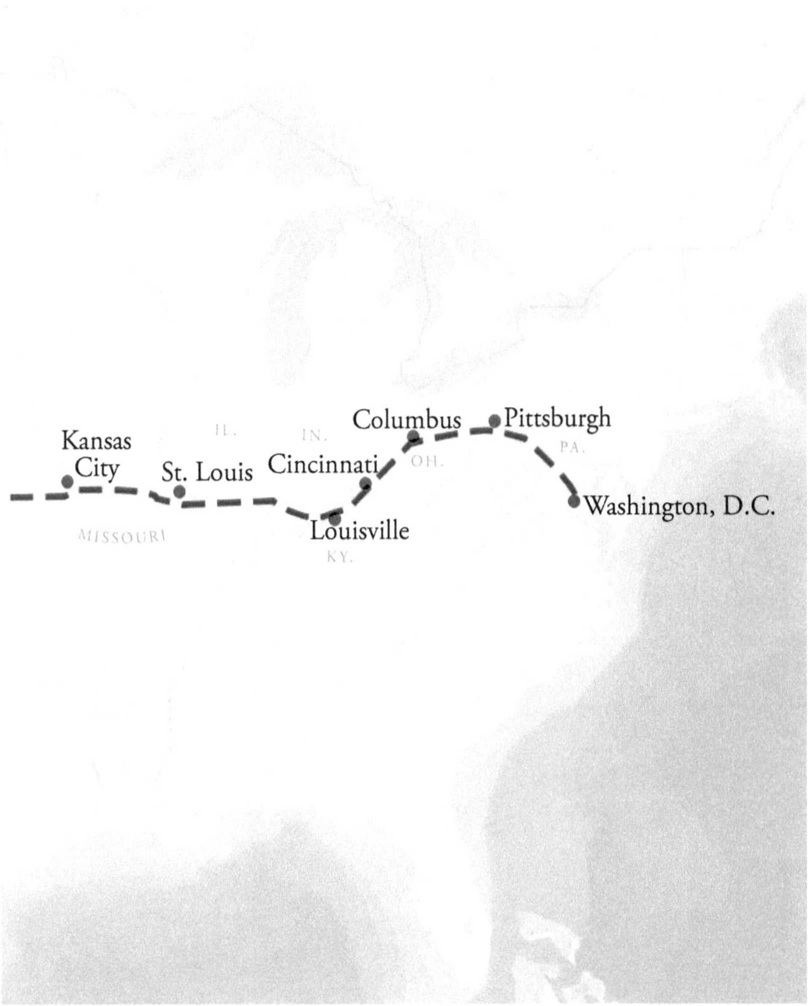
Kansas City
St. Louis
Cincinnati
Columbus
Pittsburgh
Louisville
Washington, D.C.
MISSOURI
IL.
IN.
OH.
KY.
PA.

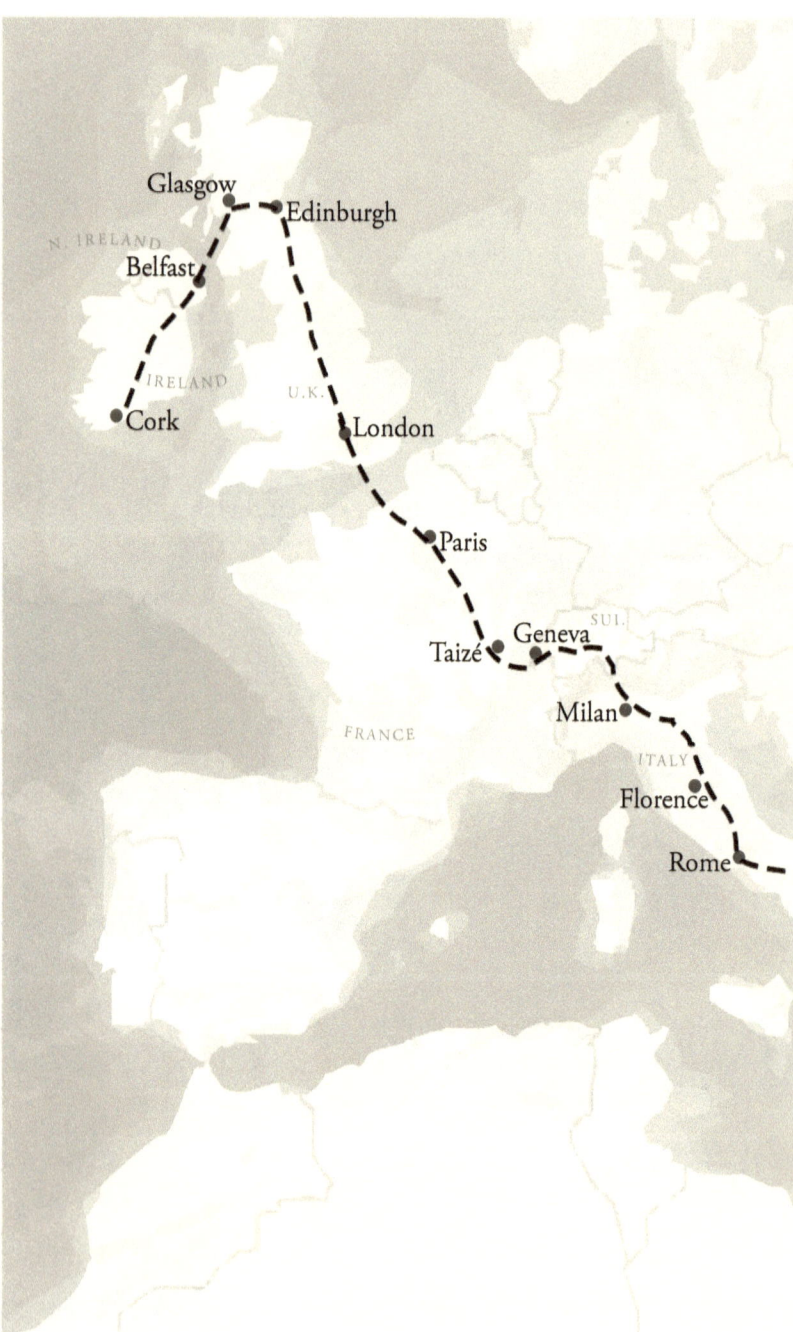

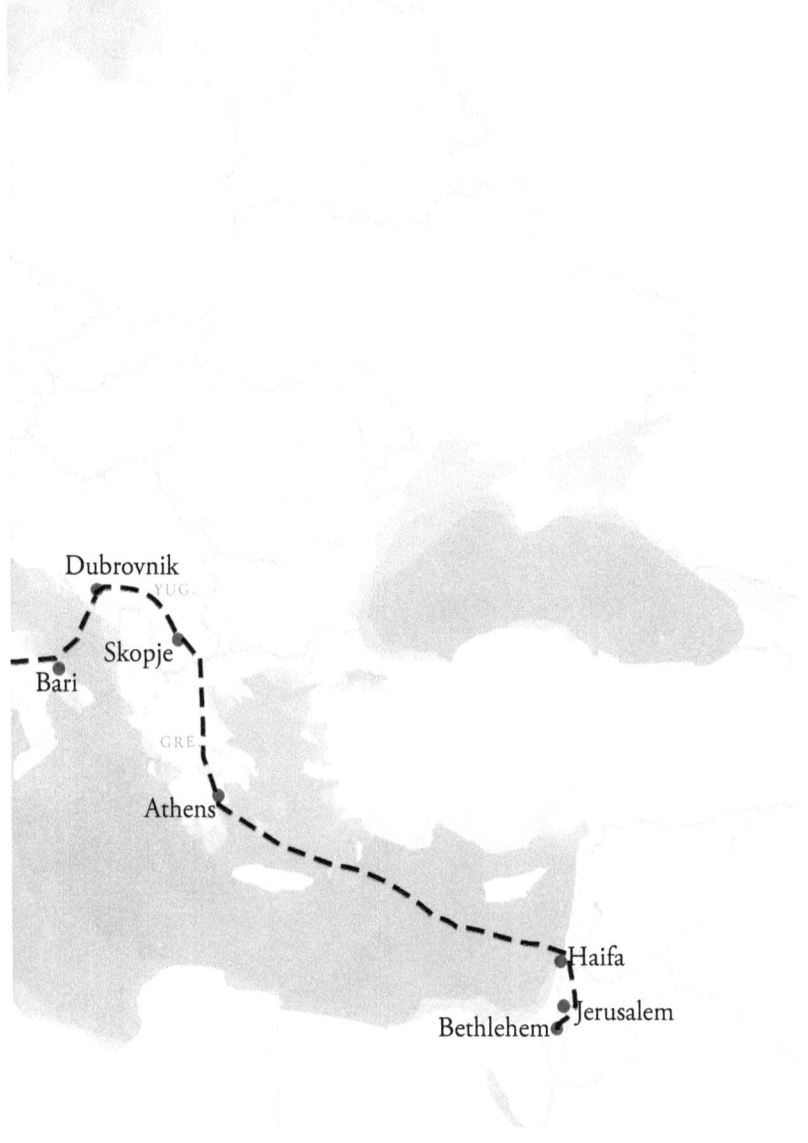

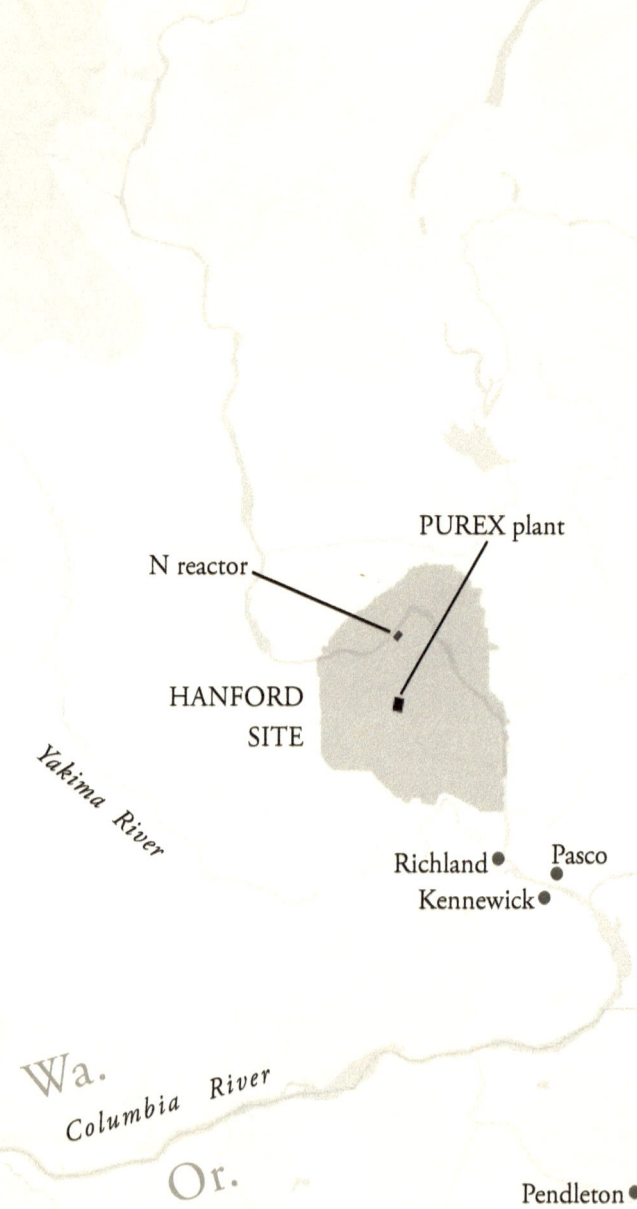

Spokane

Fairchild
Air Force Base

IDAHO

Washtucna

WASHINGTON

Walla Walla

OREGON

Dedication

To my fellow pilgrims, without whom I would not have been able to even imagine this journey.

To my fellow downwinders—not just those exposed to radioactive contamination downwind from Hanford, but those in Japan and throughout the world—for all who have died, for all who have suffered, and for all who continue to fight for recognition and justice.

To the people this book will inspire to join in the pursuit of the truth, to seek answers to the remaining questions, and all who persist in demanding a full accounting of what nuclear weapons have cost the human family.

You are all my heroes!

Author's Note

This book recounts my adventures along two trails. Beginning on Good Friday 1982, nineteen other pilgrims and I walked 6,700 miles for peace and nuclear disarmament across the United States and nine other countries. The Bethlehem Peace Pilgrimage concluded on Christmas Eve 1983 in the Shepherds' Field grotto. Thousands of people joined us by walking a few hours, days, or weeks as we passed near their cities and towns.

Part two of *Atomic Pilgrim* chronicles my pursuit of the truth about U.S. nuclear weapons, especially the production of those weapons at the Hanford plutonium factory in south-central Washington State. Assisted by mentors and colleagues, I discovered our government and its contractors betrayed the American people.

Several Bethlehem pilgrims gave me access to their journals, and for that, I am very grateful. I had access to oral history interviews Michael Monteleone recorded while he worked on his documentary of the pilgrimage. I reviewed recordings of interviews done during the walk. Another source was the newsletter that the pilgrimage distributed to the thousands of people on our mailing list. I also had access to many of the 6,000 color photographs taken by Bill Cox during the walk and several hundred of my own. I accessed the Father George Zabelka Papers, 1943-1992, at Marquette University, and the Brother Fred Mercy Collection at the Jesuit Archives & Research Center, St. Louis, Missouri, to bolster my writing.

In describing the Hanford trail, I relied on the declassified documents I obtained through more than 200 requests under the Freedom of Information Act, other documents in archival collections and online repositories, interviews, court transcripts, books on the history of nuclear weapons, newspaper accounts, and the twenty-five notebooks I compiled during the two decades of my full-time involvement with Hanford issues.

Writing this book was a wonderful adventure, much like the epic journey of walking to Bethlehem. I discovered that my pilgrimage through life has been more than a search for peace. I have pursued the truth about myself as well as the human cost of America amassing its vast arsenal of nuclear weapons. Through decades of work, hundreds of companions, and years of investigation, I feel invigorated by this truth: Living one's life for others is a stupendous joy.

Trail One

Searching for Peace from Bangor to Bethlehem

1 – Becoming Fully Alive

Fr. George Zabelka and Fr. Jack Morris, SJ, on the pilgrimage's first day, Good Friday, April 9, 1982.

On Monday evening, January 12, 1981, I was alone in the two-bed-room house I shared with a friend from college. I was exhausted after getting home from my job as an operations engineer at KREM-TV in Spokane. I worked Sunday nights until 2 a.m., and my Monday shift began at 10 a.m., so I was always wiped on Monday evenings. In addition to hating my work schedule, I struggled with being bored at work. I didn't find my job fulfilling.

After fixing a quick dinner, I turned on the TV and started watching *The World of Mother Teresa* on PBS. The documentary showed her accepting the 1979 Nobel Peace Prize for her work with the poorest of the poor in the slums of Calcutta. I do not remember much else about the program except for when the reporter asked Mother Teresa how she could tell if she was doing God's will. Mother Teresa said, "Love until it hurts."

Immediately, I felt a churning deep in my gut. I was dizzy, almost sick. It was hard to breathe. What was happening to me? I was gripped by both fear and excitement. Had my life just changed radically?

I went into my bedroom and grabbed my journal and a pencil. I flipped past entries about growing dissatisfaction with my job, then sat on the floor and tried to make some sense of what all this meant.

As I wrote, I sensed my years of feeling insignificant were gone. I had longed for my life to have greater meaning and purpose. Since the assassination of Archbishop Oscar Romero in El Salvador in March 1980, I had been searching for a way to be more like Jesus and make the world better. Now, there was no going back to my old self. I knew what I had to do. I needed to give more of myself, to sacrifice for others—to "love until it hurts."

On my way to work the next morning, I mailed a letter requesting an application for the Jesuit Volunteer Corps (JVC). JVC offers young adults a domestic alternative to the Peace Corps, serving people in poverty on Indian reservations and in inner cities. Several of my closest friends from high school had spent a year or two after college serving as Jesuit Volunteers in Alaskan villages.

Once I submitted my JVC application, that act marked a clear, tangible readiness to quit my job. On one level, it seemed an easy choice, given my dissatisfaction with television. But to so quickly make a major decision was very much out of character for me. I was typically more cautious. My mom and sister worried about my rash decision to give up a good-paying job. Yes, a strange thing for me to do, but I also found it intoxicating. I felt more alive than ever before. I was thrilled at the chance to experience voluntary poverty and social justice firsthand. I rejoiced in the opportunity to follow the Jesus of the Gospels on a more profound level. For perhaps the first time in my life, I felt free from the fear instilled in me by my parents and the Cold War.

By April, the Jesuit Volunteer Corps approved my application and placed me with an agency serving senior citizens suffering poverty in the Central Area of Seattle. My new job would start in August, leaving me time to build up my savings before my TV job ended.

I was excited about moving to Seattle for one main reason. In the early 1980s, the Catholic Archbishop of Seattle, Raymond Hunthausen, made headlines with his prophetic statements against nuclear weapons. Here was a bishop who was not afraid to speak out—very much like San Salvador's Archbishop Oscar Romero whose prophetic voice against oppression was stilled by an assassin's bullet as he celebrated Mass in 1980. The U.S. Navy was preparing to deploy Trident nuclear missiles at the Bangor submarine base twenty miles west of Seattle. Fully loaded, each Trident sub could carry 192 nuclear warheads, each with a destructive force of 400 kilotons. One sub could carry the equivalent of more than 5,000 Hiroshima bombs. In June 1981, Archbishop Hunthausen declared that the Trident nuclear weapons system was "the Auschwitz of Puget Sound." His address to other Northwest religious leaders also advocated for unilateral disarmament and tax resistance.

From the outset of President Reagan's first term, the Cold War threat of nuclear war increased almost daily. Led by neoconservative hawks, the U.S. was rapidly expanding its capability to launch a nuclear first strike—to destroy Soviet missiles before they could be used. Less than two hundred miles east of Seattle, workers at Hanford prepared to restart an aging plutonium factory mothballed since 1972. The Reagan Administration resumed civil defense planning to prepare to fight a nuclear war. The Soviet Union had reached parity with the United States in the number of nuclear weapons. It seemed like another Cuban Missile Crisis loomed. Young people, me included, wondered if they should have children when the future looked so precarious.

In August 1981, I began a week-long JVC orientation that was held in Spokane. I helped pick up other new volunteers as they arrived at the airport. Bill Cox, a volunteer in Seattle the previous year, was one of the first people I met that day. Astoundingly, he told me he was helping to plan a walk to Bethlehem for nuclear disarmament. My first thought was, "What a crazy idea—walking to Bethlehem for peace. Can he really be serious?" Over the next few weeks, I discovered that Bill and other would-be pilgrims lived just five blocks from my volunteer house. They invited me to come to one of their meetings and later encouraged me to accompany them to protests at the Bangor submarine base.

In late September, we drove downtown to catch a ferry. While crossing the Puget Sound, I drank in the view of deep blue water, majestic mountains, and sparkling sunshine. Our destination was the Ground Zero Center for Nonviolent Action. Its property shared a fence with the Trident base. The Ground Zero founders, Jim and Shelley Douglass, told us of their years of protesting the Trident system and their commitment to nonviolence. They explained how the increased accuracy of these new nuclear weapons marked a significant escalation in the arms race. That night, I wrote in my journal, "Very sobering and frightening knowing the power that resides beyond that fence."

The idea of walking to Bethlehem for peace came to Father Jack Morris, a Jesuit living in Seattle, as he read an interview by Father George Zabelka in the September 1980 issue of *Sojourners* magazine. During

World War II, Zabelka served on Tinian Island as the Catholic chaplain to the men who dropped the atomic bombs.

Several weeks after Japan surrendered, Zabelka was transferred to a military hospital in Fukuoka, about halfway between Hiroshima and Nagasaki. Because he had blessed the crews before and after their atomic missions, he recalled that "the whole Tinian Island experience ... had scalded my soul. I was confused and troubled by a growing feeling of dark guilt that wouldn't go away. We hadn't been in Nagasaki more than a week when I found myself making my way to the ruined hulk of the Urakami Cathedral in Japan's most Catholic city. ... I saw the beauty and splendor of the cathedral that had been ... a symbol of peace and harmony, a place of life dedicated to the God of peace."

Accompanied by two other chaplains, he visited the victims of the atomic bombings. Seeing the children—with horrible burns over most of their bodies—hit him the hardest. George wondered about "these little children who had nothing to do with the war, why were they suffering?" This experience began a long process that led to Zabelka embracing Christian nonviolence. He served in Japan until November 1946 when he was discharged from the Army Air Corps. In the 1950s, Zabelka began serving an inner-city parish in Flint, Michigan. He became known for his preaching against racism and participated in both the March to Selma and the Poor People's March on Washington.

In the early 1970s, Zabelka attended several retreats on Christian nonviolence which challenged him to consider the implications of Jesus' words "love your enemies." He surrendered to the logic of active nonviolent love and began leading similar retreats. Reflecting on the atomic bombings and the U.S. firebombing of Japanese cities that killed hundreds of thousands of civilians, Zabelka confessed that, as a Catholic priest, he should have opposed "the utter moral corruption of the mass destruction of civilians. I failed as a Christian and a priest."

Back in Seattle, as Jack finished reading George's interview, he felt a surge of energy pulse through his body. Alone in the living room, he said out loud, "I'm going to walk to Bethlehem." He immediately felt foolish and confused. "Where did Bethlehem come from? I have no idea." But those emotions were accompanied by intense excitement. "I felt more deeply myself than I had in years."

Before reading Zabelka's interview, Jack had been communicating with a young man who had recently walked from California to Washington State to protest nuclear weapons. From Jack's previous involvement with the Ground Zero Center for Nonviolent Action, he knew Suzuki, a Buddhist monk whose order frequently made long walks for peace. The Center was founded in 1977 to foster nonviolent action to free the world from the threat of nuclear destruction.

The day Jack read George's interview was September 9, 1980, the same day that another Jesuit priest, Daniel Berrigan, was arrested with seven others at a General Electric plant near Philadelphia that built nose cones for Trident missiles. I remember reading about Fr. Berrigan's arrest the next morning on the front page of the *Washington Post* while I visited a cousin near Washington, D.C. In reading that news, a seed was planted inside me that would germinate a year later. It seemed others, both in Jesuit spheres and around the United States, were experiencing similar awakenings.

Jack quickly wrote George about walking to Bethlehem. Jack was unsure how George would react. Perhaps he would dismiss this crazy notion. Surprisingly, George telephoned three days later to tell Jack he wouldn't be walking alone. "I got your letter, Jack. It sounds like a good idea. Let's keep working on it."

Two weeks later, Jack was driving with Bill Ingalls-Cox to a meeting. Jack told Bill about a peace walk to Bethlehem.

Bill asked, "Wow, you mean in Pennsylvania?"

Jack replied, "No, where Jesus was born."

That night, Bill told his JVC housemates about Jack's idea. To his surprise, everyone was intrigued by it. Bill's fellow community members included his wife, Pam Ingalls-Cox (from Spokane), Laurie Hasbrook (Whitefish Bay, WI), Mimi Ward (Cape Cod), and Alice McGarey (New Canaan, CT). Bob Patten (Portland, OR) who lived in a different volunteer house and worked in the archdiocesan social justice office, learned of the pilgrimage soon afterward.

The young volunteers asked Jack for a meeting and within a month, they all began to organize—conducting research on the ancient practice of pilgrimage, gathering information on other continental walks, learning about the nuclear peril, and determining how to manage as an intentional community while on the road.

It wasn't long before all recognized Bob as a natural-born organizer. The son of a Presbyterian minister, he had attended Whitworth College, just north of Spokane. Easy to work with, Bob was adept at identifying logistical challenges and finding ways to meet them. Spontaneous and fun-loving, he was always game for some antics to lighten the work. A gangly beanstalk with broad square shoulders, he relished the challenge of scouring maps to figure out the best route to walk across the country while including as many large cities as possible.

After developing tentative dates for reaching major metro areas across the U.S., the pilgrims researched peace organizations and made initial contacts. Weekly meetings kept the group informed of what each pilgrim was learning. When questions arose, they were resolved by consensus, and a shared leadership model emerged.

Each pilgrim brought their own unique talents to the pilgrimage effort. Mimi's passion for peace and justice provided a steady guide for the group. Laurie contributed a fierce gentleness that advocated for including everyone's input. After majoring in English and Sociology at Boston College, Alice helped with her knack of getting to the core of difficult issues. Tall with long red hair, Pam shared Mimi's commitment to prayer and created beautiful graphics and posters for the outreach efforts. Bill added a spontaneous spark to the collective spirit of adventure, along with his creative proclivities as a photographer.

Carmelite Father Kevin Lafey was the third Catholic priest to join the pilgrims. Originally from Haverhill, Massachusetts, Kevin was working in a soup kitchen in Tacoma's Hilltop neighborhood when he learned about the pilgrimage. During the last half of 1981, he started participating in weekly meetings in Seattle with the organizers.

Meanwhile, George continued to give workshops on nonviolence around the country, taking every opportunity to mention the pilgrimage.

Steve McKindley, a Free Methodist student from Edmonds, a Seattle suburb, was studying peace at the Mennonite Biblical Seminary in Elkhart, Indiana, and attended a workshop at the nearby University of Notre Dame. He was immediately hooked on the walk. His sharp mind, sincerity, and quirky sense of humor made him a perfect collaborator.

A brochure was developed to summarize the mission of the pilgrimage and sent to potential donors and endorsers. In a section titled "Why We Walk," the brochure stated, "Our goal is to call church leaders and all peoples of faith to take responsibility for the imminent aborting of the human race, and … [to establish] a more just world order." Originally from Seattle, Dean McFalls, a recent convert to Catholicism, received one of the brochures from his spiritual director while studying theology in California. Intense with a brilliant grasp of geopolitics, Dean was fascinated by the idea of walking to Bethlehem for peace. Without delay, he wrote a letter asking to be considered as a pilgrim.

In early 1982, Mimi and Alice went on a spiritual retreat in Massachusetts. While there, they met another retreatant, Mary Jude Postel, who was finishing an English degree at Vermont's Middlebury College and wondering what was next. Raised Catholic in a Jewish neighborhood near Chicago, she was captivated by the pilgrimage's blend of activism and spirituality. Thrilled at the possibility of walking to Bethlehem, Mary Jude asked how she could join.

In telling her parents about her intention to walk to Bethlehem, Mary Jude remembered that her father Ted quashed it, declaring, "No, you're not. You're not doing that. I just paid all this money for your expensive college education, and you're going to go walking around the world with a bunch of—who are these people?"

To Mary Jude's surprise, her usually timid mother interjected: "Now, Ted, let's hear more about this."

Laurie's parents worried about their daughter's participation. With the 1978 Jonestown mass suicide still fresh in people's memories, they wondered if Laurie was being sucked into some kind of cult.

Knowing that many would be skeptical about such a far-fetched idea, the organizers solicited endorsements from religious and peace leaders. Among the earliest endorsers were Seattle Archbishop Raymond Hunthausen, the Church Council of Greater Seattle, the Jesuit Volunteer Corps, and Rev. Jim Wallis of Sojourners.

When the Jesuit Volunteers reached the end of their year-long commitment in August 1981, they found odd jobs to cover living expenses and save money for the trek. They continued meeting regularly with Jack. Bob found a large house to rent in Seattle's Madrona neighborhood and nicknamed it Lothlórien—after the Elven land in J.R.R. Tolkien's *Lord of the Rings* trilogy—the place where Frodo and the Fellowship prepared for their epic quest. The house provided the pilgrims with a place to stay, room to organize, and time to deepen ties as a community. It became a beehive of activity during the eight months before departure.

In August 1981, I began my year of service in the Jesuit Volunteer Corps and explored a spectrum of justice and peace issues including the sectarian strife in Northern Ireland and the massacre of peasants in Central America. My exploration ended abruptly on Saturday, October 17, 1981, when I went to a program offered by the Washington chapter of Physicians for Social Responsibility. Held inside the red brick edifice of Kane Hall on the University of Washington campus, the large auditorium made the diminutive lead-off speaker look even smaller than she was. Barely five feet tall, Judith Lipton, M.D., soberly presented the facts about the escalating peril posed by the nuclear arms race and how Seattle could be devastated by one nuclear weapon. Because most of the hospitals, including the regional trauma center, would be extensively damaged, those injured by the blast couldn't expect medical treatment for weeks or even months. Thus, many would succumb to their agonizing wounds and burns. Most of Seattle's major transportation routes would be destroyed or strewn with debris. Thick smoke from numerous fires would reduce visibility and choke survivors.

While distressing, Dr. Lipton's words were rather dry and clinical. I was accustomed to the threat of nuclear weapons, having grown up near two of the Air Force's Strategic Air Command (SAC) bases, each with significant numbers of nuclear bombs. Starting in grade school, I followed the daily news and considered myself well-informed about the nuclear threat. If Judith Lipton had been the only speaker that night, I doubt I would have ended up working for nuclear disarmament the rest of my life. But the second part of the program delivered an emotional punch to the core of my being—like what I experienced watching the documentary of Mother Teresa nine months before.

Four women presented a pantomime depicting the nuclear arms race between the U.S. and the Soviet Union. The title "Four Minutes to Midnight" evoked the *Bulletin of the Atomic Scientists'* Doomsday Clock setting for 1981. The Doomsday Clock represented an assessment of how close the Earth was to nuclear war. Originally set to seven minutes to midnight in 1947, the clock's hands moved closer to midnight if international tensions increased and away from midnight when countries moved toward disarmament.

Back in Kane Hall, the four women didn't speak, only moved. Out of the silence, the only sound in the auditorium was the ticking of the Doomsday Clock. With simple props and costumes, they acted out several phases of the nuclear arms race, starting with the destruction of Hiroshima and Nagasaki. One scene involved a foot race with the U.S. competing against the USSR, seeing which one could "win" by achieving "nuclear superiority." Wearing masks representing the two superpowers, the two racers portrayed the insanity of amassing ever greater numbers of weapons of mass destruction.

To depict the period of detente during the 1970s, the actors mimicked diplomats negotiating across a table from each other. But without any substantial progress toward disarmament, the Doomsday Clock kept ticking.

Improvements in missile guidance technology during the 1970s made nuclear warheads capable of destroying enemy missiles in their underground silos. This escalation led to ever greater instability as each side feared a nuclear first strike—the potential for one adversary to "win" a nuclear war by being the first to launch its missiles and wiping out the enemy's capacity to retaliate. The women portrayed this development as a boxing match.

As the actors moved from one phase of the nuclear age to the next, it became obvious there would be no winners in a nuclear arms race, only losers. The only way to win such a race was to drop out of it by disarming.

Suddenly, the stage went dark and the clock stopped ticking. It was midnight.

The silence forced me to face the nuclear danger. In my mind, I saw mushroom clouds rising from fireballs, pictures reminiscent of my childhood nightmares. My imagination filled in what my eyes couldn't—nuclear destruction rained fire and lethal radiation, leaving our Earth a silent planet, a dead orb drifting in the vacuum of space.

Why had this pantomime impacted me so profoundly? I think it had to do with the absence of words. By not speaking, the pantomime cut through all the rhetoric about the balance of power and peace through strength. In silence, the women spoke a truth that resounded throughout the hall: The arms race poses an immediate threat to all life on the planet.

My mind had dominated most of my life until that night. My brain fed on words. It craved information and vacuumed up facts. I could control words and file them away in tidy boxes inside my head. But during this performance, absent any words, my mind was defenseless. Adrift. I could only process the pantomime on a visceral level. I began to see the futility of such "rational" doctrines as nuclear deterrence. With so many nuclear weapons, every minute of every hour of every day was precarious.

For the next two weeks, I was enshrouded by the darkest, deepest depression of my life. All happiness was sucked out. How could there be a future? What point was there in feeding the hungry or visiting the sick when the launch of a nuclear missile, even by accident, could wipe out millions of people in a few hours? The dread of nuclear annihilation is a crushing weight. During those two weeks that autumn, I looked across Puget Sound from First Hill and made out the general location of the Navy's Trident Submarine Base, only twenty miles to the west.

Given the base and several Boeing defense operations in the area, it was a foregone conclusion that the Puget Sound was high on Soviet targeting lists if nuclear war broke out. Several times each day, I caught myself imagining mushroom clouds rising above the Sound and blotting out the Seattle skyline. Somehow, I managed to continue with my job. But I seemed to be moving slower, like I was wading through thick mud. I felt as if I had gained thirty pounds, seemingly overnight.

My depression got so bad that I did what any good Catholic does in a hopeless situation. I went to see a priest.

Fr. Jack Morris was one of those people who was easy to talk to. I had met him two months before at my volunteer orientation. He was in his mid-fifties and had a warm smile, large glasses, and an Irish glint in his eyes. Raised in Anaconda, Montana (the same hometown as Archbishop Hunthausen), Fr. Jack was one of the founders of the Jesuit Volunteer Corps, which began working with people in poverty in Alaska a few years before it became a state.

From the depths of my depression, I poured out my concerns to Jack. I wondered aloud about whether there could be any hope when the world was so close to nuclear Armageddon. What use was it to do good deeds for the poor when it wasn't directly addressing the main problem? I told Jack I'd been having trouble sleeping since seeing the "Four Minutes to Midnight" pantomime.

He listened carefully to my voice and my heart. After my litany of woes, Jack responded in a calm voice. "You're right. The peril posed by nuclear weapons is the greatest threat facing humankind. And as people who are called to follow Jesus, nuclear weapons challenge us to act. I understand why you're depressed. I want to suggest that rather than obsessing about the problem, you get involved with working for peace."

Jack took a deep breath and looked me straight in the eyes. "You see, this is why the pilgrimage to Bethlehem makes so much sense. It combines praying for peace with a plea for nuclear disarmament. I want you to consider joining me on the pilgrimage."

I just sat there. Many conflicting thoughts and feelings swirled inside me. I found the idea of participating in a walk spanning three continents intimidating. But walking to the Holy Land was enticing—the chance of a lifetime. I told Jack I needed to think it over.

As I pondered his invitation over the next several weeks, I bounced between being terrified and excited. The prospect of becoming a ragtag vagabond, not knowing when the next meal or shower would be, scared me almost as much as the threat of nuclear war. I enjoyed the comforts of home: a dry, warm house, a good book, an easy chair and slippers. I was not the kind of person who would leave home and walk thousands of miles, getting dusty and sweaty, sleeping who knew where.

And yet, the chance to adopt an even simpler lifestyle, so near to the one portrayed in the Gospels, resonated with deep stirrings in my heart. Since seeing that documentary on Mother Teresa, I had fallen in love with God. Spirituality was something more than what happened in church. Now my faith was much more relevant and dynamic.

As 1982 began, concerns about the burgeoning nuclear stockpiles escalated. The *New Yorker* published Jonathan Schell's three-part series *The Fate of the Earth*. Schell's reporting portrayed what nuclear war would be like. As I read each installment, I knew I had to spend more time promoting disarmament. The increasing nuclear peril was too depressing to ignore—I had to increase my involvement.

Though I hadn't committed to going, I invested more time in helping to organize the pilgrimage. We identified a need for someone to staff a support office once the walkers departed Seattle. Would it be possible for me to only work three days a week at my volunteer placement in Seattle and devote the other two workdays to supporting the walkers? Since there were no funds for staff, this would mean an income loss for my volunteer household. My housemates would have to agree to sacrifice and make up the difference. I also needed the approval of both the Jesuit Volunteer Area Director and the social agency where I was working. Luckily, everyone agreed. My housemates enthusiastically endorsed my plan—it was their way of supporting the pilgrims who frequently visited our house.

I committed myself to staffing the home base for the duration of the pilgrimage. I would support the peace walk while enjoying the comforts of home. But I wondered if I was missing a fantastic opportunity by not walking to Bethlehem. I was still torn.

With less than a month to go before the scheduled departure, the organizing intensified as the other pilgrims arrived in Seattle: George drove all the way from Michigan in his red Chevy pickup that would serve as our main support vehicle; Mary Jude flew in from Chicago; and Laurie arrived from Milwaukee. There were thirteen pilgrims in the core group, with three others slated to join by the time the group reached Salt Lake City—evenly split between women and men.

In our March 1982 newsletter, George summed up our collective anticipation to finally begin walking: "I've been talking peace for a long time. I've stressed loving our enemies and praying for those who disagree with us. I've called for disarmament and outlawing war as a means of solving conflicts. I've talked and talked and talked. There comes a time when I must commit myself to doing something, giving of myself, changing my way of life, living in a simpler way, living in community in trust and faith. What better way than a pilgrimage? Every day there will be a commitment of body and soul. Walking, physically giving of myself, praying with every step, and still talking and leafleting to hundreds, maybe thousands who perhaps could not be otherwise reached."

Nineteen months after Jack thought of walking to Bethlehem for peace, the day of departure finally arrived: April 9, 1982—Good Friday on the Christian calendar, marking the crucifixion and death of Jesus. Jack recalled, "We chose that day to draw attention to the capacity of nuclear weapons to crucify the whole world." The pilgrims chose the Navy's Trident Submarine Base as the starting point—the largest concentration of deployed U.S. nuclear weapons. After months of planning, organizing, and networking, it was time to take the first steps in what Jack described as "a two-year nonviolent assault on the utter folly of nuclear arms."

Originally built as an ammunition dump during World War II, the Trident base covers more than 7,500 acres along Hood Canal, a narrow arm of Puget Sound. Established in 1977 to be the West Coast port for Trident strategic (nuclear-armed) submarines, the base is mostly forested except for the weapons storage area, a large rectangle near the center of the base that is kept clear of vegetation for security purposes. The area is dotted with hardened storage igloos covered with dirt and surrounded by security fencing.

Known for its years of organizing protests against Trident, the Ground Zero Center for Nonviolent Action offered the pilgrims hospitality the night before the journey began. Abutting the eastern fence of the Navy base, the Ground Zero Center had a small house with enough floor space for us to roll out our sleeping bags. We enjoyed a simple spaghetti dinner.

Waking up the next morning, we found the sun shining brightly, the air unseasonably warm. The birds were singing, trees sprouted new growth, and the early flowers were in full bloom—a gorgeous spring day.

None of the pilgrims really knew what to expect. How would people respond? Who would join us for the first six miles? What would it be like for us to take our first steps toward Bethlehem? We were full of butterflies as our adventure was about to begin.

Each pilgrim was unsure if our bodies and minds were tough enough. A survivor of two serious heart attacks, could George make it all the way? Would any of us get hit by a car or fall off a cliff? Even with all the months of planning and organizing, how many things did we forget to consider? How crazy was this really?

After spending the morning rechecking all the gear, George, Jack, and the other pilgrims ate lunch before the 1:30 p.m. departure ceremony. There were two categories of walkers: the core group and guest walkers. The members of the core group were committed to walking all the way to Bethlehem. Throughout this book, I usually reserve the use of pilgrim to refer to members of the core group, though certainly every person who walked even one mile with us could be considered a pilgrim. Guest walkers accompanied us for as long as four weeks. While the guest walkers didn't participate in core group meetings, they pitched in with whatever work there was to do. They brought fresh energy to our effort and were instrumental to the success of the pilgrimage.

My role was unique, sort of a hybrid member of the core group. While I had committed myself until the pilgrims reached Bethlehem, I would remain behind in Seattle. Thus, I was a full member of the core group during the planning phase, but my full participation would be impossible once the others were on the road.

My primary responsibility the morning of Good Friday was to drive a large van and shuttle people who had difficulty walking to the departure ceremony. With more friends and supporters arriving, all of us were busy distributing copies of the Stations of the Cross, a traditional Catholic practice on Fridays during Lent—commemorating the suffering and death of Jesus. We would be praying the fourteen Stations along the six miles to the maritime town of Poulsbo, our destination that first day.

We were thrilled that five hundred people showed up to celebrate the beginning of the pilgrimage. Children in wagons and strollers, along with their parents, crowded in front of the ammunition gate on the east side of the Navy's Bangor base. Just over the security fence were the railroad tracks that delivered nuclear warheads and missile parts to the base.

Seven saffron-robed Buddhist monks from Japan stood next to a large contingent of Catholic nuns from Bellevue. Even though we were next to one of the largest concentrations of deployed nuclear weapons in the world, the crowd was jubilant, grateful to be a part of one of the longest pilgrimages ever undertaken. Pam Ingalls-Cox, one of the pilgrims, remarked, "The first day of the pilgrimage was like a wedding."

As the time for the departure ceremony approached, several television crews and newspaper photographers scurried to find the best angle, carefully negotiating their way through people who were pressed against the fence. On the other side of the fence, military guards kept silent watch. The crackle of shotgun blasts from the nearby gun club firing range mingled with hymns as our supporters began to sing "Amazing Grace" and "Were You There When They Crucified My Lord."

Taking the microphone in his hand, Jack offered the opening prayer. "O God of Bangor, God of Bethlehem, giver of all who ask, bless us on our way. We deliberately choose to begin our journey on this day when the universal Church remembers how you sent your son, Jesus, to bring peace and healing to our broken world. We thank you for this wonderful turnout of fellow peacemakers and ask that you guide and protect us as we make our way across America and Europe to Bethlehem in Palestine, birthplace of the Prince of Peace. Let us all labor together to turn swords into plowshares. Amen."

Next up to the microphone was Fr. George Zabelka who, at sixty-seven, was the oldest pilgrim. Recounting how he had supported the U.S. effort in the Second World War, he said, "We were military men then and, when the planes returned, we felt that we had done what was necessary to end the war." Recalling the devastated ruins of Hiroshima and Nagasaki, George continued. "I have seen with my two eyes how nuclear weapons decimate whole cities. The devastation was incredible. In whatever buildings they had left, there were thousands of burned people, with scabs over their faces, suffering in absolute silence—rows of them—dying each day by the hundreds. Many were old people and children. I asked myself, why was it necessary to kill or burn them?"

Zabelka confessed, "I'm an old man now, but I am driven by my silence then to shout now as loud as I can to bring a halt to the use and manufacturing of all nuclear weapons. I see our pilgrimage as a sign of hope, a belief that together, we, the ordinary, little people, can change the course of history."

Finally, it was Archbishop Hunthausen's turn. In blessing the pilgrims, he said, "Nuclear weapons are in place around our earth, waiting like silent demons, to blow us back into the dark chaos unknown since the beginning of creation." Looking out at the hundreds of disarmament supporters, Hunthausen exhorted, "Now is the time to stand up and be counted!"

Anticipation rippled through the assembly. The speeches were finished. The time to move had come. As the pilgrims took their first steps away from the Trident base, the exuberance of the crowd began to fade. Conversations wound down and settled into a prayerful silence. This was not a protest march. It was one long prayer for peace and nuclear disarmament. The fate of the planet hung in the balance. Would prayer and nonviolence be enough to stop the arms race which was feverishly amassing ever greater numbers of warheads? Could humanity's drift toward the nuclear abyss be averted?

Then drums broke the silence. Buddhist monks from the Nipponzan

Myohoji order started to beat their drums as they joined in behind the pilgrims. The monks chanted, "Na Mu Myo Ho Ren Ge Kyo" (In Respect of All Life). After listening to their voices and drumming for several miles, I noticed the cadence of the chant matched the rhythm of waves lapping the seashore. I felt at one with all of nature.

I found in walking that my whole body, mind, and spirit resounded with the rightness of putting my fears about the nuclear peril into action. Integrating my ache for peace with the movement of my body made power course through me. It was intoxicating.

I felt like a batter who swings at a pitch and connects with the ball at the bat's sweet spot—a perfect hit when the ball explodes off the bat and takes flight over the outfield fence for a home run. The exhilaration of multiple factors coming together perfectly at the exact right time, this was my experience on those first six miles. Over-the-top joy!

Buoyed with such elation, my body felt lighter. The walking motion was so natural, as if I were gliding along the road. What a difference from the heaviness of being depressed six months before. Now it seemed as if anything was possible. The lightness of hope.

Praying the Stations of the Cross accentuated the experience. The fourteen Stations were spaced about every half-mile along the route. Pilgrims would stop at each Station and read the text Jack had written. For example, the second Station read: "JESUS BEARS HIS CROSS. He leads us to choose to bear the cross of loving our enemies and never seeking revenge or retaliation. The Cross of non-violence alone will save the world from nuclear destruction."

Upon reaching St. Olaf Church in Poulsbo, the pilgrims enjoyed a potluck dinner at the parish—the first in a long line of similar meals throughout the route. As for me, I had to switch from being a walker to a driver. After ferrying people back to where they had parked their cars near Ground Zero, I returned the borrowed van to the Mount Saint Vincent nursing home in West Seattle and then, getting into my car, drove home to my volunteer community.

2 – Growing Up in Fear

The author's dad, Lt. Bernard Thomas, in WWII,
(second from right in top row).

I am a child of the Cold War—that period of history when the peril of nuclear war infected American society. One of my earliest memories of the Cold War was when I was in second grade. I grew up in Chewelah, Washington, a town of 1,500 located about forty-five miles north of Spokane. I lived in a small two-bedroom duplex with my parents and younger sister. On the evening of September 10, 1962, while I watched the black-and-white television that sat in our living room, a grim "News Bulletin" graphic appeared on the screen, interrupting regular programming. A disembodied voice announced, "A plane from Fairchild Air Force Base [near Spokane] has crashed." My stomach tightened. Had the plane carried nuclear bombs? Were any of them damaged? The announcer continued, "The plane was a KC-135, a mid-air refueling tanker. There is no information yet on casualties. We will bring you more information when it is available."

My stomach relaxed. The crash involved a tanker and not a bomb-carrying B-52. I remember feeling a profound sense of relief. This astonishes me because I was only seven years old! It was a month before the Cuban Missile Crisis. How could the fear of nuclear weapons have permeated my childhood?

A short while later, the announcer provided further details: "The plane was carrying forty-four people: four crew members and forty airmen. There were no survivors. The tanker struck the side of Mount Kit Carson in poor weather, twenty miles northeast of Spokane."

Throughout the 1940s, 50s, and 60s, American culture vibrated with fear. Even people who lived through that era may find it difficult to recall how completely fear infiltrated American society, since it has been more than thirty years since the collapse of the Soviet Union. Many schoolchildren practiced "duck and cover" drills by dropping under their desks and covering their heads with their arms. These drills forced children across the country to contemplate the megadeath of nuclear annihilation. The loss of any human life is tragic, but the scale of nuclear war is beyond comprehension.

The production, testing, and deployment of nuclear weapons have shadowed me all my life, born as I was in Great Falls, Montana, home to the Strategic Air Command's Malmstrom Air Force Base. Malmstrom's F-84 jets were among the first fighters to carry nuclear weapons. When I was five, my family moved to Spokane. Ten miles west of Spokane was Fairchild Air Force Base. As part of the Strategic Air Command, B-52 nuclear bombers were stationed there. Each dark green B-52 had eight jet engines that belched thick black exhaust, especially during take-offs. The combination of high decibels and low frequencies of those eight engines would rattle windows as they flew overhead. When the bombers were particularly low, the whole house would vibrate. Some Spokane residents referred to the noise as the "sound of freedom," but I found it menacing—a constant reminder of America's readiness to wage nuclear war and bring the world to an end.

On long missions, the wings of the B-52s would be so ladened with extra fuel that the wing tips had to be supported by their own set of wheels to prevent the tips from scraping the runway during take-off. During the 1950s and 1960s, B-52s were always loaded with nuclear bombs when they flew, and when B-52s crashed with nuclear bombs aboard, there was always the risk of catastrophe. The most serious accidents occurred near Goldsboro, North Carolina (1961), Palomares, Spain (1966), and Thule, Greenland (1968). While the nuclear bombs didn't explode, significant radioactive contamination occurred that necessitated massive clean-up efforts. Following the Greenland incident, the Air Force changed its policy and banned aircraft from carrying nuclear weapons during peacetime flights.

Growing up, I enjoyed watching movies, and several, such as *Them!* and *The Day the Earth Stood Still*, vividly portrayed the nuclear peril.

Other films such as *Strategic Air Command*, which starred Jimmy Stewart, and *Fail Safe* depicted the Air Force's round-the-clock war footing.

Another ever-present reminder that the nuclear threat was real was the weekly wailing of the Civil Defense sirens, every Wednesday at noon. One summertime Wednesday, I was visiting my Aunt Jo in Spokane. I was in the backyard cleaning out the concrete birdbath under the shade of several large trees. I glanced at my watch and saw it was nearing noon. I steeled myself in anticipation of the weekly reminder that we lived under a nuclear cloud. The fear of nuclear war was built into Cold War culture, haunting many of our waking moments.

If air raid sirens blew at any other time during the week, people were to go immediately to the nearest Civil Defense shelter. Each large building was required to have space reserved as a shelter, and the entrance was marked by a yellow and black placard designating the building as an official "Fallout Shelter." The placards also indicated the number of people the shelter could hold in the event of a nuclear attack. Through propaganda campaigns, the federal government encouraged people to build their own bomb shelters in their basements or backyards.

There was a companion fear that haunted Americans who lived through the Cold War: the fear of communism. The two fears had a dangerous symbiotic relationship, each feeding off the other. Anyone who questioned the U.S. nuclear policy or who advocated for disarmament was quickly branded a communist sympathizer or perhaps even a Red spy. To be a patriotic American, one had to accept the escalating peril of nuclear weapons. Knowing that the end of the world was possible was part of growing up during the Cold War. I remember newspaper headlines emblazoned in large, bold type like these: "Communists Threaten West" and "Reds Abhor Freedom." Before every meal, my Catholic family included a petition to our prayer: "For the failure of communism."

Our family meals were also the most frequent occasion for what Dad called "hair-raising experiences." He was the chief disciplinarian, and his preferred method of punishing my sister and me was pulling our hair. He would grab a bit of the hair on the back of my neck between his thick, muscular thumb and index finger and then yank. Instantly, pain would encompass my brain and course up and down my spine. How I wished I was a turtle so I could escape inside a protective shell. While I'm sure Dad thought he was being a good parent by instilling discipline in my sister and me, what we learned was fear.

Dad was a powder keg. We never knew when something would set Dad off and he would strike out at one of us. The slightest wrong move would set it off. And then BOOM! Such was sharing the same space with my dad.

My dysfunctional family was practiced at pretending there wasn't anything wrong—that it really wasn't all that bad. After all, we did enjoy eating homemade fudge, playing Yahtzee, and in the summers, going to the drive-in theater in Deer Park where we watched *The Love Bug* and *Son of Flubber*.

My parents didn't show affection toward each other and frequently argued. They were devout Catholics, so divorce was not an option. When things got bad, they would go see a priest. Sometimes things were better for a while, but soon the arguing and angry outbursts returned. Dad loved living in Chewelah. Mom hated it. We made a good show of being a loving family during family reunions or in church on Sundays. But tension simmered below the surface.

The times when we did enjoy being happy made Dad's unpredictable outbursts even more frightening. Just when we were lulled into thinking our lives could be normal, something would set Dad off, jerking us back into our dysfunctional reality. ZAP! A lightning bolt of pain as Dad grabbed the hairs on my neck.

And oh, how I wanted to cry. Dad didn't want to hear about it: "No son of mine is going to be a crybaby." Often, I was punished twice: once for the original offense and again for crying about the pain and the shame.

Then Dad's angry frustration would drive him to turn on his heels, storm down the long hallway, slam the back door, stomp down the back stairway to the garage, and seek escape by driving someplace. When Dad and Mom argued, these confrontations would end the same way—with Dad disappearing for several hours. I never knew where Dad went to cool down. Sometimes I felt as if he might not ever come back. Part of me wanted it to be so.

While Dad was the primary inflictor of pain, Mom had her own method. Dad had a large, cluttered Army-surplus desk wedged into the kitchen. Inside that big oak desk, there was a wooden ruler in the center drawer. Whenever Mom felt like one of us needed a reminder to comply with her orders, she would open the drawer and grab the ruler to paddle our behinds. That drawer made a telltale screech as it was pulled out. As my sister and I grew wiser, the mere sound of Mom opening that drawer was enough to get us back in line.

Since his death in 1987, I have come to better understand my dad and the psychological scars he suffered in the Second World War. He served as a bombardier in the U.S. Army Air Corps. As a kid, I asked him what his war experience was like. But silence was his only response. When I approached draft age, I was desperate to talk with Dad about war. My choice to go to Vietnam or Canada loomed. All I learned was he had flown B-26 bombers.

Dad was twenty-six years old when he was drafted in the spring of 1942—nearly the same age I was when I walked to Bethlehem. After training camp, he began active military service in the Army Air Corps shortly before Thanksgiving of 1943. He was assigned to the 344th Bombardment Group, which flew twin-engine B-26 Marauders over northern Europe as part of the Ninth Air Force. The targets included bridges, railroad yards, and launching sites for V-1 rockets.

As the bombardier, Dad's job was to navigate the plane to the target and then, using a bombsight and mathematical calculations, determine when to drop the bombs. He had to consider such factors as altitude, speed, and wind. During bombing runs, he sat in the plexiglass nose cone. He flew twenty-five missions before the D-Day invasion. He played a role in liberating France, the Battle of the Bulge, and the push into Germany before the final victory over the Nazis.

An article from the March 3, 1945 issue of *The Spokesman-Review* quoted from a letter he wrote about his visit to the front lines in Belgium. The infantrymen used one foxhole "to fight from and the other they sleep in. The men I talked with had been in the lines for eight days in a row." With some snow drifts waist high, he reported the soldiers were "fighting the cold as well as the enemy." The article ended by noting that "Lt. Thomas [was] credited with 53 missions as B-26 bombardier."

The various photos of Dad during the war show a handsome man with thick black hair, gray eyes, and a medium build. In pictures during training, his expressions hinted at a youthful playfulness. But in photos taken after he was first wounded in May 1944, his face is noticeably somber. Gone is any hint of exuberance. There are two rows of service ribbons decorating his chest, reminders of the action he had already seen. One group photo, dated October 13, 1944, shows Dad and six other men standing in front of their B-26. They had christened their plane "Little Chick." Dad seems to be forcing a smile.

I also have a series of aerial photographs of a railroad bridge over the Loire River, just east of the villages of Les Ponts-de-Ce and Saint-Maurille which sit across the river from each other. This area is roughly 150 miles southwest of Paris. A sequence of eight numbered photos records one of Dad's bombing runs. The photos were clearly taken from a high altitude; B-26 bombers usually flew their missions between 10,000 and 15,000 feet. No clouds can be seen.

The first frame shows the bridge intact. In the second, smoke is rising from several bombs exploding along a line that intersects the bridge. From the shadow cast by the plume, it seems to be late afternoon or early evening. One of the bombs detonates on the north bank of the Loire in what seems to be a farmer's field. By the fifth frame, the entire bridge is obscured by billowing smoke and debris.

In viewing a recent satellite image of the same area, I could make out a line of six pilings where the bridge once spanned the Loire. There is no sign of the old railroad line.

I also have some of his war medals. There is a Purple Heart with nine Oak Clusters, which means he was wounded in combat on ten separate occasions. He was awarded the Distinguished Flying Cross for "extraordinary achievement while participating in aerial flight against the enemy" (as described in the official commendation). Less than a month before the

D-Day invasion, he was wounded by anti-aircraft fire while still fulfilling his assigned duties. Amazingly, he flew another mission later that day and was wounded again. The commendation noted that the next morning, he flew "still another mission skillfully scoring devastation against the enemy despite pains from his previous day's wounds."

In addition to his physical wounds, he also knew the loss of buddies who were not as lucky—those who didn't return across the English Channel. Another injury was knowing his bombs had sometimes killed civilians.

In interviewing my sister for this book, I learned Mom once told her that Dad had a troubled conscience that literally ate away at him, causing him to spend the final months of the war in a hospital recovering from a perforated ulcer. Ulcers plagued him the rest of his life—the result of struggling with dropping bombs on Germans. Since his grandfather was a German emigrant, I sometimes wonder whether Dad was tormented by the prospect his bombs may have killed some relatives.

Without Dad sharing anything with me about his war experience, I can only guess about his inner suffering. I do know many men of his generation believed it was unmanly to cry. They were told: "Buck up. Don't stand there sniveling. Get on with it." So, even when they were subjected to the brutal violence of a world war, Dad and his peers could only stuff their pain deep down.

While Dad had faced flak from Nazi anti-aircraft guns, my mom had her own secret pain. It was nearly fifteen years after her death when I learned of her wounds from World War II. My Aunt Jo had recently moved into a nursing home. She was the last of her generation, and her basement housed the family's archive of old photos, letters, and memorabilia. My sister Mary, a few of our cousins, and I gathered in my aunt's house to go through her possessions before selling her house. My cousin Jack brought up boxes from the basement and set them throughout the wallpapered living room.

In one large box of old photos, I came across a wood-framed 8x10 color photo of a handsome Army officer in uniform. I had seen similar portraits of my dad and uncles. But this officer was a complete stranger.

"Hey, Jack. Who is this guy?" I asked.

He said, "Oh, don't you know?"

I shook my head.

Jack replied, "He was engaged to your mom. He was killed in action. I think his plane was shot down."

I was stunned. I heard Mary gasp. I turned to look at my sister. Her mouth was open, her eyes wide. This was news to her, too. Mom had never mentioned anything about him.

Jack added, "Your mom's heart was shattered. She was very depressed for a long time afterward." How could Mom have carried such heartache through the rest of her life without revealing even a hint of it to her children?

The Second World War had deeply wounded both of my parents. I imagine they thought it was possible to lock all their anguish, grief, and fear in a box and throw away the key. I'm sure they wished they could bury the demons of war. But Father Richard Rohr, OFM warns, "If we do not transform our pain, we will most assuredly transmit it—usually to those closest around us: our family, our neighbors, our work partners, and, invariably, the most vulnerable, our children."

In August 1969, at my mother's urging, my family moved back to Spokane from Chewelah so I could attend Gonzaga Prep, an all-boys high school run by the Jesuits. Prep was the alma mater of Dad and most of my male relatives. For me, the transition was hard. I knew none of the other students. I went from having three classmates in the eighth grade to 210 of them.

Over the next dozen years, a tug-of-war unfolded within me. On one side was my parents' conservative politics, the pre-Vatican II Catholic Church with its own brand of fearmongering, and Eastern Washington's xenophobia. Pulling me in the opposite direction was the much more engaging Catholicism that emerged from the Second Vatican Council and the anti-Vietnam War and Civil Rights movements.

In the 1964 presidential campaign, my parents enthusiastically supported Republican Barry Goldwater. They even took my sister and me to one of his campaign rallies. One morning, we arrived at the Spokane airport and made our way out to the tarmac. I remember shivering as we waited for Senator Goldwater's plane to arrive. I do not remember being inspired by anything he said that day but came away excited at seeing a presidential candidate in person. The rally's fervor spurred my sister and me to start wearing Goldwater campaign buttons on our coats. After the resounding defeat Goldwater suffered in the November election, my classmates ridiculed me.

During the 1960s, my parents made disparaging remarks whenever Dr. Martin Luther King, Jr. appeared on TV. Their comments gave me the impression there was something evil about people advocating for social change. My parents considered protesters to be threats to law and order. The population of Chewelah was nearly all white. There was only one person of color in my grade school, Ray Flett, a member of the Spokane Indian Tribe and a classmate of mine. When my family drove past the Japanese section in Spokane, I recall my parents making derogatory comments.

Chewelah was typical of most U.S. small towns in the sixties. The townspeople were suspicious of outsiders. One Sunday afternoon in summer when I was ten or eleven, a wave of panic coursed through town on rumors that the Hells Angels motorcycle gang was about to invade Chewelah, bent on wreaking all sorts of havoc. Some of the neighbor kids raced by on their bikes, doing their Paul Revere duty to alert the town of danger. I heard the alarm in their voices and saw their contorted faces. I am still amazed at how quickly fear seized our small town—mothers hurried their children inside, closed the drapes, and hunkered down. As is the case with most rumors, this one ran its course and fizzled within an hour or two. The bikers never came.

My Jesuit high school education presented me with a more expansive view of the world. I relished being constantly challenged to think for myself, form my own opinions, and discern my place in the world. I was being pulled in a much different direction.

Inspired by Vatican II, my religion teachers at Prep revealed a radical Jesus who challenged social injustices. The new Jesus of *Godspell* and *Jesus*

Christ Superstar was an actual person I could relate to. In English classes, we read such anti-war classics as *Johnny Got His Gun* and *All Quiet on the Western Front*. As I approached eighteen, I took a political drama class that included the *Trial of the Catonsville Nine* about the burning of draft records—captivating discussions ensued.

By my senior year at Prep, the tug-of-war grew more forceful: my conservative upbringing pulling me to the right, and the cries for social change pulling me to the left. 1972 was the first presidential election in which eighteen-year-olds could vote. One month before election day, on the afternoon of my eighteenth birthday, I walked six blocks to the fire station and registered to vote.

Several months earlier, I attended a rally for Democratic Senator George McGovern at Gonzaga University. But after McGovern abandoned Senator Thomas Eagleton as his running mate (when Eagleton's history of depression became known), I wondered whether Republican Richard Nixon might be a more reliable leader. I felt torn between the "safe" small-town values and my growing awareness that significant societal change was necessary. In November, when it came to marking my ballot, I succumbed to my white conservative upbringing and voted for Nixon.

Instead of going off to college and escaping my dysfunctional family, I lived at home during my four years at Gonzaga University. (My parents' house was next to a dorm.) I drifted through college, guided more by my work-study assignments than any career plan. I ended up with a broadcasting and theater degree and took a job as an operations engineer at KREM-TV in Spokane. Once the excitement of my first full-time job faded, I settled into a comfortable routine that included bicycling and stamp collecting. In the 1980 presidential election, I voted for Ronald Reagan. Like many Americans, I was concerned about the 1979 Soviet invasion of Afghanistan. It seemed Reagan promised security.

Among the downsides of a secure lifestyle are stagnation and a loss of vitality. After a few years at the TV station, I started to realize how lonely and unhappy my life was. The boredom I experienced at work nagged me. I longed for something meaningful, something to make the world better.

I began meeting with a Jesuit priest who had been one of my college professors. Father Dave Leigh listened as I told him how dissatisfied I was with my work. I wasn't finding it fulfilling. I yearned for a sense of purpose. He encouraged me to volunteer at the House of Charity, an overnight men's shelter. According to him, "The experience of meeting people in poverty will be good for you."

Several nights each month during that winter, I drove downtown and parked my car near the elevated railroad tracks that bisected Spokane's business district. After being let in by a shelter staff person, I climbed the dilapidated stairs to the second floor. A small landing at the top served as the intake area. There was a wooden table on which sat a clipboard to log in the men as they arrived. Next, they would enter a much larger room with mattresses spread out on the floor. My job was to monitor the men while they slept and defuse any disagreements before they escalated into fights. Come morning, I woke the men up before they headed back onto the streets. In my brief interactions with them, I learned of the despair of people who had spent too much time on the unemployment line or were trapped in alcoholism.

Fr. Dave also suggested I volunteer several hours a week at the Spokane Peace and Justice Center, located in a large two-story house near Gonzaga University. I helped with mailings and spent time reading books and magazines in its small library. The directors Joe and Mary Ellen Gaffney-Brown exposed me to information and viewpoints missing from the evening news. My eyes were opened by authors such as Susan George (*How the Other Half Dies: The Real Reasons for World Hunger*) and Penny Lernoux (*Cry of the People: The Struggle for Human Rights in Latin America*). These were amplified by the 1980 assassination of St. Oscar Romero, Archbishop of San Salvador, as he celebrated Mass and, eight months later, the horrific murder of four American Catholic women who served oppressed people in El Salvador. I struggled to understand why my fellow Catholics were being killed by death squads allied with the U.S.-supported regime.

All this inner turmoil subsided with Mother Teresa's "love until it hurts" and the joy I experienced as a Jesuit Volunteer. But the struggle between personal comfort and living for others would return.

3 – Waiting for My Turn

Rocky Flats prayer vigil.
(Photo by Bill Cox)

Milepost: 6 – April 10, 1982

Saturday began as another sunny spring day. Grabbing the newspaper from the porch, I unfolded it and was thrilled to see that the start of the pilgrimage was the lead story on the front page, accompanied by a large photograph. The headline in the *Seattle Post-Intelligencer* read, "Peace pilgrims begin Bangor-Bethlehem nuclear arms protest." *The Seattle Times* also chose to run our walk as its lead story, using the same photo under the headline, "Pacifists start Bangor-to-Bethlehem trek." We had wondered how the news media would cover our walk. This was an auspicious beginning.

Laurie sent the articles to her parents who were among the most worried that the pilgrimage was some kind of cult. When her parents saw the newspaper clippings, they were "very supportive from then on. My dad had worked for the *Milwaukee Journal* his entire professional life. If the editors of *The Seattle Times* thought this was worthy of front-page coverage, it must be a pretty good thing." The parents of other pilgrims, including my own, stopped worrying about cults.

Meanwhile, back in Poulsbo, the other pilgrims began trekking the twelve miles to the Winslow ferry dock on Bainbridge Island. Along the way, they stopped at the grave of Chief Seattle in the Suquamish Tribal Cemetery, located on the Port Madison Indian Reservation. Steve Old Coyote, one of the tribe's medicine men, met the pilgrims and led them to the gravesite. As pilgrims encircled the grave, Old Coyote lit a cedar smudge and used an eagle feather to fan the fragrant smoke, first over the grave and then over the pilgrims. He said, "All of nature whispers peace." Presenting the pilgrims with four colorful pouches filled with herbs, tobacco, and feathers, he made a request: "You will honor my people by carrying these all the way to Bethlehem." Pam took charge of fulfilling this request (in 1984, she returned to the tribal cemetery with soil she collected from Bethlehem's Shepherd Field). After several more hours of walking, the pilgrims boarded a ferry to Seattle. Reaching the other side of the Puget Sound, they climbed several of Seattle's steep hills on their way up to St. Joseph Church where Jack had been an assistant pastor in the 1970s.

Well before sunrise on Easter Sunday, the pilgrims gathered in a dark church for the start of Mass at St. Joe's. Afterward, there was a special sendoff prayer for the thirteen members of the core group, including me. One woman from the parish, Bunny Wilburn, embroidered a patch for each pilgrim. On a bright yellow background, a white dove holding an olive branch in its beak filled the patch's center. Around the border of the four-inch circular badge, in dark purple lettering, were the words, "BETHLEHEM PEACE PILGRIMAGE—Seattle, Wa. 1982." The pastor, Fr. Pat Hurley, SJ, read a special blessing while each pilgrim was presented with a badge. To accentuate the festive atmosphere, each pilgrim was also given a brightly colored balloon, donated by Pam's aunt. Then the pilgrims proceeded down the long center aisle and out into a drenching rain. Nearby, a woman parishioner was heard saying, "Holy thunder, and they intend to walk all the way to Bethlehem! God bless 'em."

Thirty minutes later, our first crisis hit. For the walk across the U.S., we had two support vehicles: George's old Chevy pickup and Pam and Bill's red Volvo station wagon. We used these to carry our tents, backpacks, literature, banners, and sleeping bags. The truck towed a small yellow trailer that carried our food and cooking equipment. To pick up more food for lunch, both vehicles planned to stop at a grocery store. As the pickup and trailer pulled into the parking lot, Alice followed in the Volvo. Alice said, "I was too excited, and I wasn't paying enough attention at one point. I slammed into the back of the trailer and smashed it up."

A quick transfer of food into the back of the pickup allowed lunch to be delivered down the road to the pilgrims. When pilgrim Bob Patten heard the fate of the trailer, he smiled and said, "God's reality therapy."

Marcus Groffman, a former Jesuit Volunteer who had considered joining the walk, hauled the mangled trailer to his house. The next Saturday, Marcus (with me assisting) patched the torn fiberglass and made the trailer roadworthy again. Marcus delivered it back to the pilgrims before they reached Portland.

As for me, I spent that rainy Easter morning walking with the pilgrims several miles from the church until Cherry Street. Ten blocks to the east lay my volunteer house. It was time for me to bid them farewell. It was here on a wet sidewalk that our paths parted. They had chosen to walk. My part was managing the home base. The steady rain shortened our goodbyes.

In "holding down the fort" in Seattle, my chief responsibility was producing *Pilgrims' Progress*, the newsletter sent to our supporters. The pilgrims would mail their articles to Seattle, and I would type and lay out the newsletter. After several thousand copies were printed, I assembled volunteers to label and organize the mailing. My other tasks included forwarding mail to the pilgrims twice a week, maintaining the mailing list, depositing contributions, asking volunteers to write thank-you notes, handling the bank account, answering correspondence, and responding to messages left on the answering machine. This machine was a vital link to our families and contacts along the way. In 1982, there were no cell phones, social media, email, or even the internet as we know it now.

For the pilgrims, they realized that the exhilaration of the first two sun-drenched days was over. Walking that Easter was no parade. Instead, the weather tested their mettle and rain gear. There was a new sensation as socks and shoes became sodden and squishy. The damp seeped into their leg muscles which started to stiffen. Easter's eighteen miles from Seattle to Des Moines matched the total of the two previous days' mileage.

The walkers trudged through the rainy and noisy city streets. With each mile, there were fewer houses and more trees as the urban landscape transitioned into a suburban one. Recalling that Easter, Alice said, "We were just drenched, like really wet rags, but it was fine. You just keep walking—once you're wet, you're wet. You don't get any wetter. It was actually quite enjoyable." Late in the afternoon, the pilgrims arrived at

St. Philomena Church in Des Moines. The parishioners greeted them with cheers and ushered them into the parish hall where basins of warm water and Epsom salts were waiting. As soggy shoes were peeled off and dripping socks hung to dry, the pilgrims eased their feet into the basins. The soothing water calmed the pain of the first blisters. Volunteers applied first aid to those feet in the worst shape. Caring thoughtfulness brought welcome relief.

You might be wondering why I didn't walk more when the pilgrimage was near Seattle, especially since the first day had been so exhilarating. At the time, I belonged to two communities: the pilgrims and my volunteer housemates. During her volunteer year, Carolyn, an Episcopalian from Portland, was so inspired by Archbishop Hunthausen, Jim and Shelley Douglass, and Jack that she was drawn to join the Catholic Church. Carolyn had made her profession the night before at the Easter vigil. To celebrate, my volunteer community held a big brunch on Sunday.

In the days after the pilgrims left Seattle, intense feelings inundated me: excitement, anxiety, elation, sadness, infatuation, doubt, wonder, and confusion. I oscillated between desperately wanting to join the others on the road and being tempted by the security of staying put in Seattle.

Another pilgrim who was uncertain about whether to walk was Fred Mercy. A religious brother in the Jesuits, Fred was very much the reluctant pilgrim. Jack was Fred's best friend and urged him to join the pilgrimage. But prior to the first day of the walk, Fred had no interest in having anything to do with the walk. He had no experience with the peace movement and wasn't sure what he thought about nuclear deterrence.

Somehow, Jack persuaded Fred to walk the first two days, from the Bangor gates to Seattle. The experience was positive enough that Fred kept walking. Then Pam coaxed him into walking as far as Portland. By then Fred was hooked on the pilgrimage. Within two weeks of departing from Bangor, the core group welcomed Fred as a Bethlehem pilgrim.

About the same time, I decided I wanted to join the pilgrims in August at the end of my JVC commitment. When I called them about my decision, they said they needed to discuss it. I was surprised to hear that. I thought I had a reserved slot. However, the constant stream of different guest walkers and being constantly on the move had stressed the pilgrims. They discovered life on the road was harder than expected. Some wanted to limit the size of the core group. Commitments had already been made to have several others join the core group in June.

My gut tightened with an awful sinking feeling. Now that I finally had decided to walk, here was an unexpected roadblock. Even though no decision had been made, I felt sick that I might have missed the chance of a lifetime by dithering. Having them review my participation felt like a betrayal.

There was nothing for me to do but wait, so I focused on my tasks in Seattle. Days passed—no word from the pilgrims. What was taking them so long? Why hadn't I accepted Jack's initial invitation to walk all the way? Finally, Bob called. They wanted me to come to northeastern Oregon and walk with them for several days. There was a ray of hope, but it felt like they had placed me on probation.

Milepost: 467 – May 7, 1982

Four weeks after they left the Trident base, I caught up with the pilgrims outside of Pendleton, Oregon, walking through dry, desolate lands. There were towering outcroppings of basalt amid range grass and pockets of sagebrush. With few trees and sparse clouds, the sun beat down relentlessly. Fairer-skinned pilgrims had spread white zinc oxide cream on their noses, chins, and cheeks. With their broad smiles, zinc-oxide makeup, and ragtag clothing, they looked like a band of clowns.

Another clear memory from that day was watching a red-tailed hawk dive to the ground in front of me. It landed off the right side of the two-lane road, grasping a writhing snake in its talons. There was blue sky, miles of open space, and a stiff wind. Nearing the Umatilla Indian Reservation, we met two tribal members who guided us along a trail to their cultural center. The trail climbed several steep hillsides, stretching our leg muscles with thirty-degree slopes. While the spring rains had transformed the grasses to a lush green, the hills were devoid of trees except for the cottonwoods along creeks and streams.

I enjoyed the walking even more than I had delighted in it that first day. But there was a bit of an edge to my interactions with the pilgrims. The past four weeks of walking twenty miles a day had hardened them. Meanwhile, I felt as if I were under a microscope. Were they waiting for me to say or do something unbecoming of a pilgrim?

After two and a half days, I returned to Seattle. The pilgrims met to decide my fate. Following some discussion, they agreed unanimously that I could join in August. I rejoiced. I had not missed my chance to walk to Bethlehem. Now I needed to find someone willing to serve as the homebase coordinator. Within a few weeks, Charlene Collora stepped forward to take over my tasks. She was a longtime friend of Jack's and a former Jesuit Volunteer.

During my remaining three months in Seattle, my relationship with my volunteer community deepened. The transformation which began with that documentary on Mother Teresa was continuing. My life felt brighter. I began feeling a special affection toward Carolyn. I had little inkling of the loss I would soon feel after leaving Seattle and thrusting myself into the pilgrimage firsthand.

I still had much trepidation about whether I could hack the deprivations on the road. Could my body handle walking over 100 miles each week? Could I put up with living with dozens of other people in tight quarters on a 24/7 basis? Would I allow the journey to change me? Would others accept a different me? Desiring to be one with Christ in poverty is one thing—actually living it is something else again.

One of my biggest worries was how I would keep myself and my clothes clean. Would strangers accept me if I stank or wore grimy clothes? How often would I be able to shower—once a week? Could I relate to a community three times bigger than my volunteer household? Was I brave enough to relinquish control over so many aspects of my existence? These and other anxieties filled my head as the day of departure approached.

Milepost: 993 – June 7, 1982

Meanwhile, on the road to Bethlehem, the pilgrims crossed from Oregon into Idaho, through Boise, and entered Mormon country. Mimi Ward from Massachusetts wrote about her experience of Holbrook, a small farming town in southern Idaho:

"As I came into its center, time took a breath as past, present and future ran together in the simple everyday life of this Mormon community. Occasional abandoned buildings stood silently. ... I made my way to the house of our contact, Larry Nalder. His very pregnant wife, Bernice, came to the door. She was surrounded by lots of little ones who greeted me with eyes in awe of a stranger. She told me they were planning to parcel out the pilgrims among several host families.

"A few minutes later, Larry joined her and confessed, 'We're taking a great risk by providing you a place to stay. Many townspeople believe that your group might be backed by communists.'

"Larry continued, 'After praying about it, we decided to trust you. We want to see for ourselves before judging, and besides, we never know how or when Jesus will return—we need to be open to strangers.'"

The next morning, the folks of Holbrook lavished the pilgrims with gifts of nine dozen eggs, fresh raw milk, homemade butter, and cheese.

That same week, President Reagan met with Pope John Paul II at the Vatican. Afterward, he told reporters that he was now on a pilgrimage for peace. Given the policies and actions of his administration, I shook my head when I read the news. The U.S. rhetoric about the Soviet Union had become increasingly bellicose amid an unprecedented peacetime increase in military spending. Reagan ordered the development of several new nuclear weapons systems as well as resurrecting the B-1 bomber and the neutron bomb which President Carter had canceled.

The arms race was never far from our thoughts. Steve and Alice flew from Salt Lake City to New York to be among the million people who rallied in Central Park on June 12 to draw attention to the U.N. Special Session on Disarmament. The main goal of their trip was connecting with European peace representatives participating in the rally. Those contacts proved helpful when we got to Europe.

After more than two months on the road, the pilgrims stopped to pray at the Hercules plant, located in Bacchus, Utah, near the southern tip of the Great Salt Lake. The factory made solid fuel rocket motors for the Pentagon, including for its Trident missiles.

Mary Jude Postel reported, "It was the lunch hour when we arrived, and employees were strolling freely in and out of the main gate of the huge plant. We spread out along the road, and leaflets in hand, offered to share our concerns with anyone who cared to stop. Most did; curious about the pilgrimage and our point of view, they engaged us in friendly conversation.

"Then a woman drove in and stopped her car next to Steve. She slipped a piece of paper into his hand and drove into the plant. Steve called us over and we gathered around him as he read the letter aloud: *'Greetings to all of you: I'm sorry I cannot physically protest with you today but in my heart I am. I fully agree with this cause and I'm working with local groups in Salt Lake City to further it. I feel like a hypocrite working here but with this economy I must support my children and this place pays better than most. It's a Catch-22. I so want to meet and talk with you, but we are all under constant surveillance. Thank you for stopping at Hercules along your way. Good luck on your journey; My thoughts will be with you. Peace and love.*

"We stood in silence. Pam said a prayer for the woman. As we trailed off to pilgrimage around the plant's fence, a security officer accompanied us in a car, snapping pictures. The sheriff's department contingent was by then five cars strong at the main gate."

Mary Jude continued. "Something is so very wrong here. We are told that nuclear weapons protect our freedom. Yet the price of these weapons is the very freedom they are supposed to protect."

Later that afternoon, eight pilgrims drove into Salt Lake City to the headquarters of the Church of Jesus Christ of Latter-Day Saints and were escorted to the twenty-fifth floor. They met with four LDS leaders, including the Director for Special Affairs. Fr. Zabelka pitched our idea for an interfaith council to proclaim that war was immoral. While the LDS leaders listened attentively and asked good questions, they were noncommittal about supporting such a council. The hour-long meeting concluded with both delegations offering prayers for peace.

At the Catholic cathedral, George met Dick Sherwood who had been a B-29 pilot on Tinian Island. On August 6, 1945, he flew his plane over Hiroshima two hours after the atomic bombing on a photo reconnaissance mission. Sherwood told George of flying only a few hundred feet above the carnage and seeing the squirming survivors in the wreckage. As Sherwood recounted his experience, he broke down in tears. After Sherwood's crew returned to Tinian on August 6, they joined other crews in pledging themselves to work for peace so that such a horror would never be repeated. While in Salt Lake City, George stayed at Sherwood's home. Afterward, George frequently included Sherwood's eyewitness account in his presentations and interviews.

Two other members of the core group joined in Salt Lake City, Janet Horman and Helen Claire Ferguson. They were friends studying to be United Methodist ministers at Garrett-Evangelical Theological Seminary in Evanston, Illinois. They interrupted their studies to be part of the pilgrimage. Janet grew up in Plantation, Florida, while Helen Claire was from New Jersey and Pennsylvania. Unfortunately, after two weeks on the road, Helen Claire developed severe foot pain that limited her to only walking a few miles a day. When the pain became too intense, she would drive one of the support vehicles.

After Salt Lake City, the pilgrims headed east along Highway 40 and entered a long stretch where they had to camp due to the distance between towns through eastern Utah and western Colorado. During this stretch, they started walking at 6:00 a.m. and stopped for lunch around 11:00 a.m. to avoid the hottest part of the day when the mercury rose above 100°. They drove ahead to a campsite to rest. In the evening, they drove back to where they stopped in the morning and walked the remainder of that day's miles. They delighted in frequent sightings of coyotes and prairie dogs.

As the miles went by and the landscape unfolded before their eyes, Mimi wrote, "I'm in love with the experience we call the U.S.A. I'm in love with windblown wheat fields and the arid expanse spotted with sagebrush and mustard. I'm in love with wild asparagus, with the shapes of the mountains and the iridescent colors of common ground cover. I'm in love with the singing meadowlarks and the soaring hawks and the laboring blue herons. I'm in love with the farmers and the small-town people who, in profound and simple ways, express their concern over thermonuclear war—with all its complexities. I'm in love with all those normal people we meet who don't think we are crazy to be walking to Bethlehem as a prayer for peace. I'm in love with God who created it all and saw that it was good."

Milepost: 1623 – July 15, 1982

The thin air of the Rocky Mountains heated quickly as the pilgrims crossed the Continental Divide at Berthoud Pass, elevation 11,300 feet—the highest point of the walk. The mountains also brought an onslaught of thousands of no-see-ums and mosquitos, resulting in "very scratchy, itchy" bites as George recorded in his small notebook.

Two days later, as they neared Denver, the pilgrims stopped to pray in front of the Rocky Flats Plant, where the U.S. Department of Energy took plutonium from Hanford and machined it into the precise configurations needed for America's nuclear weapons. Watched closely by two armed guards and a sheriff's deputy, the pilgrims sat on the ground at the plant entrance. Between them and the guards was a chain-link fence with yellow "No Trespassing" signs. The pilgrims offered prayers, sang songs, and shared reflections on ending the nuclear arms race.

Since the next morning was Sunday, the pilgrims were invited to be speakers in eight churches throughout the area. Later, at a picnic lunch in a park, they were joined by U.S. Congresswoman Patricia Schroeder, who endorsed the pilgrimage. Rep. Schroeder asked the pilgrims to urge citizens to hold their elected representatives accountable. She said most politicians campaign on a pro-peace platform, "but seldom stick to [it]." The pilgrims encircled Schroeder and, raising their hands over her, sang their blessing song.

As they headed farther east and left the mountains, they entered the Great Plains. As George noted, "The country here is flat and gently rolling wheat fields harvested and open fallow fields—just nothing around—miles and miles of nothing…unbelievably vast and empty."

Something else happened as the pilgrims crossed America—Steve became smitten with Mimi. However, as Mary Jude recalled, "she wanted nothing to do with it. He carried a torch for her for miles. I mean literally miles and miles and miles and miles. I remember one time in Kansas, it was my turn to cook. I opened the back of the pickup truck to get something out and Steve and Mimi were in there. They were just kissing, but I remember saying, 'Ooh, sorry.' I turned around and thought, 'Yay! He made it. He won her over somehow.' It was beautiful to watch that relationship flower. That was a great part of the walk—Mimi and Steve's romance."

While the pilgrims were trekking across Colorado and Kansas, I was helping organize a rally to protest the arrival of the first Trident submarine. I met regularly with Jim and Shelley Douglass and others in the basement cafe of the Elliott Bay Book Company in Pioneer Square. On Sunday, August 8, the "Resist Trident, Celebrate Hope" rally was held at Point Julia on Hood Canal, west of Seattle. With over 6,000 people protesting the arrival of the first Trident sub, I was glad to represent the pilgrims since we had started our walk at the base. The deployment of the Trident sub and its hundreds of nuclear warheads strengthened my resolve to endure whatever challenges lay ahead on the road to Bethlehem.

A week later, I said goodbye to Carolyn and my five other housemates. Carolyn gave me her set of dark brown Rosary beads to carry to Bethlehem. All my housemates gave me a tan bandanna on which was written, "I have been nurtured by the warmth of the sun, the soil, and the company of a friend." Each of them had signed their names as well. I wore that bandanna every sunny day to protect my neck from sunburn. With tears streaking my cheeks, I drove to Spokane. I was awestruck by how close our volunteer community had become in one year.

After spending several days visiting family and friends, I boarded a Greyhound bus for the three-day trip to Kansas City. The bus passed through Boise, Salt Lake City, and the seemingly endless expanse of Wyoming and Nebraska. Switching buses in Omaha, I thought of the nearby headquarters of the Strategic Air Command (SAC), which oversaw all nuclear weapons deployed through the Air Force, including Malmstrom in Great Falls and Fairchild near Spokane.

Could I hack it as a pilgrim? Was I making a mistake? How many days before my next shower? I was about to be tested like never before.

4 – Walking at Last—Through a Field of Missile Silos

Pilgrims' peace banner flying below the Gateway Arch, St. Louis.

Milepost: 2323 – August 27, 1982

Traveling fifty-five hours by bus was exhausting, but it enabled me to cover the distance it had taken the pilgrims four months to walk. One of our supporters in Kansas City came to the bus station and drove me out to meet the pilgrims as they walked into the city. It was a wonderful reunion though a bit soggy, as they had gotten drenched an hour earlier by an afternoon thunderstorm.

It felt good to stretch my legs following the long bus ride. And to be walking with the pilgrims on our way to Bethlehem was profound joy. After four months of longing to walk for peace, I had bodily joined our quest for disarmament. The pilgrims welcomed me with open arms and wide smiles.

After a few miles, we stood before the Bendix plant—a sprawling complex of over 300 acres that manufactured most of the non-nuclear components for U.S. nuclear weapons. Employing 6,500 people, the plant shipped components to the Pantex plant near Amarillo, Texas, the final assembly point for all U.S. nuclear weapons. Along the sidewalk in front of the Bendix plant's main gate, we held a prayer vigil. As workers drove out of the plant, many of them blared their horns or shouted "get a job" or "go protest in Russia." While such reactions were discouraging, they knew our purpose. More depressing were the people who drove by without any recognition. Were they aware of the nuclear peril?

Three days later, heading east across Missouri, the urban environment gave way to rich farmland approaching harvest time. A few white clouds dotted the blue sky. The sun shone brightly. Around mid-morning, I was walking with Steve and Bookda Gheisar, a guest walker who had joined the group in Logan, Utah. The songs of meadowlarks and red-winged blackbirds delighted us. The humid air felt heavy. Off the north side of the highway and up a six-foot embankment, we saw a high-security fence not more than a hundred feet from the roadway.

Always the wary one, I stayed on the shoulder of the highway while the pair of more curious pilgrims scrambled up the embankment for a closer look. They couldn't see much except for a thick concrete slab surrounded by gravel which filled in the rest of the double-fenced enclosure. We were nearing Whiteman Air Force Base, the command center for 150 Minuteman II missile silos scattered across west-central Missouri. Given the security fencing, we guessed that we had found one of them. Each Minuteman II missile carried a nuclear warhead with the explosive equivalent of roughly eighty Hiroshima-size bombs.

From the shoulder, I cautioned the other pilgrims to be careful. I wondered whether they should be getting that close.

Just then, an Air Force Jeep pulled up at the far end of the silo enclosure. One young soldier jumped out of the front passenger seat. He raised his M16 rifle and pointed it in our direction. The three of us froze. The driver picked up the radio handset and reported to his commander, "We have two individuals, a man and a woman. They're just outside the security fence. Appear to be unarmed."

In a surprisingly calm voice, Steve told the guards, "We're walking for peace. We mean no harm. We are praying for a world without nuclear weapons." The Air Force personnel said nothing. The rifle pointing at us spoke loudly enough. The situation simmered in a tense standoff.

Over the next few minutes, a dozen other pilgrims joined me along the highway shoulder and began praying—our eyes fixed on our two companions and the faceoff with the Air Force security detail. How would this end?

Soon, a police car approached from the east. It was the county sheriff. He pulled his car onto the shoulder, stopping a few feet in front of me. As the sheriff got out of his car, I moved toward him. He was about fifty years old and a bit pudgy.

The sheriff inquired, "Who are you and what is your intent?"

I told him, "We're walking to Bethlehem for nuclear disarmament.

We noticed the fenced area and wanted to see it better. This morning we started walking from the town of Lone Jack and are staying in Warrensburg tonight. We want to spend a few minutes praying before continuing our walk."

The sheriff acted as if we were hopelessly naïve, albeit with a kindly attitude that said, "Such crazy kids these days." He shook his head in disbelief. He eyed me carefully and looked up at the Air Force detachment. He said, "Well, that's all fine, but I want you to move along. You're making the Air Force nervous."

After saying goodbye to the sheriff, we shared prayers before resuming our walk east and ever closer to Bethlehem. Soon we heard the pounding thump-thump-thump of an Air Force helicopter approaching. It shadowed us for the next hour. Apparently, the Air Force was still nervous.

Steve remarked, "Wow, I can't believe how paranoid they are." I reflected on the 150 missile silos and their combined destructive power of 12,000 Hiroshimas. It was impossible to imagine such killing power.

The next day, we stopped to pray at the main entrance to Whiteman Air Force Base. The launch crews for the 150 silos were housed there. Whiteman had fifteen underground launch centers, each controlling ten missiles.

Today, the missiles are no longer there, having been decommissioned in the 1990s after the Cold War ended. The current mission of Whiteman is the 509th Bomb Wing, the same military unit that dropped the atomic bombs on Hiroshima and Nagasaki during World War II. The 509th now flies the B-2 stealth bomber. Each of the twenty B-2s can carry sixteen nuclear bombs. A single bomb has a maximum destructive force of 1.2 megatons. Thus, the B-2 bombers can deliver the equivalent of more than 25,000 Hiroshimas, double the destructive potential of the Minuteman II missiles the bomb wing replaced.

Our walk was not total gloom and doom. We didn't spend the whole time confronting the unthinkable. Through the ingenuity of local organizers, we had some delightful accommodations. West of St. Louis lay the small town of Gray Summit, Missouri, and on its outskirts was the research farm for Ralston-Purina (think pet food and Chex cereals). The farm conducted nutritional research on dogs, cats, pigs, chickens, cows, mink, catfish, and horses. The farm had a conference center with sleeping quarters for sales representatives who attended their training sessions. Arrangements had been made for the pilgrims to stay the night with hotel-like amenities: mattresses, clean sheets, and pillows—a real treat. It beat sleeping in tents or on the concrete floors of school classrooms and church basements.

The conference center had a kitchen and dining room where we enjoyed a large breakfast of eggs, bacon, hash browns, pancakes, and of course, Chex cereals. The tables were bedecked with red-and-white checkered tablecloths (part of the Purina logo). We welcomed this morning feast that contrasted with the simple bowl of oatmeal, our default breakfast on the road.

To top it all off, a guide took us on a tour of the farm. Being a research operation, most of the large animals had plastic ports in their sides to allow sampling of the various stages of digestion. My clearest memory was when the guide demonstrated how Purina could control the color of egg yolks by varying what the chickens ate. Collecting three ordinary-looking eggs, he broke one open and placed the contents on a clean white plate. The yolk was the familiar yellow we all expected from a chicken egg. Next, he cracked the second egg and put the contents onto the same plate. Instead of being yellow, this yolk was a bright green! I couldn't keep my jaw from dropping. Then the guide broke open the third egg and added it to the plate. Its yolk was a deep, dark red. The chickens who laid these eggs were definitely not free-range.

What was it like to walk twenty miles a day across the country, mostly along the shoulder of busy highways? Out West, wider shoulders made the walking more pleasant. As we moved across the Plains and into the Midwest, the shoulders narrowed, and the traffic increased. As each vehicle blew past us at 50 to 60 mph, we waved and smiled. Then we braced ourselves for the whoosh of the pressure wave. When it was raining, the spray added another coating of road grime.

There were usually several guest walkers joining us while two or three pilgrims would be away from the walk, either organizing the next segment, attending a wedding, or taking a few days off from the grind of the miles.

While most of the movement was slow, only three or four miles per hour, it was relentless. Six different towns each week; eight to ten hours on the road each day; breakfast, pack, walk, lunch, walk some more, unpack, greet people at potluck, present program on nuclear peril, bedtime. Next morning, we would get up and repeat. That left little time for anything else.

Constant motion, a constant stream of new people to relate to—the daily grind wore us down. If we were hosted by a church or town, we all slept in one room, like the social hall or cafeteria. If there were smaller rooms available, then Pam and Bill, being the only married couple in the core group, got priority. The rest of us would lay our sleeping mats and bags on the floor with our backpacks nearby. When you share one large room with twenty or thirty people, there is no privacy. Everyone can see and hear everything. Several of the pilgrims were loud snorers, so sleep would be interrupted at least once during the night.

At one point, Bill was convinced that I was one of the snorers, which I always denied. Bill had a cassette tape recorder, and one night he recorded me while I slept. The next morning at breakfast, he came over to me with a triumphant look on his face. "Okay, Jim, now I have proof that you snore," he said as he held his tape recorder out to me. He rewound the tape and then hit play. All that I and several nearby pilgrims could hear was the white noise of tape hiss. Bill shook his head in disbelief. He had been sure he had captured me snoring. Perhaps he failed to hit the record button in the dark. Whatever the case, I felt exonerated.

As pilgrims, we were with other people on a round-the-clock basis. Usually, my only opportunity to be alone was on the road. As one of the faster walkers, I enjoyed the exhilaration of a brisk pace. By walking fast, I could distance myself from the others and find a bit of solitude.

In those weeks after Kansas City, my body was tested by the miles, the variety of foods, and the weather. Living most of my life in the Pacific Northwest had not prepared me for the heat and humidity of the Midwest. Even though I had trained by walking four to six miles a day, it was not enough to get me in shape for averaging twenty miles a day. Before long, my feet spawned blisters. With daily punishment, my blisters developed blisters. Having good shoes, two pairs of socks, and ample application of moleskin didn't prevent blood-stained socks. By the fourth day, I had to ride in the pickup for the afternoon.

For most of the previous year, I had yearned for this chance to be part of the walking contingent. Now that I was living it, I was surprised how quickly I was beset with stinging doubts about continuing the journey. My previous jobs had provided my mind with nearly constant stimulation which I now lacked—walking through farmlands for eight to ten hours a day didn't keep my mind busy. My dammed-up emotions from childhood trauma began demanding attention. I feared what lay hidden inside me.

In response, I manufactured a dilemma so I could put off coming to terms with my past. I began questioning whether the pilgrimage was the best way to promote disarmament. Was there something else that would be more effective than walking? I imagined there was a job back in Seattle that would make better use of my skills.

At the time, I didn't see my situation clearly. All I knew was that part of me wanted to remain on the walk—and another powerful force was desperate to escape. I yearned to be at peace, but that would take much longer to find.

A Jesuit Volunteer I had known in Seattle had grown up in St. Louis and returned there after our JV year ended. As we neared St. Louis, I called to invite her to join our rally at the Gateway Arch. The comedian and civil rights leader Dick Gregory would be among those speaking. The city issued a proclamation declaring that Sunday as Bethlehem Peace Pilgrimage Day.

She asked me what our route would be after the rally. I told her our plan was to cross the Mississippi River and walk through East St. Louis. Interrupting me, she warned that it wasn't safe. East St. Louis was an area she avoided. She didn't even like driving through there because of the danger. She always made sure her car doors were locked. She was alarmed that we planned to walk through it.

I couldn't believe what I was hearing from a fellow volunteer. We had just spent a year together in Seattle going to the same retreats focused on social justice and serving people in poverty. I almost didn't know what to say.

She told me she wouldn't attend the rally and hung up. I couldn't help but shake my head in disbelief. Her reaction seemed over the top, irrational. What kind of danger could East St. Louis pose? Was there something there that our planning hadn't accounted for? Even so, any danger there would pale in comparison to the threat of nuclear war, right?

After the Sunday rally ended, civil rights activist Dick Gregory led us away from the Arch, across the Mississippi River, and into Illinois and East St. Louis. We saw people sitting on their porches enjoying the sunny afternoon. They were intrigued by our peace banners. Many recognized Gregory, and his presence gave our mostly white group instant credibility. People left their porches and eagerly joined our procession—within blocks our numbers swelled to over 350. My volunteer friend had missed a life-affirming experience.

For Helen Claire, hearing Dick Gregory and walking through a majority-minority community was joyous. The only African American member of the core group, she was committed to walking all the way to Bethlehem, but foot pain continued to plague her. She took a break from the walk for several weeks and sought medical treatment and rest.

Milepost: 2600 – September 12, 1982

The first signs of autumn greeted us as we crossed southern Illinois and Indiana: cool mornings and birds flying south.

The most surprising aspect of walking across the United States was how people openly welcomed us into their homes and churches. The ready hospitality was something I thought had been relegated to some bygone age. Given how dusty and sweaty we would get, coupled with long periods between showers, we were not the most attractive lot.

I remember particularly one Midwest couple who looked to be in their fifties. They lived in a white, two-story farmhouse that was set back from the road about 150 feet. One Sunday afternoon, as they sat on their front porch, they watched several pilgrims pass by. This piqued their curiosity; I imagine it was unusual to have people walk along their rural road. They called out to me, "Hey, come here, young feller. Where are you folks going?" As I approached, I said, "We're walking to Bethlehem for nuclear disarmament." Instead of being skeptical or cautious (as I would have been), they insisted I come inside their house for some refreshments!

Before I could say "thank you," I was sitting at their kitchen table with a hefty piece of homemade chocolate cake and a glass of water. Within a few minutes, one of them had invited two other pilgrims, Pam and Bill, from off the road—treating them to cake as well. For the next half hour, we conversed about our experience of walking across the country. They shared their fears of nuclear war and lamented the shrinking support for family farms while Congress threw money at defense contractors. Relishing the last brown crumbs on our plates, we told the couple we had about five more miles before reaching that day's destination. They wouldn't let us leave until they gave us a bag of carrots and potatoes from their garden. After several rounds of thank-yous and goodbyes, we returned to the road, reinvigorated by their generosity.

While this sort of encounter didn't happen every day, it happened often enough that I learned how much I had in common with people throughout the world. After walking across the Great Plains, Steve wrote about the overwhelming friendliness, generosity, and openness of rural America: "It was almost as if we'd entered a subculture which specialized in loving kindness: food was brought to us, potlucks appeared out of nowhere, cafe waitresses picked up the tabs, and civic swimming pools were opened late at night for our use!"

Interwoven into the pilgrimage, too, was the opportunity for adventure. There was a new horizon every day. Walking up hills and down into valleys, the landscape was one long cavalcade of beauty. The colors were different in each region, the clouds varied, the terrain shifted from gentle to flat to steep. The people changed as we went. Quaint local accents ebbed and flowed, and complexions shifted. But nearly every town or village greeted us with smiles and curious eyes. Their expressions seemed to inquire, "Who are these people walking so many miles?"

Nearly all the people we met were just average folks. Even with mayors, pastors, and bishops, we met them as fellow human beings. That is the biggest advantage of walking. We were not part of a barnstorming campaign with a fancy retinue of supporters or staff. We were just like the people we met—simple, humble people. We seamlessly entered their everyday lives by putting one foot in front of the other.

We gave people hope. But we always received more in return: food, a roof over our heads, and a deeper faith in the innate goodness of every human person.

It was a journey I couldn't have made alone. This is the consensus of all twenty of us within the core group. Consequently, we knew we needed to make a significant investment in our mobile community. The love and support of our intentional community enabled our witness for peace. If we were advocating for the nuclear powers to eliminate their weapons and live together in peace, then we had to set a good example.

There were many opportunities each day for us to get on each other's nerves. Negotiating limited space, accepting (or at least ignoring) each other's aggravating quirks, and coping with pilgrims who snored. Additionally, we had to adjust to the ever-changing lineup of guest walkers. We learned to forgive. We sacrificed for peace.

To deepen our shared commitment, we took turns handling nearly all chores. Everyone had a chance to be part of the three-person leadership team. The team was responsible for making day-to-day decisions such as logistical adjustments to our route and schedule. The team interfaced with local contacts and news media. Every four or five weeks, we elected new leadership.

We took turns driving the support vehicle, George's red Chevy pickup. A typical day began with the morning driver waking up everybody at 6:00 a.m. The morning driver also brewed coffee and cooked a pot of oatmeal. After breakfast, we packed our personal gear. At 7 a.m., pilgrims and guest walkers gathered in a circle as someone began singing a peace song. The current leader provided directions for the day's walk and briefed us on the arrangements for dinner and the evening program. A lifelong news junkie, I listened to BBC news on a shortwave radio and, during circle, I reported on major international security developments. Circle was also a time to introduce any new guest walkers. Frequently, a pilgrim would read aloud a few paragraphs from a book on peace.

The driver also washed the breakfast dishes, made sure there was enough food for lunch, loaded all the gear into the vehicle, and ran errands. Then the driver would meet us along the road.

After finding a place protected from traffic and weather, the driver laid out a large tarp and set out the food, usually loaves of bread and jars of peanut butter and jam. When available, cheese, fruits, and vegetables joined the spread.

Fr. Jack commented in his memoir, "The noon stop was a combination of gladness that another length of road was behind, gratitude for food and health, joy at being together sharing laughter and chatter, and just plain relief for a chance to recharge the old body through food and rest."

We began each lunch by reciting the World Peace Prayer:
"Lead us from death to life, from falsehood to truth;
Lead us from despair to hope, from fear to trust;
Lead us from hate to love, from war to peace;
Let peace fill our hearts, our world, our universe."

The actual eating of lunch sometimes turned chaotic. We tried to walk at least twelve miles beforehand, so most pilgrims were ravenous. If we weren't careful, a feeding frenzy occurred. With as many as forty hungry hikers, the food tarp could get very crowded. After meeting to discuss the problem, we decided that the core group would wait until after the guest walkers had gotten their food.

There was one occasion during a picnic lunch when Dean was taking the last hardboiled egg and asked if anyone else wanted to share it with him. Sometimes we were considerate of others to a fault. But the constant checking first with others could get on people's nerves. On this day, it was too much for George and he snapped at Dean: "Just go ahead and eat the bloody egg!" Everybody sat in shocked silence. We were all surprised to hear George raise his voice.

Another person would drive in the afternoon. After loading up the lunch dishes, the driver would go to the town where we would stay that night, unload the vehicle, wash dishes, and meet our hosts to work out last-minute details.

Most nights, the church hosting us organized a potluck dinner followed by a presentation by the pilgrims about the dangers of the arms race. In more remote areas, there could be more than twenty miles between towns. In those instances, we camped out and fixed our own dinner—transforming the afternoon driver into a cook.

Every week, the core group members would hold a sharing meeting to say how each of us was doing. It served as sort of a relief valve for our community—a safe place to vent frustrations and share joys. The most important ground rule was that no one could say anything about another person unless they had talked privately with that person before the meeting.

A few times, we decided to cancel a sharing meeting to make room in our busy schedule for something that seemed more pressing. In every instance, we regretted it. The meetings served as communal reconciliation services. It was palpable how we all felt lighter and refreshed afterward. The meetings knitted our bonds tighter.

Being on pilgrimage is more than a physical journey. It is also an interior one. As the miles accumulated, things continued to bubble up inside me. My psychological pain hurt more than blisters, aching muscles, or inadequate food. As the walk pulled and stretched me in so many ways, I became obsessed with finding some way to escape.

The lack of privacy, the lack of control, being around so many people, my fear that the journey was asking me to sacrifice too much—all these were disrupting my carefully constructed system of defenses. Each day of the pilgrimage tore down my interior walls and beckoned me to be more vulnerable. I was being disarmed, and it was torture. Staying on the pilgrimage that first month was one of the hardest things I have ever done. At times, I wondered if I was losing my mind. As the battle raged within me, I couldn't keep the struggle hidden.

During one of my first sharing meetings, my internal debate about whether to remain on the walk or leave became so intense that I confessed, "As for me this week, this [pilgrimage] is a great opportunity to be truly poor, but it is extremely hard. I have pushed myself to the limits and I feel I am about to break apart. I am thinking about returning to Seattle and working for disarmament there."

The next morning as Circle ended, Jack said, "Hey, Jim! How about you and I walk together this morning? There is something I want to discuss."

"Sure, Jack. Just let me finish packing and I'll be with you in a minute."

I stuffed my sleeping bag in its sack and tightened the yellow straps that lashed it to the bottom of my rust-colored backpack. Dropping it off at the side of the pickup, I fastened my fanny pack and walked over to where Jack waited for me. Several other pilgrims had already stepped onto the road to begin our trek to the next town. At first, Jack and I walked in silence, waiting to create some distance between ourselves and the other pilgrims.

After a few hundred yards, Jack began, "So, it has been about three weeks since you joined in Kansas City. You've walked nearly 300 miles by now. How's your body holding up?"

"Okay, I guess. My blisters are turning into calluses, and my legs are not as stiff. Overall, I am enjoying the daily exertion."

"I'm glad to hear that. But I think there is something you're missing. Your comment at the sharing meeting last night about going back to Seattle concerns me. Is there something else bugging you?"

"As I said at the meeting, my intellectual skills aren't being well utilized. I feel I could be more effective back in Seattle. Most of the day is just walking. We reach only a few dozen people most days."

"While that's true, you must consider the impact we're having by our physical statement and our commitment to walk all the way to Bethlehem. And the dozens of people we meet each day add up. We've been on the road for what, five months? In that time, we've met thousands of people.

Multiply that by all the people who've seen us on television, heard one of the radio interviews, or read an article in the newspaper. There is no way we can say just how effective we are being. But you can see the impact we're making on people's faces."

Jack was right, but I didn't want to admit it. I didn't want to give him any opening into the source of my inner anguish. The lack of privacy, the constant traveling—being in six different towns every week, having to relate with a large community combined with meeting dozens of new strangers every day. It all left me feeling very vulnerable. How could I endure the additional emotional nakedness of sharing with Jack my trauma that I had held back since childhood? I thought the abuse was best left in the past. If I tried to recall it, I feared it would only cause me more suffering. I thought I might lose control.

Jack knew better. He was a wise spiritual guide. Growing up with his two brothers in the hardscrabble town of Anaconda, Montana, he likely had similar experiences.

I can't remember how persistent Jack was in his probing. Knowing Jack, he was probably dogged. But there could have been something in my responses that revealed my strong reticence. "Jack, there is nothing in my past that is impacting me now. All of that happened long ago. I don't need to deal with it."

It would be another eight years before I found out I was so wrong, and Jack was so right. It took a violent personal tragedy before I was forced to start the long process of unpacking my childhood trauma. The process will probably never be complete, but much healing occurred over the next decade.

Why did I refuse his offer of help on the way to Bethlehem? Jack had already helped me so much since our first meeting when I was so depressed after watching the "Four Minutes to Midnight" pantomime. Jack also had led me through a private weekend retreat back in December. And every time he said Mass or gave a homily, I was inspired. Jack embodied everything I wanted in living out the Gospel message. He was a living prophet proclaiming Jesus' message of compassion and the radical challenge to love our enemies.

My renewed determination to stick with the walk evaporated after a few days. Before I knew it, the torment of doubt, fear, and uncertainty returned. I continuingly manufactured rationalizations to convince myself (and, if I was lucky, Jack) that returning to Seattle was the right answer for me. During hours of walking, my thoughts were consumed with developing persuasive arguments for why I had to leave the walk and return to Seattle.

5 – Surrender to Carrying My Cross

The author carrying a banner on the walk to the White House.
(Photo by Bill Cox)

Milepost: 2892 miles – Sligo, Kentucky (October 2, 1982)

So, how did I decide to stay on the pilgrimage? I cannot remember any one moment that clinched it, but it was shortly after I talked to Carolyn, one of my JVC housemates, by phone. Carolyn was one of the many factors I felt were pulling me back to Seattle. While I was too shy and inept to court her before I left, I obsessed about a future relationship with her during the long hours walking across the Midwest. It took me several attempts to reach her. This was years before cell phones, and with me being almost continually on the move, I couldn't leave the number of a payphone on her answering machine. But finally, we did connect.

"Hi, Carolyn," I said.

"Oh, hi, Jim. Where are you now?"

"We're in Sligo, Kentucky—staying at a United Church of Christ church. It's so good to hear your voice. How are you?"

"It's a beautiful fall day here in Seattle. Lisa and I went for a long walk after work. Wait 'til you see our apartment. It's just off 15th Avenue, so it's an easy walk to the grocery store, a wonderful bookstore, and some great vegetarian restaurants. How are you doing?"

"I wish I was doing better. I am enjoying the walking. My blisters have turned into calluses. But the hardest part is living with twenty other people. And I miss you."

"Well, I miss you, too. But you and I talked a bit about this before you left. We really do not know about the future. That's why we agreed to make no commitments. Now I can imagine how hard the pilgrimage is," she continued, "but it is so important. I'm very proud you are on it. You're making a powerful statement for nuclear disarmament."

"Thanks, but, um, I'm wondering if I could better use my skills back in Seattle—like a job with PSR or the Freeze Campaign. I feel I'm wasting my talents by just walking."

"Jim, remember how much you've been yearning to be part of the walk. You spent so much time organizing it before leaving Seattle and all you've wanted to do since April is to go out on the road and be part of the whole thing. Listen, I need to go now. I'm glad you called. I pray for you and the other pilgrims every day. Remember, your peace effort is very important. I'll write soon."

"Thanks, Carolyn. Take care."

Hearing her voice brought back many happy memories of the wonderful volunteer year we had together. But it was also painful as it emphasized how distant we were from each other. And with every step I took, the distance would keep increasing for another fifteen months. Even though I desired to be close to her, it was not to be.

As I reflected on what her gentle voice had said over the phone, I realized I was in the place I most wanted to be: walking to Bethlehem. I started to accept the pain of separation from Carolyn as part of the sacrifice I had chosen. A kernel of inner peace began to grow within me. Rather than struggling to find a reason to justify my return to Seattle and escape the noise, disruption, and vulnerability of the road, I embraced the hardships as part of what I needed in order to grow. Change is hard. Growth always entails some pain. Like an athlete or musician, becoming a better person requires discipline and sacrifice.

The doubts, fears, and anxieties didn't disappear. They would come back to haunt me whenever new blisters appeared or my tendonitis flared up.

My conversations with Jack and Carolyn helped, but what kept me on the road to Bethlehem was a gentle whisper deep in my heart, beckoning me to something much more important than a committed relationship or a fulfilling job or even a cozy corner of comfort. This quiet voice arising from the core of my being offered me the inner peace of living my truth. In relinquishing my selfish desires, I chose to do whatever I had to do to make the world safer and more just. I accepted my personal responsibility as a global citizen. I followed the gentle whisper because in doing so, I would fulfill the mission I was meant to live out: ending the nuclear arms race.

As we walked through downtown Louisville, Kentucky, we passed a hotel just as Dick Gregory was coming out. Even though he was on a tight schedule, he lingered for several minutes while we updated him on our experiences since that rally in St. Louis. One of those "small world" experiences.

After Louisville, we began walking northeast along the Ohio River. Flat farmland gave way to rolling hills and trees changing color. In the early mornings, mist clung to the river.

I was surprised at how much money we found along the shoulder of the road. Once I found a $20 bill. About every other week, one of us would find enough coins or dollar bills to buy an order of French fries at the next roadside cafe we passed.

Helen Claire returned after consulting with doctors. The pain was being caused by the long bone in each foot tearing away from ligaments and tendons. She could no longer walk even a short portion of the day without great pain. As she recalled years later, "This beautiful group of people, my fellow pilgrims, had become like family, and I grieved about having to say goodbye. ... My heart and mind were, and continue to be, filled with so many incredible memories of being on the Bethlehem Peace Pilgrimage that my disappointment about having to leave quickly dissipated. ... I'm grateful for the gifts and graces of each fellow pilgrim and how they uniquely contributed to the cause for peace."

After those torturous first weeks, I started to relax and enjoy the journeying. I still had recurring spasms of doubt and uncertainty, but I was able to recognize them and keep them in perspective. The constant movement, the large community of diverse personalities, and the grind of all those miles still exhausted me. But most of the tormenting fear and doubt abated by the time we reached Ohio. I began to understand that I couldn't serve my own comfort while living my life in service for my sisters and brothers around the world.

On the evening of our rest day in Cincinnati, several of us went to a pub. At the back was a large patio with a band playing. The air was still warm. We found a table and sat down with a pitcher of beer.

After a while, Mary Jude said, "Okay, Jim—let's get up and dance."

As was my shy habit, I said, "Thanks, but I'm not any good at it. I'll just sit here."

"Oh, come on," she pleaded. "It'll be fun."

I tightened my shoulders, saying, "I'm feeling sore and stiff from all the miles we put in this week. I just want to sit."

Then, with a mischievous smile and a glint in her eyes, Mary Jude grabbed my arm and pulled me out of the chair and onto the dance floor. I felt naked and inadequate. I wanted to run back to the table.

But Mary Jude just laughed at my nervous reluctance. "Move, Jim. Loosen up. Have some fun." Her exuberance melted my stiffness, a defensive wall I'd built up long ago. But on the pilgrimage, it was preventing me from fully living. Through the love from my fellow pilgrims and other people I met along the way, I was being liberated to become my true self. I began to enjoy the dancing.

The next morning, Mary Jude and I left on a weeklong advance trip to organize the last U.S. segment from Pittsburgh to D.C. We drove Pam and Bill's troublesome maroon Volvo station wagon. It had intermittent starter problems and had to be parked on top of an incline so we could start it by rolling downhill. Luckily for us, the Volvo didn't break down again until after the advance trip.

While Mary Jude and I drove east, the other pilgrims walked through western Ohio. On October 10, they held a vigil outside the fence of the Monsanto Mound Laboratories, part of the nuclear weapons production complex. It was operated for the U.S. Department of Energy and produced parts for nuclear weapons. The plant operated from 1948 until 2003, and part of the site is still a contaminated Superfund site.

Meanwhile, Mary Jude and I organized the final U.S. stretch, stopping in towns spaced about every twenty miles and searching for a church to host the pilgrims for a night. We wanted to arrive in D.C. a few days before the annual meeting of the U.S. Catholic Bishops. The focus of their gathering was discussing the second draft of a pastoral statement on nuclear weapons. The Reagan administration was worried about what the bishops might say, especially given the prophetic statements by Archbishop Hunthausen and the other so-called peace bishops. We planned to hold a three-day prayer vigil and fast at the Capitol Hilton where the bishops would meet. In addition to standing vigil in front of the hotel, we would lobby the bishops to make a strong statement against nuclear weapons.

Mary Jude and I returned to the group in Columbus, Ohio. It was a great relief to have all the arrangements worked out. After the success of the advance trip, I felt more secure in my pilgrim role. Even though the trip had been hectic, I enjoyed that week with Mary Jude—traveling with only one other person rather than the whole contingent of pilgrims.

Milepost: 3127 – October 16, 1982

Columbus, Ohio was home to the factory where Rockwell International built the B-1 bomber. It was the first strategic bomber to incorporate stealth technology—making it easier to evade radar detection. The B-1s would replace lumbering B-52s, which were increasingly vulnerable to Soviet air defenses. Led by local peace activists, we walked six miles from the Catholic Worker house and held a prayer vigil outside the plant. Many workers entering or leaving the plant blared their horns as they passed us. Some flipped us off, their faces contorted by anger. They felt that our peace advocacy threatened their jobs.

Another four days of walking found us at Salt Fork State Park in eastern Ohio. Camping out meant no potluck or program. There were no locals to interact with. We could enjoy being by ourselves. The trees had lost their leaves, and we bundled ourselves in our warmest garments. After pitching our tents, we gathered around a campfire that took a bit of the sting out of the late October chill. We relished singing songs and sharing stories. Looking now at photos taken that evening, I notice how happy I was. I'm holding a songbook. Mary Jude is standing on my right, and Alice is to my left with her arm around my shoulder. All of us are beaming with joy. Together we had endured months of pain and hardship. With less than a month before finishing our walk across the United States, we felt exuberant.

As the days became shorter, I walked past modest small-town homes. Toward evening, warm lights glowed inside. Some houses abutted narrow sidewalks, inviting me to peer inside. I saw pots steaming on the stove, their wonderful aromas wafting into the crisp air. Everything reminded me of normal life, of being rooted in one place. I longed to have my own place where I could settle into a comfy chair and not have to wonder what the sleeping accommodations would be that night.

On November 1, the feast of All Saints, in Uniontown, Pennsylvania, we experienced one of our biggest potluck dinners. There was a huge crowd, at least 150 people, assembled in the parish hall. Tables upon tables were laden with hearty casseroles, delicious chicken, glistening vegetables, and plenty of steaming potatoes. To top it all off, there were three tables covered with mouthwatering desserts. After walking an average of twenty miles a day, we didn't worry about having seconds, or even thirds—even of desserts.

Prior to dinner, George's homily at Mass had given everyone much food for thought. So, as we enjoyed the amazing spread, we discussed that day's Gospel passage with the townspeople: "Blessed are the peace-makers." What did these words mean for Christians living in a country with tens of thousands of nuclear weapons? How can we love our enemies while possessing nuclear arms?

Walking is the best way to see the country. I marveled at the contrast between the flatness of Kansas and Missouri (where you can see for ten miles in every direction) to the lushness of the Ohio River Valley, with thick mists mushrooming out of the river and clinging to large deciduous trees. I felt more connected to the American experience and better able to savor the writings of Nathaniel Hawthorne and Henry David Thoreau. I better appreciated the complexities of our nation's struggles.

In the fall of 1982, America's industrial heartland was fast becoming known as the Rust Belt as steel mills closed and corporations moved jobs overseas. I sensed the dark clouds of economic and psychological depression sweeping into the middle-class towns along our route. "For

Sale" signs marked many homes. After seeing large four-bedroom houses on the market for $10,000, I didn't need an economics degree to feel the anguish as life savings and dreams evaporated. I imagined the devastated towns dissolving into dust and being scattered by the winds.

Seeing kids in these depressed towns with patches on their knees brought back memories of my childhood, when Mom sewed patches on my hand-me-downs from cousins. Dad earned a meager salary, as Chewelah's economy was tied to the roller-coaster price of magnesite. The dilapidated plant south of town was the backbone of the town's vitality, and it suffered a string of closures during the 1960s. The final closure came in 1968. When hundreds of the best-paying jobs vanished overnight, townspeople were devastated. I knew the pain of Rust Belt families.

These communities hungered for federal aid, but the Reagan administration was hell-bent on slashing such aid to finance its buildup of nuclear weapons.

One colorful crisp day, Sunday, November 7, found us walking along the towpath of the Chesapeake and Ohio (C&O) canal, from Cumberland, Maryland to Paw Paw, West Virginia. We rejoiced at being able to walk nearly an entire day's distance along something other than a narrow shoulder. For weeks, we had trekked along highways 22 and 40, through the coal country of Indiana, Ohio, West Virginia, and Pennsylvania. A nearly continuous procession of trucks laden with coal blackened the roadsides as the trucks rumbled past us on their way to power plants or the last of the steel mills. The coal dust soiled our handkerchiefs as we blew our noses after a day's walk in America's industrial midsection. I had a better understanding of the misery of miners who had contracted Black Lung disease from their years underground.

Hiking along the towpath, we reveled in the absence of coal trucks, coal dust, and the whoosh of traffic. The fall colors, the rustling of leaves, and the quiet of nature were most enjoyable.

But what cemented that day in our memories were the several dozen young adults from the nearby Bruderhof community who accompanied us. The women wore ankle-length skirts and dresses and had scarves or caps covering their heads. They buoyed us with rousing hymns and practiced harmonies, filling the idyllic atmosphere with resounding song. Such beauty lifted our bodies as well as our spirits—it seemed as if we floated along the towpath.

A few days later, Bill and I came upon a man raking leaves in his suburban yard. In his sixties, he had already seen some of the pilgrims walk past his house. Curious, he put aside his rake and greeted us. After answering his questions about what we were doing and why, he said, "I can't believe you've walked clear across the country. Your message of peace is one we desperately need to hear." He continued, "I want to support your effort." He pulled a $100 bill from his wallet, saying, "This will have to do for now. I'll follow it up with a check. Thank you for doing something to stop the arms race."

Bill said, "We are deeply grateful for your contribution. It helps our group in many ways. May you be blessed." As we headed along the road, the man returned to his raking.

The next week, Charlene in our Seattle office informed us that the man had sent a check for $700. He was one of thousands of people who supported us throughout our sojourn. Before we left Seattle, the mountaineer Jim Whittaker donated two tents. The Birkenstock store donated a dozen pairs. Individuals and religious communities receiving our newsletter contributed. Across the U.S., we sold BPP T-shirts at our programs—these proceeds were enough to cover our airfare to Europe. Each member of the core group chipped in $50 per month for purchasing food and gas.

After more than 3,500 miles since leaving the Trident submarine base on Good Friday, we were on the outskirts of Washington, D.C. The weather had turned gray and cold. We found shelter at a Friends Meeting House. Inside, there were beautifully curved pews made from very dark wood that was almost black. The Quaker house was only a half mile from the headquarters of the Central Intelligence Agency (CIA) in Langley, Virginia. We marveled at the irony of a religious community dedicated to peace being just down the road from one of the Cold War's most tainted agencies.

Earlier that day, as we walked along State Highway 7, Fr. Peter Henriot, SJ, briefed us on the second draft of the U.S. Bishops pastoral letter on nuclear weapons. Henriot suggested talking points for us to use in our encounters with the bishops.

Henriot's assessment was my first substantive introduction to Catholic Social Teaching, a collection of papal and other church pronouncements dating back to 1891. Such teaching sought to apply Gospel principles to contemporary issues. Little did I know then that I would devote half of my career to the study, development, and promotion of Catholic Social Teaching on such pressing issues as immigration reform, climate change, and economic justice. Another benefit of my meeting Henriot—he would serve as a key mentor after the walk.

Early Saturday morning, with several dozen supporters, we walked past the entrance to the CIA, across the Potomac on the Chain Bridge, and arrived at Georgetown University for a noontime rally. Following an evening prayer service at Luther Place Memorial Church, we rolled out our mats and sleeping bags in the church hall.

Milepost: 3566 miles – November 13, 1982, Washington, D.C.

The next morning, we gathered at St. Matthew's Catholic Cathedral with several hundred other peacemakers for a march to the White House. After crossing in front of the North Portico along Pennsylvania Avenue, we rallied across the street in Lafayette Park, decrying President Reagan's buildup of nuclear weapons. From there, the large crowd walked a few blocks north to the Capitol Hilton. Our pilgrim group began a vigil and fast, urging the bishops to broaden their condemnation of nuclear war to include a declaration that even nuclear deterrence was immoral.

Later that afternoon, we joined an all-night vigil led by the Benedictines for Peace. At the start of every hour until the next morning, there were Scripture readings, hymns, and prayers concerning the many social costs of the unbridled nuclear arms race. A recurring chant throughout was a verse from Psalm 34, "Seek peace and pursue it." During those hours of prayer, I fell in love with that phrase and adopted it as my mantra, repeating the short prayer over and over as I walked the rest of the way to Bethlehem. Even now, I silently chant this verse whenever I go for walks.

At 8:00 the next morning, the vigil concluded as the bishops began their meeting. For the Bethlehem pilgrims, we continued our fast and vigil until the meeting adjourned on Wednesday. We took turns holding peace banners on the sidewalk in front of the hotel, engaging bishops in the hotel lobby, and taking turns resting in a room upstairs.

Whenever we encountered a bishop, we related our experience of walking across the country and how so many Catholics and others were proud of them for tackling the arms race. Across America, we saw in people's faces how relieved they were that religious leaders were speaking out against nuclear weapons.

On the second day of our fast, I was waylaid by a stomach bug and became dehydrated. By that evening, I was so weak that I fainted. Bob and Steve revived me and helped me down to the pickup truck. They took me to the emergency room of George Washington University's Medical Center. The staff hooked me up to an IV. After the infusion of fluids, I felt better and was steadier on my feet. Returning to our room in the hotel, I began to eat some soup and bread. The other pilgrims continued their fast.

The bishops' meeting ended in a standoff between the so-called peace bishops who held that even the possession of nuclear weapons was immoral and the conservatives who were adamant that the U.S. must maintain a strong deterrent. Over the next six months, a third draft was prepared. On May 3, 1983, the bishops approved *The Challenge of Peace: God's Promise and Our Response.* While the document was not all I was hoping for, it endorsed active nonviolence as a morally responsible position while tolerating deterrence only as long as progress was made toward eliminating nuclear weapons.

We stayed in D.C. for several more days and discussed preparations for the European leg. Of most consequence, we decided to increase the core group from 15 to 19 pilgrims. After prayerful discernment, we invited: Mary Frazel who had just completed her JV year and was a close friend of Bob's; Maureen Casey, a grandmother and a nurse treating drug addicts in New York City; Anne Galisky, who took a break from studying history at the University of California; and Bookda Gheisar, an Iranian college student from Utah. Each had been a guest walker during our walk across America.

The pilgrims dispersed to spend the holidays with family and friends. I spent Thanksgiving with my cousin Dick and his family near D.C. Then I visited my three former JV housemates who lived on the East Coast: Amy in Boston, Diane in New Jersey, and Mary who was in graduate school at Columbia in New York. Mary and several of her classmates were planning a peace walk of their own for the following summer. Calling themselves the Plowshares Pilgrimage, they planned to walk from D.C. to the Pantex plant outside of Amarillo, Texas—the final assembly point for all U.S. nuclear weapons. I briefed them on my experience of walking across the country, including how to treat blisters. I spent Christmas in Spokane with my family and visited Carolyn in Seattle before flying back to the East Coast.

"Oh, you don't want to go up there," the older woman behind the drugstore counter told me. I had asked her which bus route to take to North Broad Street in Philadelphia. It would be my home for the next two months. I explained that I already had friends living there, a three-story row house that the Christian Brothers offered to us rent-free as a place to organize the walk across Europe. I finally convinced her, and she directed me to a bus stop across the street.

It was a cold, gray day at the beginning of January. After twenty minutes, I saw the 5300 block, pulled the cord, and got off. Looking around, I understood why the drugstore clerk was confounded about where I wanted to go—it had all the earmarks of a neighborhood in decline.

My home for the next two months was at the corner of North Broad and West Fisher Avenue. No one was home, and the door was locked. Wandering around the neighborhood, I discovered a library a few blocks away. I would spend much of the next two months researching the Middle East. I also found a Catholic church on the other end of our block, Our Lady of Hope Parish. It was a gray stone edifice that struck me as imposing and uninviting.

Walking back to the row house, I rang the doorbell again. Alice had returned from her job and let me in. In the living room, I noticed an old black & white TV. "Where did that come from?" I asked Alice. She replied, "Oh, Steve traded the yellow trailer for it with some of the neighborhood kids. They moved it down the alley and are using it as their clubhouse."

About half of the ten pilgrims who stayed in Philadelphia needed to work to save money for the rest of our trek. Steve worked in a butcher shop, Mary Jude assembled cheesesteaks, Laurie worked at a daycare, and Alice looked after an elderly woman.

Bob, Jack, Anne, Janet, Dean, and I had sufficient savings or financial support and spent those two months organizing the European leg. The pilgrims with outside jobs pitched in as they could. Tasks included obtaining international driving permits, deciding what communal gear to bring, recruiting people to organize regions or entire countries, and poring over maps to identify a route and set dates for the major cities. Alice and I determined how to manage our group funds while on the other side of the Atlantic. Of interest to everyone was learning more about Northern Ireland which was still torn by sectarian violence.

Our biggest effort focused on determining our route from Rome to Bethlehem. Janet, Anne, and I formed a committee to gather information on Greece, Turkey, Syria, Jordan, Israel, and Palestine. In 1983, the internet was under development, so we made frequent visits to the public library to learn about these countries. Through peace organizations, we identified other sources of information and assistance. For the Middle Eastern countries, we wrote to embassies to request permission to walk as a group through their territory.

While in Philadelphia, Richard Attenborough's *Gandhi* came to movie theaters. Excited to catch the first showing of this epic about the prophet of nonviolence, Dean and I walked six miles to a downtown cinema. Block after block after block was a desert of vacant lots and boarded-up houses. The acres of blight were evidence of America's failed policies. Intermittently, Dean and I saw small groups of men huddled around fires kindled in rusted trash cans. What had been miles of vibrant neighborhoods showed the aftermath of white flight and society's abandonment of people living in poverty.

The movie was not only inspiring, but certain scenes were absolutely thrilling. The one that sent energy coursing through my body was the Salt March in which Gandhi led hundreds and then thousands of his supporters across 240 miles to the sea and, in defiance of the British authorities, made salt by evaporating salt water, thus avoiding the tax the British imposed on salt. Having recently walked across the U.S., I knew how invigorating and transformative walking for a cause could be. This was not just a well-made film about a historical figure. Walking to relieve poverty by abolishing nuclear weapons was my life.

The film also depicted the harsh poverty that gripped most of the people of India. As Dean and I emerged from the theater and back out onto the streets of Philadelphia, I immediately connected India's poverty and the bleak urban landscape. So much human misery was depressing. With Reagan pressuring NATO allies to ramp up their military spending, I wondered if we would see similar scenes in Western Europe.

We didn't have to wait long—our flight to Europe was scheduled for the end of February. The second half of our adventure was about to begin.

6 – Grand Irish Welcome

A marching band with pilgrims' peace banner.
(Photo by Bill Cox)

Milepost: 3566 – February 1983

On February 21, a few days before leaving for Europe, I noted in my journal how my anxiety had ramped up. What hardships would I face over the next ten months? Could I hack it? The worst of it was feeling like I didn't belong anywhere—being constantly uprooted with no place to call home. The previous weekend, I had gone up to New York City for a meeting and then out to Long Island to give a presentation. The rest of the year would be spent walking across Europe and the Middle East. I had become a vagabond—the thing I had dreaded the most before the walk began. But later that day, I realized I felt fully alive. Being on this epic pilgrimage was a blessed adventure—made profound by our mission for peace.

On February 25, ten months until Christmas, we flew to Europe to begin the second half. Since we wanted to maximize our time in English-speaking countries, we planned to walk through Ireland, Northern Ireland, Scotland, and England before setting foot on the continent. Our first stop was Dublin where the Irish Jesuits hosted us in Rathfarnham Castle. While sightseeing in Dublin, I was struck by the different colored doors of the houses, which were mostly constructed of gray stone.

Since the entire core group had not been together since November, we spent two weeks getting reacquainted. Half of our time in Dublin was spent learning about the European peace movement that was protesting the deployment of U.S. nuclear weapons (Pershing II and ground-launched cruise missiles), slated for late 1983.

During our orientation, on March 8, President Reagan gave a major speech to the National Association of Evangelicals, declaring the Soviet Union was "an evil empire" and "the focus of evil in the modern world."

European leaders were caught between millions of protesters in the streets calling for nuclear disarmament and their NATO commitments to base American nuclear missiles in Western Europe. Even in neutral, non-nuclear Ireland, we felt international tensions rise.

During the rest of our time in Dublin, we were briefed by a bishop, staff from Pax Christi Ireland, and others on "The Troubles," referring to the Protestant-Catholic conflict that had claimed 2,417 victims by the end of 1982. We spent a day at a farm run by the Glencree Centre for Peace and Reconciliation that gave Catholic and Protestant youth an opportunity to know each other as human persons rather than members of conflicted communities. Since we would spend a week walking through Northern Ireland, our safety depended on a clear understanding of the situation. There were many tripwires that could spark trouble. One basic vocabulary lesson was the name of certain towns. For example, Protestants who were loyal to the British crown used Londonderry to refer to Northern Ireland's second-largest city. Catholics called it Derry.

Residents of Northern Ireland were also divided in their choice of passport. For Protestants, they opted for British passports. Many of the Catholics I met in Northern Ireland carried passports as citizens of the Republic of Ireland.

The day before we began walking in Ireland, I stayed in Cork with a man in his thirties who lived in a modest but comfortable house. It was my introduction to the simple life most Irish had in the years before the 1990s: he had no phone in his house. To use a phone, he had to walk a block to the nearest payphone. While he wasn't as poor as the Travellers (Irish nomads), his standard of living was significantly lower than the average American at the time.

But what the Irish lacked in consumer goods, they more than made up for it in the enthusiastic welcome that they lavished on us during our two-week sojourn through the Republic. The Saturday before beginning the European leg of the pilgrimage, George was interviewed on the *Late, Late Show* with Gay Byrne, the Johnny Carson of Ireland. The show was the most popular program on Irish television—three-quarters of the country tuned in each week.

We set out from Cork on St. Patrick's Day. As a result of George's fifteen-minute appearance on the *Late, Late Show*, we were given the red-carpet treatment. This included meetings with the Lord Mayors in Dublin, Cork, and Dundalk, nearly daily parades welcoming us into towns with brass bands, bagpipes and drums, hundreds of schoolchildren playing tin whistles, and talent shows complete with step dancing. Jack recalled he was given so many whiskeys one night at a pub that he had to dump out the last one.

I was surprised how quickly being back on the road brought back the exhaustion I experienced those first trying weeks in the U.S. An ocean and a continent now separated me from the Pacific Northwest—I felt isolated. On the second day of walking in Ireland, I wrote in my journal, "Am I wasting my time and talents? I don't want to continue on the walk. If I leave, will I feel that I've failed?" I recognized how difficult leaving would be for me and the other pilgrims.

As the group started off on the third walking day in Ireland, I called out to Jack, "Can I talk with you?"

"Sure, Jim. Ah, isn't walking in Ireland grand? Have you ever seen such green fields?"

"Very true. It's obvious how it became known as the Emerald Isle. But I am having a surprisingly rough time of it. It's hard for me to relate to the expanded core group, and then there are scores of new people we meet every day. Being always on the go is draining me of energy."

"I'm sorry you're struggling again. What's eating you?"

"I feel much as I did during that first month after starting in Kansas City. It's hard for me to do without much control over my life. I'd rather have a job and a place of my own. I'd like to know when my next shower is going to be. I'm having those doubts again about whether I could do more for peace back home rather than just walking."

"I am beginning to understand you better now. I can see why you enjoyed working at the television station. There were all those sophisticated machines to manipulate, and your day was filled with mental distractions. This walk is about as far removed from that control room as I could imagine."

"True enough, Jack. It might be a great feat to walk to Bethlehem, but I feel like an astronaut on a spacewalk who's running out of oxygen. Last night, I felt very close to burning out. I don't know how long I can hang on."

"I get it that someone like you finds it hard to give up control. Technology masks our essential nakedness before God. To be intimate with our Creator or any loved one entails surrendering. Do you know that the word Muslim means one who submits to God? This is the wisdom of all the great religions. By ourselves, we are never complete. It is only in giving of ourselves to others that we experience fulfillment."

"That reminds me of that documentary on Mother Teresa. She said, 'Love until it hurts.' That led me to quit television and join the Jesuit Volunteer Corps. But why does it have to hurt so much?"

"It's part of the ultimate paradox. Jesus talks about it in the Gospels. 'Those who want to save their life will lose it, and those who lose their life will save it.' In surrendering ourselves, we triumph. This is not how the world thinks, but the path of sacrifice brings authentic joy."

That afternoon, after covering fifteen miles, our pilgrim group neared Cahir. Hundreds of townspeople came out to walk the final miles with us. They had a fruit and juice stand set up for us. In another mile, the town's brass band (including bagpipes) joined, turning the last stretch into a parade. Soon, a troop of Girl Scouts entered the throng. Shopkeepers came outside to cheer us on as we passed. Cahir's enthusiasm swept us along. School children lining the streets clamored for our autographs. My doubts evaporated as this small town welcomed us as heroes.

The evening's program was an amazing collaboration—pilgrims shared about the perils of nuclear weapons and showed the Maryknoll film, *Gods of Metal*, while the townsfolk treated us to Irish music and dancing. One song I remember was a tribute to the forty shades of green from Cork to Larne, which, coincidentally, described our route across the Emerald Isle. The high school girls presented a play about peace.

Later that night, I sat on a bed in a small cubicle in a boarding school and journaled, "What a difference a day can make! As low as I was last night, I am as high tonight, sky high! God, this pilgrimage is a gift and I thank you for giving it to me—help [me] to be worthy of it."

My doubts and fears returned from time to time. I desperately longed for an intimate relationship with a woman. I yearned for more control over my life. So how did I find the strength to remain on the road?

There were three main factors. The first was my relationship with God. The pilgrimage was an incredible opportunity for me to grow and mature. From somewhere inside me, I surrendered myself to God. In being a pilgrim, I relinquished all control to God. It both hurt and freed me.

The second factor was my close bonds with my fellow pilgrims—forged over the past year and thousands of miles. I didn't want to let them down or give them any reason to doubt their own participation in the walk. I didn't want to do anything that would weaken our peace witness. The need for disarmament was too urgent.

Finally, I delighted in the physical act of walking. There was a hypnotic rhythm to the swinging of my arms with each stride. In spending most days exposed to the elements, the undulations of the land imprinted on me, I slowly felt at one with nature. Getting up each day and rejoining the road for peace, laying my body down for nuclear disarmament at a crucial point in world history, these daily decisions remained monumental to me. Accepting all the pain and uncertainty was my way of paying the price for peace. All three of these, like a three-legged stool, provided me with enough strength to go beyond what I thought I could endure.

On March 23, Reagan announced his Strategic Defense Initiative (SDI) or "Star Wars" as labeled by the media. We were in Portlaoise when the news hit the Irish papers. That night I stayed with Seamus, a man about fifty years old. I have a clear memory of that house because the back of it looked out on Ireland's highest-security prison, flooded with light all night, surrounded by high walls and barbed wire.

During a dinner that included lamb, Seamus inquired, "Now, Jim, can you help me understand your president's pie-in-the-sky idea? I mean, how can more weapons ever make the world safer?"

"Thank you for giving me this wonderful meal and a place to sleep tonight. As for Reagan, I'm scratching my head the same as you are. I've no idea where this scheme came from. It's obviously aimed at Europeans in the hopes NATO will agree to base American nuclear missiles later this year. But it would be much safer to eliminate nuclear weapons."

"What I can't fathom is how you Americans can accept paying such high taxes for this preposterous idea."

"I don't think that most Americans will buy into Reagan's dream. As our pilgrimage group walked across the U.S. last year, we found enthusiastic support for freezing the arms race. The average American wants peace just as much as you."

"I'm not sure about that, mate. Your Congress is bankrolling Reagan's huge expansion of nuclear weapons. Our view here is that Americans are dangerously ill-informed."

"You've a point there, Seamus. As a nation, we've not invested enough effort in diplomacy."

Based on my discussion with Seamus that night and others in the following days, Reagan's speech didn't win over any Europeans. The Irish reaction to Reagan's idea was decidedly negative. Instead of placating U.S. allies, the speech only magnified people's alarm about the burgeoning nuclear arsenals.

The U.S. leadership seemed blind to Europe's reality and how strapped individual and national budgets were. Reagan proposed spending billions on something that was more science fiction than any serious peace effort. With our route through the UK, France, Italy, and Greece, we would be spending most of the next six months in NATO countries. We wondered how well we would handle the controversies which lay ahead.

Most Irish families struggled to make ends meet, so we could only guess at their sacrifice when our host families splurged and welcomed us with hearty dinners complete with roasted lamb. Was this the only meal with meat that week? Or was it the only serving of meat for the month? That we were so warmly welcomed testified to their generosity as well as their fondness for America.

Indoor spaces had a bone-numbing chill to them as any kind of heating was expensive, or "dear" as they termed it. The Irish all wore thick sweaters inside their homes. They shared with us their astonishment at

American television where actors often wore short-sleeved shirts inside, even in winter with snow falling outside. The Irish shook their heads in disbelief and couldn't understand how Americans could waste so much energy or afford such high heating bills. Irish bedrooms were even chillier. But each host cared for us by placing a hot water bottle underneath a thick comforter.

In the village of Trim, we stayed at a school run by the Sisters of Mercy. It was there that Jack received a letter from the Jesuit community in Damascus, Syria. Back in Philadelphia, Jack wrote to them for advice about walking through Syria. In an alarming tone, the Jesuits warned against venturing into Syria at all, most especially on foot. As if to drive the point home, an accompanying note explained that the letter had been smuggled out of Syria.

Given how stern the warning was, it's amazing we continued to consider the Turkey-Syria-Jordan route as a possibility. I was one of the strongest proponents of that option because it provided the longest, least-interrupted walking path to Bethlehem. I wanted our pilgrimage experience to match that of the first century as much as possible.

But the letter from Damascus had an immediate impact. After lunch the next day, the core group held our weekly business meeting. Pam described it as "uneasy." After discussing other items, Alice proposed researching alternative routes through the Middle East—perhaps one through Yugoslavia and Greece before arriving in Israel and the Occupied West Bank. Janet, Anne, and I now had to research a second route and another country—one ruled by communists.

On Sundays in Ireland, we split up in pairs, going to different churches to give short presentations about our pilgrimage. Hundreds of people attended each Mass, crowding into every pew. Parents nudged their small children to scrunch together and make room for others. Everyone listened attentively to what we were doing and why. After Mass, they poured out of the church and into the parish social hall, giving us an opportunity to share more details and listen to their perspectives.

Spring's numerous showers deposited silvery drops on the grass that glinted during frequent sun breaks. There is a saying in Ireland that there are four seasons in every day. To me, with the squalls marching across the island from the North Atlantic, it seemed there were four seasons in every hour: a period of vigorous rain would be followed by forty-mile-per-hour winds that drove cold hail into our cheeks. After a brief snow flurry, the wind would hustle the clouds over the horizon and the sun would return, bringing warmth. Such variety invigorated our walking.

As we walked into the towns of Callan, Trim, and Dundalk, we were swept up by the wholehearted welcome of the townspeople. Each town's marching band uplifted us and eased the last miles of the day. Hundreds of schoolchildren cheered us on, holding signs reading, "Cead Mile Failte" (A Hundred Thousand Welcomes). Hundreds of broad smiles lined the sidewalks. They greeted us as heroes, with children asking for our autographs. It reminded me of newsreels from World War II when Allied troops were welcomed with happiness and relief by villagers liberated from the Nazis. We were astounded by the enthusiasm and generosity of the Irish.

With all the smiles, gifts, and parades, Ireland was by far the most welcoming country along our route. We never heard anything but words of encouragement, wonder, and gratitude. I began telling my fellow pilgrims, "If any other country tops Ireland in hospitality, we'll settle down and never get to Bethlehem."

It seemed like the only person in Ireland who we didn't meet was the Prime Minister (in Gaelic, Taoiseach). However, I did meet with the sister of Charles Haughey, who had been the prime minister twice: 1979-1981 and 1982. A brother of theirs was a Jesuit priest at Gonzaga University in Spokane where my mother was a switchboard operator. What's more, Fr. Haughey lived next door to my parents! So, when I was in Ireland, I called and arranged a brief meeting one afternoon with their sister Eithne Haughey as the pilgrimage passed through Dundalk.

One day, Fred and I were walking along a quaint Irish country lane hemmed in on each side by hedgerows six feet high. We heard a car approaching from behind when suddenly a lorry appeared around the curve just ahead.

"Dive, Fred!" I yelled.

We plastered ourselves onto the scratchy wall of branches. The whoosh of air from the passing lorry pressed us further into the hedgerow. My heart jumped into my throat.

With our legs shaking, Fred and I carefully disentangled ourselves from the hedgerow. "Whew!" Fred exclaimed. "What just happened?"

I staggered back onto the roadway. "I can't believe it—only a few scratches. You okay, Fred?"

"Yeah, I'm fine. Wow, that was close."

How was it that we had not been hit? Equally amazing, the two vehicles had not collided. I looked down the road. The truck had disappeared. Turning my head in the other direction, I saw the car 200 feet down the road and backing up.

The car pulled alongside us, and the driver got out. Shaking his head, he looked at us in disbelief, "I don't believe it. I thought you two were goners."

Fred said, "Thank you for coming back to check on us. We are grateful nobody was hurt." As the car drove off, Fred and I started walking again toward that day's destination.

That was the closest brush with death I experienced on the walk. Getting struck by a car was an ever-present hazard, and several times cars nearly brushed one of my hands as they raced by at highway speeds. Each of us accepted the risks, adopting the attitude of those who go off to war—we had gone off to peace.

7 – A Week in a War Zone

Good Friday, 1983, in Northern Ireland.

Milepost: 3796 – April 1, 1983

On Good Friday, exactly one year on the Christian calendar since setting off, we walked across our first international border. Intellectually, our minds knew the political significance. But beyond a few border security buildings and related signage, the countryside looked much the same: the same climate, same flora and fauna, same air.

As we had done the previous year, we prayed the Stations of the Cross during our walk from Dundalk to Newry, a total of thirteen miles. We prayed half of the Stations in the Republic and half in Northern Ireland. A group of about 150 supporters accompanied us, a mix of Catholics and Protestants from both sides of the border. Jim Thorn, a local carpenter, made a five-foot oak cross for us to carry as we processed. As we marked the suffering and death of Jesus, we reflected on the tragic violence that had rocked Northern Ireland since 1969. More than 2,400 people had been killed by 1983 in the conflict between Protestants and Catholics.

The gray skies threatened rain—a sharp contrast to the bright sun one year earlier. The gloomy weather and the deaths of so many made the day feel heavy. The first day of our pilgrimage had seemed like a wedding. This one was more like a funeral.

I felt my gut tighten. The guards wore thick bulletproof vests and toted automatic rifles. At the security checkpoint, guards scrutinized our passports and searched our bags. The authorities were especially alert to any terrorist who might try to sneak in with our peace contingent. The guardhouse had thick, tinted glass. I noticed the other pilgrims tense up. Nobody smiled. We wondered what the next week in the North would be like. For most of us, it was our first taste of a war zone.

Walking through Northern Ireland in 1983 certainly entailed risks. We were an ecumenical peace group traversing a region sharply divided along sectarian lines. Both sides were heavily armed, and tens of thousands of British troops occupied the territory.

I had a typical American understanding of the conflict before I crossed the border: Protestant loyalists desperately clung to their Britishness while Catholics yearned for justice after centuries of oppression. What I discovered on the ground was much more complex. The paramilitaries on both sides preyed on the suffering of both Catholic and Protestant underclasses for their own political objectives. Only low-income neighborhoods were segregated along religious lines, enmeshed in poverty and hatred. The Provisional Irish Republican Army (IRA or Provos) drew inspiration and military training from Marxist and Leninist terrorists. Some pilgrims visited the Sinn Fein (the IRA's political wing) office in Belfast and were surprised to see posters emblazoned with the hammer and sickle. When more well-to-do families provided us hospitality in safer neighborhoods, we discovered that Catholics lived alongside Protestants, as in most residential neighborhoods throughout the United States.

There were still differences. The Protestant family I stayed with in Belfast gave me directions to get to where other pilgrims were staying. I had no problem following their directions, walking there on a bright sunny afternoon. After eating dinner there, a Catholic offered to drive me back. I gave him the address and described the two-mile route I had taken. His brow creased and his jaw tightened as he considered the directions.

"I can take you there but not by the way you came. Go ahead, get in my car." As we drove along dark streets, he explained, "Because of the Troubles, the security forces cordon off certain streets after nightfall to isolate sectarian areas. That is why I couldn't follow the same route you took this afternoon. 'Tis the reality of living in Belfast."

Every night in the North, I stayed with Protestant families. Like my interactions with Catholics that week, my interactions with Protestants were eye-opening. Their generous hospitality still had a distinctive Irish flavor, but it was clearly strained by the atmosphere of violence and hatred.

One family who hosted me invited a friend of theirs over one evening. Amazingly, he worked as a guard at the Maze (also called Long Kesh), the high-security prison on the outskirts of Lisburn. About 60% of the prisoners were Catholic, the rest Protestant. Nearly all the guards were Protestant. Two years before, ten Catholic prisoners died during a hunger strike at the Maze. Bobby Sands was the first to die (May 5, 1981). Taking turns to join the strike, nine others starved themselves over the next four months. The strikers demanded that the British treat Catholic inmates as political prisoners.

I had followed news accounts of the hunger strike, and now I was talking with one of the guards. Over the next hour, he patiently answered my questions about what his job was like. "Aye, these jobs are among the best in Ulster," he said. "A man can easily provide for his family. But if you happen to be Catholic, it's a problem."

I said, "But I thought sectarian discrimination was now illegal."

"Right you are. And there are a few Catholics who work with me. But they are often marked men."

"What do you mean?"

"You see, any Catholic foolish enough to get a job at the Maze risks being visited by the Provos [members of the Provisional IRA]. They make it clear that if he doesn't quit his job, either he or a family member will be kneecapped, or worse."

"I've heard about kneecapping. What exactly is it?"

"It's when a paramilitary enforcer fires a bullet into the back of a guy's knee. His limp marks him as a traitor."

"What happens if the Catholic guard doesn't take the hint—because his family is so poor?"

"The Provos will do whatever it takes to enforce their rule. I've seen family businesses, like pubs, get torched. The IRA and other Catholic paramilitaries are cruel and relentless. But to be honest, the UVF [Ulster Volunteer Force], the UDA [Ulster Defense Association]—the paramilitaries that control the Protestant ghettos—are no angels. Their methods are just as brutal."

That night as I lay in a comfortable Protestant bed provided by my host, my mind sifted through the new insights. I tried to make sense of all the complexities, nuances, and paradoxes of a war zone. The tall walls of hatred were suffocating, even as I succumbed to merciful sleep.

In a small van, our Pax Christi Ireland organizers gave us a tour of the Shankill and other Belfast ghettos where paramilitaries ruled their respective turfs like so many gangs or drug lords. The endemic poverty was rich soil for extremist groups.

Depressing. Block by block, mile after mile of decrepit housing. Here and there were charred remnants of firebombings. At some windows, weary people peered through slits in their drapes, assessing whether they dared risk a dash to the grocery store to restock.

Suddenly, a dark green Saracen (an armored vehicle used by the British army) appeared on the road to the right of the van. As it passed, I saw the rear doors were pinned back and four soldiers with automatic rifles were poised to jump out when given the order. On the other side of the Saracen was a grassy hillside. Looking uphill, I saw a few scattered trees, still barren, and broken branches littering the ground. A young boy, no more than seven or eight, ran to one of the branches. Grasping it with both of his small hands, his body bent with the weight of the substantial branch. With all his might, he hurled it at the Saracen. It crashed on the road, just shy of its mark. Astoundingly, the soldiers didn't even flinch. Through this brief and reckless act, I glimpsed the hatred that boiled in this boy's defiant heart.

In those few moments, I better understood the daunting task of restoring peace in communities wracked by years of violence and injustice.

Because of the threat of car bombs, no vehicle traffic was allowed to enter Belfast's downtown shopping district. Every pedestrian entering the area had to pass through a metal detector, and each handbag and backpack was searched by hand. Since nearly all the security staff were Protestant, our tour guides told us that Catholic women would often put broken glass in the bottom of their handbags so the security personnel would cut their hands on the shards while searching the bags. Such was the hatred between two Christian communities during the decades of the Troubles.

After just a week, I felt relieved to leave Northern Ireland and board a ferry from Larne to Stranraer on the Scottish Coast.

8 – Scotland & England: More Nuclear Subs, More Rain, and a Princess

Buddhist peace pagoda in Milton Keynes, England.

Milepost: 3860 – April 8, 1983

After the ferry docked in Scotland, we boarded a train to Glasgow. While seeking to exit the station, I asked an attendant for directions. He began speaking to me, but my ears failed me. His Scottish brogue was so thick I couldn't understand a word he said.

On our rest day, we drove the van to the Faslane peace camp, roughly forty miles northwest of Glasgow, near the British submarine base. The peace campers were protesting the United Kingdom's nuclear missile submarine force. At the time, the British had older Poseidon missiles and submarines, but preparations were underway to deploy their own Trident missiles and subs in the 1990s.

The day we visited Faslane was April 9, one year since we had left the Bangor Trident Base. Here we were, next to another Trident base on another continent. Geographically, the two bases are strikingly similar. Both are situated along a narrow arm of water. Faslane lies on the Gare Loch which opens into the Firth of Clyde. Bangor sits along Hood Canal, a branch of the Puget Sound.

Climbing out of the van, we crossed a strip of dried mud in front of several trailers. Farther on was an improvised shack with plastic sheeting for walls and a dirt floor. Inside, a small fire crackled in a rusting steel barrel. A dozen dilapidated chairs surrounded the fire. Two of the peace campers, Louise and her husband Les, seemed to be the connecting force for an otherwise anarchic community.

Later, carrying two large peace banners, we walked a short distance along the highway to the south gate of the submarine base, glimpsing the waters of Gare Loch. We gathered in a small circle to the right of the closed gate. Through thin clouds, faint sunshine highlighted the white steel fencing of the base. A stiff, chilly breeze billowed our blue banner and swirled our long yellow one. Mary Jude and Laurie led us in prayer. On the other side of the eight-foot fence, we could see the tops of several buildings on the base. I reflected on being half a world away from the Trident base near Seattle and realized the far reach of U.S. nuclear weapons technology, here in an isolated cove on the Scottish Coast. The weapons of mass destruction at both bases endangered the entire planet.

Later that day, during the weekly business meeting, several pilgrims voiced reservations about walking through Syria and Yugoslavia. After brainstorming other alternatives, we agreed to study three routes for our pilgrimage after Rome:

The new possibility entailed walking through Greece, crossing the Mediterranean Sea to Alexandria, Egypt, and trekking across the Sinai Peninsula to approach Bethlehem from the south. This would fulfill some pilgrims' dreams of retracing the steps of the Hebrew people in their exodus from Egypt (though I worried about finding enough water in the desert).

The second option would take us to Yugoslavia which was then still one country under communist rule. After walking south through Greece, we would cross to Haifa, Israel. This route included walking in both Israel and the Occupied West Bank.

Our original plan would traverse Greece, walk along Turkey's Mediterranean Coast, through Syria and Jordan, and finally approach Bethlehem from the east. This would provide the longest walking distance.

Over the next four months, finding consensus on the route would prove elusive, threatening to split our community apart.

During April, the United States Navy's Pacific Fleet conducted its largest exercises since the Second World War in the North Pacific near the Soviet Union's Kamchatka Peninsula. Forty ships, including three aircraft carriers, took part. At least six aircraft violated Soviet airspace as part of the new aggressive posture of Reagan's Pentagon. On April 18, in the volatile Middle East, a massive explosion destroyed the U.S. Embassy in Beirut, killing fifty-seven people. The world seemed to be sliding into greater violence.

Great Britain's cold, wet spring took a toll on our pilgrim community, many people suffering bad colds or flu symptoms. One day, as I was walking with Jack, he shared his concern about George: "His color hasn't looked good since we left Cork. I think he could well die on the journey."

A few days later, I walked alone through a desolate Scottish moor, silent except for the wind. Suddenly, an explosion of noise obliterated the solitude. Two NATO fighter jets crested the ridge behind me, flying unbelievably low, showering me with the thunder of their afterburners. I jumped and ducked at the same time. I could hardly breathe.

After my heart started beating again, I understood an aspect of the Cold War that most Americans never experienced. NATO and the Soviet Bloc both bulged with technologically advanced war machines. The guns were loaded. The triggers cocked. Normally, we were geographically removed from this reality. But not now, and not for the rest of the pilgrimage.

Milepost: 3981 – April 17, 1983

On the day we crossed Hadrian's Wall (the Roman border between Scotland and England), Janet and Bookda boarded a train to London, where they planned to gather more information about the Mideast route. They planned to visit the embassies of Turkey, Syria, and Jordan.

Meanwhile, we were so cold—showered with snow, hail, and sleet. The calendar said it was supposed to be spring, but the weather was stuck in winter. As we trudged through wet snow, sheep bleated in the white-coated fields. Even as our teeth chattered, we marveled at the newborn lambs. It seemed like a strange time to be giving birth. Shepherds rushed from field to field, helping ewes in distress.

In northern England, we spent several nights in community centers where the only source of heat was coin-operated electric heaters mounted on the ceiling. Precious little warmth made its way to the floor where we lay shivering in our sleeping bags. As the group's treasurer, I was responsible for plugging coins into the heaters. I was awakened at least every two hours by pleas from the other pilgrims for more heat. I feared running out of coins before morning. I felt relief when a new day dawned.

Our impact in England was significantly diminished by the failure of our regional organizers, who did not give enough advance notice to the towns along our route. With only a day or two to prepare, the townspeople responded generously by providing food and shelter but lacked enough time to publicize events. Slapped together at the last minute, our meetings drew thin turnouts. It was frustrating to miss these opportunities, knowing that England was our last English-speaking country.

The disappointment felt heavier because of the incessant rain. The combination of wind-driven rain and the gritty spray from speeding trucks defeated our rain gear. Our drippy experience was confirmed by banner headlines displayed at news kiosks: "Wettest Spring on Record." Thankfully, many gracious pub owners took pity on us and allowed us to bring our lunch food into their establishments so we could eat out of the rain. Warm pints of ale never tasted so good.

Due west of Harrogate in North Yorkshire, the U.S. National Security Agency (NSA) operated the largest intelligence-gathering installation outside the States. Ostensibly a Royal Air Force base, the Menwith Hill site is dotted with two dozen white domes; from high above, it may look like a golfer's practice green. On our rest day, a bunch of us piled into the van and drove to this highly classified electronic surveillance (i.e., spy) base. Buffeted by a raw wind, we huddled together at the main entrance for a short vigil. Even though hundreds of Americans were based there, I felt alienated from those on the other side of the fence.

At our evening program in Ripon, George declared, "My purpose on this pilgrimage, across these thousands of miles, is to convince people that we must get rid of war. We cannot dis-invent nuclear weapons. We must adopt a whole new way of thinking. As President Kennedy said, 'If we don't end war, war will end us.' We must stop glamorizing war."

Then Laurie rose and shared, "One of my uncles was only seventeen years old when he was killed during the Battle of the Bulge. I am glad to now be making a sacrifice for peace just as so many have made sacrifices for war."

A fortnight later, we visited the International Centre for Reconciliation at Coventry Cathedral. Before the altar, in the charred shell of the original cathedral (destroyed by Nazi bombers), we all lined up for a group photo. It was the first time that all nineteen of us were together in one place since we'd started walking in Europe. And it would be the last time the core group was together for the rest of the journey.

Just then, our local contact rushed in and asked for Maureen Casey, the only pilgrim who had children. Maureen had a phone call that no one wants to receive. Maureen's son-in-law was calling from a hospital in Atlanta. Her daughter, Lisa, had been in a bad auto accident and was near death. "How soon can you fly back to Atlanta?" he asked her.

The question stunned Maureen. It was the day before Mother's Day. Given the seriousness of her daughter's condition, she desperately wanted to be at that hospital. She had been walking so her grandkids could live in a world free of nuclear weapons. Now her dream of pilgrimaging across Europe evaporated.

After making a quick round of goodbyes, Maureen was whisked off to the airport. Nobody knew when we would see her again.

After walking two more days, we entered Milton Keynes which provided another chance to connect with Buddhist monks of the Nipponzan Myohoji, the same order that had walked with us near Seattle. A peace pagoda had been completed at Milton Keynes in 1980, like the one planned for the Ground Zero Center for Nonviolent Action neighboring the Bangor base. In Milton Keynes, two monks, Saka Maki and Handa, and a nun, Nora, met us on the road and guided us to the beautiful pagoda.

It was wonderful to experience again the rhythmic energy of their drumming. The soothing cadence of their chant, "Na Mu Myo Ho Ren Ge Kyo" (In Respect of All Life), felt like a balm to our rain-weary bodies.

Arriving at the peace pagoda, I marveled at the gentle curves of the dome, encircled by a broad promenade. On top of the dome was a dark spire, capped with a large gold ornament. In front, a large niche held a standing Buddha, shimmering in gold. The pagoda was surrounded by a field of grass—leaving no doubt about the pagoda being the center of attention. A half circle of trees provided a beautiful backdrop for it.

The founder of Nipponzan Myohoji, Nichidatsu Fujii, was inspired to start his order after meeting Mahatma Gandhi in 1931. Fujii dedicated his band of monks to promoting nonviolence. Now, there are over eighty peace pagodas around the world, including ones in Hiroshima and Nagasaki. Other monks began constructing a pagoda near the Bangor Trident Base in 1981, but it was destroyed by arson the next year, less than two months after our pilgrimage began. After two decades, the monks restarted the project and expect to dedicate the pagoda in 2025.

Our solidarity with this band of Buddhist monks reiterated the centrality of peace in each of the world's great religions. That this order of monks began in Japan helped connect us with the cities devastated by the first atomic bombs. As the roadside resounded with their beating drums, I imagined the wind spreading our dream of peace.

Over the next two days, we visited two nearby peace camps, Molesworth and Greenham Common. The joint U.S.-UK bases were slated to house 160 nuclear-tipped, ground-launched cruise missiles by the end of 1983. When we arrived at Greenham Common, the scene was chaotic. Police were dragging several women away and forcing them into vans with barred windows. Unlike the other peace camps, the campers at Greenham Common were all women. At the other bases, the campers were content to simply camp near the entrances. The women of Greenham Common used a variety of protest methods to invite arrest, attracting much media attention.

We continued to gather information on our route after Rome. We had already received written permission from Syria, Jordan, and Israel to walk through their countries. We had yet to hear back from Turkey. During our weekly organizing meetings, a member of the route committee provided an update. We hoped with enough information, a group consensus would emerge. During our visit to the peace pagoda, Nora shared her own experience of being in Turkey. She counseled us to find a different route—the women would risk harassment or worse.

On May 14, we walked twenty-three miles from Dunstable to London. The pouring rain drenched us by noon. Continuing in the afternoon, we only got wetter. Several pilgrims considered it the wettest day of the journey. The rain magnified the back and leg pain that Jack had been suffering for several weeks.

During the two nights we stayed in London, I received hospitality from John Lahr, his wife Anthea, and their son Chris. John was the son of Bert Lahr, the actor who portrayed the Cowardly Lion in *The Wizard of Oz*. The walls of their London flat were festooned with Richard Avedon photographs of his father and other Hollywood luminaries. Another brush with celebrities happened when we walked into Canterbury. The streets were lined with thousands of people waiting for Princess Diana. A large red helicopter flew overhead and set down in a nearby field. A short while later, a black limousine drove by. Seated in the back seat, Princess Diana waved, delighting those lining the streets. Two days later, we walked from Canterbury Cathedral to the white cliffs of Dover overlooking the English Channel. I wondered how walking through non-English speaking countries would impact our mission and community.

9 – France & Switzerland: Approaching Burnout

Vigil outside United Nations, Geneva.

Milepost: 4399 – May 23, 1983

After the ferry docked in Dieppe, we stepped onto the continent of Europe. These lands had seen so many wars over the centuries. As we began our five weeks of walking in France, we noticed that many older buildings had small pockmarks on the exterior walls. These were usually one to two inches in diameter and about half an inch deep. They had been made by bullets in World War II, four decades earlier.

A typical day on the walk was a whirlwind of activity. In France, it was more like a tornado. Gerard Daechsel volunteered to be our organizer for France. He was an American expat who had been part of the 1960s Walk to Moscow and had settled down in France. Gerard was a man on a mission—he was determined to maximize our walk's impact, even setting up breakfast meetings with mayors. During our five weeks crossing France, Gerard never left any stone unturned when it came to speaking opportunities. Hardly an hour went by without some sort of interview or event.

There was one afternoon when several of us arrived early at our host community. There was nothing scheduled, and several of us relaxed by tossing around a Frisbee in the courtyard outside the community center. A few minutes later, Gerard walked by.

"What do you think you're doing?" Gerard yelled.

"We're just relaxing a bit," Steve explained.

"You can't. You should be folding brochures or something useful."

"Gerard, you can't be serious. We've been eating, breathing, even sleeping disarmament for more than a year. We've walked over 4,000 miles through all kinds of weather. We need to relax occasionally."

Gerard set his jaw and ground his teeth. He shook his head, turned sharply on his heels, and walked away.

We couldn't believe it. How could he be so driven as to not allow time to relax? I felt sad for him. Being so intent on only one thing must have left him very dry inside. No wonder his body seemed so stiff all the time.

On another afternoon, Gerard dragged some students from a military academy off the street and asked us to present an impromptu program. The students were so impressed by the pilgrimage that they skipped dinner and violated their bedtime curfew to learn more about our experience of walking for peace.

But Gerard's wall-to-wall scheduling drained us. Anne confided to Fr. Jack, "I am so tired that I am close to crying. There is no time to relax—there's just constant engagement with people." Additionally, the strain of not being able to speak French showed that we would need to rely more on each other for the rest of the way. Laurie was the lone pilgrim fluent in French, having spent her junior year in Aix-en-Provence (southern France). Thus, she carried the additional burden of always being asked to translate.

When we stayed in people's homes, we felt the language barrier acutely. George wrote about one of his overnights with a French family: "I experienced culture and language shock. This will be a great problem for our group especially in Near East. Mental tension growing in me and group, was very tired tonight … real torture trying to explain [to his hosts] what I wanted."

On top of the other strains, I was beset with my worst bout of hay fever in years. I had been plagued with hay fever since childhood. As a boy in Chewelah, there was an alfalfa field a half block from our house, and each spring it brought suffering. In France, the itchy eyes and sinus pressure made me miserable. Abundant spring rains had caused severe flooding in France. As the waters receded, flowers bloomed in the warm June air.

The older people we met shared their stories of what it was like under Nazi occupation. For years, they lived in fear under the Gestapo. They recalled how Jews and others of their neighbors had been crammed into railroad cars and transported to Auschwitz, Buchenwald, and other cogs in the Final Solution. They shared memories of bombs exploding and tanks blasting through the narrow streets of their towns and villages. Some had joined the Resistance. They whispered about others who had collaborated with the enemy.

They took us to military cemeteries where allied soldiers were buried and expressed their gratitude for all that the United States and Canada had done to defeat Hitler. The graves gave silent witness to the human toll of war. I gazed out on the expanse of green grass, dotted with white grave markers, row upon row upon row. So many dead—such eerie silence. Observing some of the grave markers, I noticed the birth and death years on the markers. Nearly all were in their late teens or twenties. I was twenty-eight years old then and realized I had already lived longer than most of the ones buried.

Growing up, my Aunt Jo had told me about my uncle Clarence who served in the Marines during World War I. By the time he got to Europe, the Armistice had been signed, ending the war. Instead of being involved in the fighting, his unit was assigned the grisly task of cleaning up the battlefields. His job included removing bloated bodies left behind. I cannot imagine the stench.

I thought of my dad. During the Second World War, he dropped bombs on France and other countries across northern Europe. I wondered how many of his mates had not come back. Perhaps one of his classmates was buried in a cemetery I had visited. Four decades after my dad's warfighting experience, I was walking across the same lands for peace, frequently alongside people from West Germany.

Ten days later, we entered the streets of Paris, on our way to the Arc de Triomphe, which commemorates those who died for France in the French Revolution and the Napoleonic Wars. We had planned to gather under the massive arch for prayer, but security guards wouldn't allow it. They were nervous about any large group near this national symbol.

We lingered around the perimeter of the arch long enough to meet several new guest walkers. Among them was a French Capuchin priest who had heard about our pilgrimage that morning and decided to check us out. Father Benoit Charlamagne was barely five feet tall, wiry, and buzzing with energy. The tip of his left index finger pointed off at an odd angle. His graying hair was unkempt, as was his scraggly beard. His dark eyes sparkled with joy and compassion. This was a priest who was fully alive.

From the Arc de Triomphe, we walked along the Champs Élysées until we crossed onto the Île de la Cité where we stopped in front of the Notre Dame Cathedral. Like centuries of pilgrims before us, we entered to pray.

After three months in Europe, I needed a break from the walk. I found the daily grind of miles, unfamiliar food, close quarters, and constant motion exhausting. I contacted a friend from college who lived near Trier, West Germany. Paris was as close as I would get. As the pilgrimage left Paris, I accepted a ride from Udo, a young German man we met in Ireland. Anne Galisky was also traveling to West Germany to meet with Josef Abileah, a Jewish peace campaigner, in the hopes that he could provide us some good contacts for the Middle East. George rode in the car as well, traveling to make several appearances for Pax Christi Germany.

Shortly after we crossed the Luxembourg-West Germany border, they dropped me off in Trier, which I would later learn was the birthplace of my great-grandfather. My college friend, Loye Berg, was married to Erich, a captain in the U.S. Air Force. A year earlier, I had attended their wedding in Spokane. He had been stationed at Fairchild Air Force Base but was now at the Spangdahlem Air Base, doing aircraft maintenance.

It was my first break since Christmas, and I enjoyed staying in one place for a week. Loye and Erich lived in American housing off base near the quaint village of Herforst. They shopped at the PX (post exchange) on base, stocked with foods that could be found in any supermarket back in the States. Loye and Erich were great hosts and allowed me long periods of solitude so I could unwind.

I felt strange to be benefiting from some perks supplied by the Pentagon while on a break from the peace pilgrimage. I was careful in talking with other Americans I met there and mostly listened. I went to Mass several times at the base chapel.

The break allowed me to see the Cold War from a different perspective. F-4 Phantom jets thundered above as pilots practiced takeoffs and landings while ground crews maintained their operational readiness. The prospect of a Soviet invasion that would begin World War III was ever-present—the base was only 150 miles from East Germany.

In conversations over dinner, Loye and Erich talked about their experience of being stationed in West Germany and their anxieties about the escalating rhetoric being exchanged between the two superpowers. Most surprising was the hardship they faced. All the recruiting ads portrayed overseas assignments in the U.S. armed forces as exciting, even glamorous.

The reality was starkly at odds with the media campaigns. Erich had been deployed at other U.S. bases for six of the past twelve months. Most of the stints were three to six weeks long. The cumulative separation had strained their relationship. They knew several couples with young children who were experiencing marital problems. Children acted out due to the long absences of their fathers. Mothers endured being single parents for half the year. Twelve- to sixteen-hour workdays, living in a foreign country, and the peril of being targeted by terrorists all contributed to the strain on service personnel and their families.

Heightened East-West tensions weighed on everyone. The bellicose rhetoric from the Reagan White House was noticeably shriller than past administrations. The détente of the 1970s was gone. The U.S. had launched its largest military buildup during peacetime.

The Soviet Union's expansion since the Cuban Missile Crisis had brought their nuclear arsenal up to parity with U.S. strategic forces. The newest SS-20 missile worried NATO because of its accuracy and mobility. The vise of two opposing superpowers got tighter each day—U.S. military families based in West Germany were caught in the middle.

With the death of Leonid Brezhnev in November 1982, there was increasing anxiety throughout the world about the stability of Soviet leadership. The median age of the ruling Politburo was seventy. Yuri Andropov replaced Brezhnev as party chairman. Four months later, he suffered kidney failure, beginning a steady decline in his health. He died in early 1984, only fifteen months after Brezhnev's death. Andropov's replacement, Konstantin Chernenko, fared even worse—lasting only thirteen months as head of the Politburo, mostly in poor health and out of the public eye. He was succeeded by Mikhail Gorbachev in 1985.

I used the base library to do more research on the three routes through the Middle East. I read books on Greece, Yugoslavia, Egypt, Turkey, Syria, Jordan, and Israel and wondered which ones we would end up walking through. Each route had its dangers and unknowns. Our group hoped to settle on a route before we reached Geneva—only a few weeks away. I had to rejoin the others and share the additional information. After twelve hours and four different trains, I rendezvoused with the pilgrims in the hilltop town of Vezelay, France.

When I started walking again, tendonitis developed in both knees. I tried to log as many miles as possible, but most days I could only manage six to ten miles before I had to stop and flag down the support van. While I had already suffered tendonitis a few times on the walk, I never had it so bad. Given my week of vacation, this bout was surprising—I thought I was in peak condition. There was no choice but to limp along—another chance for me to surrender control.

At our program in Vezelay, Jack explained, "We walk because the world is on fire, and unless each of us joins in a great bucket brigade, the flames of a holocaust will engulf us. I walk for the children. I walk for their future. We must never give in to the darkness. The greatest way to peace is to believe in it and do something about it."

On the morning of June 19, the core group met about the Mideast route. Janet chaired the meeting while Anne and I reported on the information we found during our visits to West Germany. We discussed the dangers we would face on whichever route we chose. Some pilgrims wondered whether we would be targeted by terrorists. There was the harsh Syrian government and that ominous letter the Jesuits had smuggled out of Damascus. We sought consensus on our post-Rome route, but it eluded us.

That afternoon, we walked to the monastery and retreat center of Taizé. The countryside was a heart-warming green with crops growing fast in the long days of June. Every year, tens of thousands of young people flocked to this Christian monastery for retreats and spiritual renewal. An ecumenical community of monks resides at Taizé, committed to a life of prayer and solidarity with the poor of the world. Unlike most monasteries, the monks take turns living amongst people suffering from abject poverty around the world. By regularly rotating in and out of Taizé, the community maintains contact with impoverished people. This gives their prayer a deep resonance of truth; they walk the talk. Their hearts are formed by sharing in the joys and hopes, the fears and anxieties of people who are victims of consumerism, violence, and neglect.

Several monks greeted us in the village of Taizé and guided us to the monastery, a quarter-mile outside the village. To help us enter Taizé's atmosphere of prayer, they asked us to walk in silence.

The monastery bell beckoned us to prayer in the chapel. The expandable walls were wide open in the warm summer air, accommodating thousands of retreatants who spilled onto the grass. Most retreatants were in their teens or twenties from across Europe. The musical chants shifted from language to language during the verses while the chorus was often in Latin. That so many people from dozens of countries had come together to lift their hearts to God gave me new hope. Peace was possible.

The fellowship continued after leaving the chapel through conversations during the hearty meals. Even after four decades, I can still feel and hear the delightful crunch of the French bread.

Taizé's founder, Brother Roger, made time to meet with us and recounted Taizé's clandestine efforts to connect with Christians and others behind the Iron Curtain. Eastern Europe was in the grip of communism. Millions suffered from religious persecution. Taizé monks visited underground Christian communities.

From the questions we asked, it was obvious how enthralled we were with his community. Brother Roger exhorted us, saying, "Forget Taizé. You cannot stay here. You must return to your homes after Bethlehem. Your place for work is there."

After three days in Taizé, we wound our way through the rugged Rhcne River Valley in southeastern France. Sheer, dark cliffs rose high above our heads on both sides of the narrow highway. Winding back and forth along the road, white water rapids plunged down from the melting snows of the Alps. One day, a youth group from Grenoble joined and led us along narrow goat paths traversing steep alpine slopes covered with thick grasses. While captivated by the spectacular views of snowcapped peaks, I took great care placing my feet—one errant step and I could have tumbled hundreds of feet down the slopes. There were no trees or even small shrubs to arrest a fall.

Returning to the road, we neared the Swiss border—time to bid farewell to our organizer Gerard. Encircling him, we stretched out our arms and began singing the blessing song we picked up from the nuns in Federal Way on the fourth day of the pilgrimage.

Gerard started to shake with emotion. He pressed his fingers into the corner of his eyes, trying to dam his tears. Underneath his hands, I saw twin streams roll down his cheeks and into his beard. His stiff-as-a-board body seemed to soften a bit. It was clear how much the last five weeks had meant to him. We thanked him for all he had done for us.

After walking a few hundred yards down the road, we crossed into Switzerland. Surprisingly, the border guards didn't stop us or even look at our passports. What awaited us during the next two weeks in the Swiss Alps? Geneva was the center of arms control negotiations. It was also the headquarters of the World Council of Churches.

Would we finally reach a decision on a route through the Middle East? Time was getting short, as Anne had pointed out at our last meeting: "We can't put off the decision much longer. We need time to do more detailed research on whatever route is chosen." The last chance to obtain the visas we needed was in Rome. But without a decision on the route, we couldn't know which embassies we needed to visit. There were six weeks remaining until Rome.

Milepost: 4846 – June 27, 1983

After winding through the magnificent Rhône River Valley, our eyes feasted on the spectacular Alps. I found walking along Lake Geneva exhilarating. The combination of shimmering water, blue sky, and snow-capped peaks reminded me of the beauty of Seattle with its vistas of Puget Sound, Lake Washington, and the Cascade and Olympic Mountains.

Lying next to a tranquil lake, Geneva symbolizes peace for many. Switzerland is known for being a neutral country. The United Nations Conference on Disarmament is based in Geneva. Many arms control treaties have been negotiated there. During 1983, Soviet and American diplomats engaged in talks to develop the START (Strategic Arms Reduction Treaty).

Disconcertingly, we discovered that Switzerland has compulsory military service. A soldier's military rank determines his advancement in the civilian sector. Also, every home and building were required to have a bomb shelter capable of surviving a nuclear war—paid for by the Swiss government.

All the disarmament talks had not eliminated the threat of nuclear war. With the Doomsday Clock nearing Armageddon, the situation required action. To illustrate the futility of so many years of talking across negotiating tables, we walked through Geneva in silence. In addition to our regular banners, we carried one that read, "En Silence pour la Paix et le Desarmament Nucleaire" (In Silence for Peace and Nuclear Disarmament).

As Alice wrote in the newsletter: "Lunchtime rush was underway as we fell into step behind the police escort that led us through the crowded streets. I felt the uncomfortable weight of indifference and cold stares.

"Gradually through this veil of silence another side of Geneva became apparent. A businessman, hurrying along the sidewalk, read our banner and stopped. He stood there and applauded as each pilgrim passed by. A little further on, a work crew was breaking up the road surface with pounding jackhammers. As we approached, one of the men stopped his deafening drill long enough for our silent walk to file past. Continuing toward our destination of the United Nations Plaza, yet another name-less face among the crowd entered our silence. An older woman, who [stopped] to read one of our leaflets, turned and joined her steps with ours for thirty yards then without a word went on her way.

"Our walk concluded with an hour of silent prayer in front of the U.N. We had not been sitting long when a woman came over with a large shopping bag filled with cartons of juice. She placed her peace offering before us and with a beaming smile she left us.

"These simple gestures of solidarity were Geneva's gifts to our pilgrimage. In the midst of the noise and activity of the city these people joined with us in a silent prayer for peace."

The next day, a warm Friday afternoon, two teams of five pilgrims each went to meet with the START delegations for the U.S. and the USSR. Dean, Steve, Laurie, Fr. Larry Gooley (a guest walker), and I visited the U.S. disarmament mission. After waiting in the reception area, we were ushered into a small conference room. Instead of meeting with the American negotiators, we met with several of the communications staff. They regurgitated the Reagan Administration's talking points to us. Evidently, they had no interest in listening to our experience of walking across the United States. It was like they were automatons.

Afterward, we went back to our hosts and compared notes with the pilgrims who had visited the Soviet negotiators. Their experience couldn't have been more different. George, Bob, Mary Jude, Pam, and Joan Clough, a guest walker from Seattle, made up the pilgrim delegation. Instead of meeting PR staff, they met with Viktor Karpov, the lead Soviet START negotiator, along with two generals on his team and a young translator. The meeting took place in the lush garden behind the mission and lasted an hour and a half. There was an honest exchange of views on arms control. However, when George asked whether Soviet citizens could organize an independent peace group, they claimed it was possible. Knowing of the plight of Andrei Sarkarov and Aleksandr Solzhenitsyn, repeating such baseless propaganda revealed the insincerity of the Soviets. As Bob noted, "It left us with somewhat of a bad taste."

The two countries had different approaches to dealing with us. The U.S. side adhered to bureaucratic talking points. The Soviets engaged us on a personal level. Still, neither had engaged in any meaningful dialogue on ending the arms race.

The flurry of meetings in Geneva included representatives of the non-aligned (countries outside of NATO or the Warsaw Pact) movement's disarmament office and leaders of the World Council of Churches.

After Geneva, our road-tested community of peace started to run out of steam. Alice, Mimi, Pam, and Bookda sought refuge at the Grand Champs monastery, a community of thirty Protestant nuns inspired by the Taizé monks. From there, Alice wrote an alarming letter to the core group, listing all the pressures burdening us. She saw the group as dangerously close to burnout. Alice warned that we "had fallen into the trap of the world, forgotten our chief charism of love, and that we were no longer free." She quoted Thomas Merton: "'We must learn to distinguish between the pseudo-spirituality of activism and the true vitality and energy of Christian action, guided by the Spirit.'"

Alice had named what most of us knew but were trying to ignore. After all, we had been on the road for well over a year. We had walked nearly 5,000 miles. While most of our bodies were in top physical shape, collective burnout still loomed large. Why was our community facing such a crisis in these beautiful mountains?

A day's walk from Geneva is the town of Nyon—the oldest town in Switzerland—dating back more than 2,000 years to Roman times. Our accommodations were the trek's most ironic: sleeping on triple-stacked bunk beds in a new atomic bomb shelter underneath a school. Built to withstand nuclear explosions, the steel blast door was a foot thick. There were no windows. Designed for over 100 people, it felt like a mausoleum, so claustrophobic that some pilgrims opted to sleep outside in tents rather than inside the bomb shelter. The constant hum of air purifiers gave us a bleak taste of trying to survive a nuclear war—imprisoned in a black closet, a living death.

The core group held a sharing meeting that afternoon. I shared that I was feeling as good as I had since Kansas City.

Shortly after the meeting ended, Laurie came up to me with a stern face. "Jim, I need to talk with you alone."

I suggested, "How about that spot over there?"

I sat down on a log by the lake shore, but Laurie remained standing and blurted out, "Wake up, Jim! Open your eyes and look at your fellow pilgrims. Can't you see how exhausted everyone is?"

I struggled to listen. Nobody had ever spoken to me so forcefully without hitting me. Slowly, I responded. "I heard people during the sharing meeting saying how close they felt to burnout. But, as I said, we have a responsibility to carry through on our commitments. We must do all we can to raise people's awareness of the threat of nuclear war."

Laurie glared at me. "Jim, you can't be that thick, can you?" She was furious.

"I still believe we should honor all our scheduled events in the coming weeks."

Laurie implored me to think differently. "Are you listening to anybody besides yourself? We can't keep up this pace. We need more downtime."

It was hard to sit there and listen. No one had so strongly called me to account in my entire life.

After several tense moments, I struggled to understand her. I recognized that her words were respectful and loving. I began to realize my myopia. "Laurie," I said finally, "I'm sorry. I don't know how I could have been so blind. I suppose I am used to glossing over negatives and focusing on wishful thinking."

"I'm glad you're starting to see our situation. We can't keep plowing ahead just because you think we should. If we want to get to Bethlehem, we must recharge."

"Thank you, Laurie, for opening my eyes. I'm sorry for being so dense. I don't want the group to implode. Getting to Bethlehem needs all of us."

We had failed to account for how much energy it took to be in different cultures and languages. Because of the language barrier, we were having to rely more heavily on each other—even as we were getting on each other's nerves more readily. Some pilgrims were doubting whether we could survive as a community all the way to Bethlehem, still six months away. Even conversing with someone in accented English required more effort. Gerard had over-scheduled us in France. Additionally, the French and Swiss people were much more engaging than the English had been.

They wanted to talk with us while we walked, when we stopped, during dinner, and into the evening. We had little chance to rest. Walking across the United States and stopping in small towns, we had only one program a night. But the population density was greater in Europe, and so we had more engagements. One night in Lausanne, Switzerland, we had programs in four different churches. This was soon after our three-day blitz of activity in Geneva.

Another stressor was everyone's frustration at not being able to reach consensus on the Mideast route. How would we get to the Holy Land: (1) Turkey-Syria-Jordan, (2) Greece-Egypt-Sinai, or (3) Yugoslavia-Greece-Israel? Regardless of which option we chose, each posed serious risks to our health and safety. Nerves frayed. Tempers flared. The thirty-seven days of rain in England and the waves of illness had not brought us this low. Some pilgrims started to despair that we might not make it to Bethlehem. The core group was at a breaking point.

We had to do something fast. Something drastic. We stopped walking.

The next day in Montreux, we canceled all events for the next three days. We needed a vacation. Our Swiss contacts arranged for us to stay in a beautiful chalet with stunning views of the Alps. It was called "Notre Abri" (Our Shelter), a place for members of Alcoholics Anonymous to come. As George noted, it was "a dream place."

Never had the whole group taken a vacation. Spreading out through the large chalet, we found comfortable chairs and curled up with good books. Our hosts brought us delicious food. We relished sleeping in. Some played cards. Pam offered haircuts. We took in one big collective deep breath and relaxed. The alpine air refreshed our lungs and healed us.

Having battled fatigue and stomach pain since Paris, Jack had already visited several doctors. Laurie was utterly exhausted and slept much of the three days. Fred had a bad cold and was running a fever. On the final vacation day, Jack took Fred to a hospital where he was treated for dehydration.

The three days of rest in the Swiss chalet, with the beauty of the mountains and warmth of the sun, eased some of the exhaustion. But the challenge of crossing the Alps loomed in the days ahead. Most worrisome of all was how many more meetings it would take before we could decide about the route. The magic of our peaceful harmony was fraying.

What we really needed was a three-week vacation or a resolution to the route quandary. Somehow our muscle memory kicked in. We kept walking, mostly because we had no other option. We couldn't afford to stay in one place. We soldiered on. With every step we took toward Rome, the urgency to decide grew.

Ascending the Alps took four days. I loved walking uphill. My knees didn't enjoy going down the other side, but I was captivated by the challenge of climbing. The year before, I had missed out on traversing the Rockies because I was still in Seattle, so I looked forward to the Alps.

Interspersed with the climb to the Great St. Bernard Pass, the core group scheduled three discernment meetings about the route after Rome. The core group learned about the discernment process from Jack and Fred, the two Jesuit pilgrims whose founder, St. Ignatius, developed it in the sixteenth century. The process encourages people to consider the available information surrounding a possible action, ponder motivations, and attend to any misgivings. Through listening to the views of everyone involved and using periods of silent reflection, this process enables people to reach decisions with confidence, allowing them to act.

The day before the first meeting, I journaled, "Our motivations for choosing [the route] have changed significantly. No longer is it just a matter of danger, physical injury, jailing, deportation, or being co-opted by governments, etc. The main issue now is whether or not the group can walk that number of miles and still reach Bethlehem with our psyches and emotions in one piece."

After walking from Martigny to Bourg St. Pierre, a long thirty-one-kilometer (nineteen-mile) day, gaining 3,000 feet in elevation, the core group gathered in a large room at 7:30 p.m. Serving as the facilitator, Bob began by saying, "Let us trust each other's motivations for whichever route they favor. With these meetings, may we rebuild trust within our community." The format called for each pilgrim to share the route they favored and why.

Laurie went first. "I favor the original Turkey route because it would provide us the chance to walk the most miles. I look forward to just being a pilgrim on a spiritual journey without any programs or outreach efforts. I am well aware of the danger of terrorism in Syria. Perhaps we will need to take a bus through there. But Bethlehem is on the West Bank, one of the most volatile areas in the world. I am relying on what the people from the World Council of Churches said that walking through Turkey should be reasonably safe."

For Kevin, he believed "the needs of the group should be our highest priority. I am not sure that walking through Turkey is something we are up to. I am not looking forward to six weeks of camping in Turkey. My preference is going through Yugoslavia."

I went next. "Personally, I still favor the Turkey route. On a group level, maybe we need a break from walking. I was the leader during those last weeks of walking in the United States. I remember how tired we got. We could bus through part of Turkey and Syria. Maybe we could spend part of that time volunteering in a refugee camp in Jordan or in the West Bank."

Steve preferred the Turkey option, even though "we do not know what will happen when we reach the borders of Turkey and Syria. I know it is a risk they could revoke their earlier approvals and leave us stranded at the border. But I do not want a long boat ride across the Mediterranean at the end of the walk." He added: "Besides, any other route is not guaranteed to be less stressful."

Jack spoke next. "Both the Jesuits in Damascus and the Little Sisters of Jesus have cautioned us against going through Syria." He reminded us that, "Fundamentally we are a group. We need to have more respect for our weaker members. The Turkey route is too long. Thus, I say we go through Yugoslavia and Greece. That way, we'll be able to walk from Nazareth to Bethlehem."

Janet followed in her Floridian accent: "I still want to go through Turkey and Syria. After spending the last six months learning about these exotic countries, my curiosity is piqued. That said, I want more than anything else for us to remain as a group."

Everyone quieted as George took his turn. "We are talking too much about what each individual wants. I feel strongly that the emphasis must be on how the group can fulfill our mission. All you young people can easily click off twenty-mile days, but those of us who are older need less mileage and more rest days. The Turkey-Syria option is too tiring and time-consuming. For us to go there, we will experience even greater culture shock. We need to seriously weigh how that will impact our mental health."

After a period of silence, Alice spoke. "The most important thing is continuing. I have lost trust in us as a group. I do not know if changing the route is going to help. We must prioritize whatever contributes to us being people of peace. The Yugoslavia-Greece route will give us the best chance for doing that."

Several others expressed support for walking through Greece and taking a ferry across the Mediterranean to Alexandria. They talked about how meaningful it would be to retrace the steps of the Exodus of the Jews from Pharoah's Egypt, crossing the Sinai, and into the Holy Land.

On the final day of climbing the Alps, a large youth group from Grenoble, France joined us, providing refreshing energy and lifting our spirits with their singing. They were also familiar with the network of trails (some only narrow goat paths) which allowed us to get off the highway. This provided a true alpine experience: verdant meadows, jaw-dropping views, and row upon row of jagged peaks.

At the top of the Great St. Bernard Pass (elevation 8,119 feet), we were hosted by a community of monks—complete with the kennels for the famed rescue dogs. The second Mideast discernment session was held that afternoon. We spent forty-five minutes writing our individual response to what people had heard the night before. We hoped the reflection and writing exercise would allow something to emerge that could resolve our impasse. That night we bedded down in the comfortable pilgrim quarters that the monks offered. Early the next morning, we walked past the kennels and, after several hundred yards, crossed another international border into Italy.

10 – Italy: The Fateful Decision, Papal Snub, and a Wedding

George meeting with reporters at the Vatican.

Milepost: 4974 – July 12, 1983

After walking across the border and entering Italy, descending the Alps was grueling. Down, down, down we went, encountering many hairpin turns. With no shoulders, one side of the road was a sheer rockface and, on the other, a steep drop-off. There were no guardrails, only regularly spaced cement posts that may have prevented cars from falling but not pilgrims.

Thankfully, there was little traffic. But the numerous blind curves tested our mettle. If we were not pressing close to the rocky cliffs, we were gingerly treading close to the edge, trying not to imagine how many hundreds of feet down we would plunge if our steps went awry. Hour after hour, the winding descent continued. The pounding of each jarring step took its toll. Muscles and tendons tightened with the relentless downward motion. Finally, we reached Aosta, our first overnight stop of our ten-week trek through Italy. From the pass, we had descended more than 6,000 vertical feet over thirty-one kilometers (nineteen miles).

The next rest day, I stayed at the home of an older woman who had worked for Olivetti (the typewriter manufacturer) in Ivrea. My journal reads, "I am currently immersed in the trough of yet another depression. This one was brought on by an upset stomach … heat, a new language and culture, … and the current crisis and tiredness of the community. … I don't *want* to walk any further because of the physical discomforts. … I fear that I will not be able to withstand the stresses, pressures, and demands of all types over the next five and a half months. … If I would just become sick or injured, then I could go back to the States. I want to go back home, but I don't want to be responsible for the decision."

Later that day I wrote, "No matter which way we decide to go, the interpersonal trust is, for me, the highest priority. At present, this level of trust is not high enough for me. No matter which way we go, we will have to entrust our very lives to each other in a more significant way than we have done already."

A few hours later, I admitted to myself that "I have lost a large part of my faith and trust in God. I do not feel as close to God as when I started." And yet, I continued writing, "In short I need a retreat, a revitalization, a re-inspiration. Fill my cup, Lord." I got up the next morning and joined the other pilgrims in the discipline of walking for peace.

Leaving Ivrea, we started crossing the vast plain of northern Italy where we were often hosted by Waldensian congregations. The Waldensians broke off from the Roman Catholic Church around the time of Saint Francis of Assisi, several hundred years before the Protestant Reformation.

The cool mountain air was behind us—now it was hot and humid. Without many trees, the sun was relentless. As we had done in Kansas, we altered our walking schedule and tried to cover all or most of each day's mileage before noon. If there was any distance remaining, we would walk it in the evening. But the weather was not the only challenge.

In the town of Santhia, the stone church had a basement whose cool refuge promised a good night's sleep. All was well for about twenty minutes after we turned out the lights. Then the silence was broken by the high-pitched whining of mosquitoes. Quickly, the peace pilgrims waged a counterattack against the winged invaders by slapping at them. How did the mosquitoes get into the basement?

Wave after wave of aerial intruders violated the cool sanctuary. First one pilgrim, and then another, and then more surrendered to the inevitable. The mosquitoes had conquered the basement. The pilgrims retreated to the muggy stillness outside while fending off the relentless mosquitoes. Frantically, tents were erected in the dark. After a few pesky stragglers were dispatched by more slapping, the pilgrims tried to sleep in the humid heat of a Lombardi summer night. Morning came too early. Disgruntled by the interrupted sleep, we commiserated with each other about our bloodshot eyes and aching heads.

The first thing I did that morning was consult my Italian phrasebook for the word for mosquito. I found zanzara—a very apt name—sounding just like the pest's buzzing. Armed with this information, I stopped in the first store I saw during that morning's walk and asked for zanzara repellent.

Later that day, we learned why the mosquitoes were so plentiful. The agricultural lands surrounding Milan were used for growing rice. The shallow water of the rice paddies provided an ideal breeding ground for mosquitoes.

On our way to Novara (west of Milan) on July 19, we stopped for lunch in the shade of an abandoned, half-finished commercial building alongside the highway. It was a sweltering afternoon. This was meant to be our final discernment meeting on the Mideast route. Tensions were high as Alice led the discussion. Tempers flared. Janet and Laurie were in tears. As the meeting grew more intense, Anne said, "I feel like leaving the group." At one point, Fred, one of the most easygoing pilgrims, stood up and leaned over Dean. Fred pointed his finger and said, "You young people still don't get it, do you? Us older pilgrims can't keep up this pace. If we go through Turkey, we'll have to average twenty miles a day. We can't do it. You want to break the group apart?"

The drawn-out process was driving us away from consensus rather than toward it. Was our pilgrim community self-destructing? Barely ten days after the alpine vacation, the route quagmire now threatened our very existence. The meeting ended without any decision on the route.

A week later, we held yet another meeting in Reggio-Emilia, now only three weeks until Rome. The meeting ended after two and a half hours with still no decision, but Kevin jotted an optimistic entry in the group journal: "Hope is that one more half-hour meeting should do it."

During the rest day at a youth center in Reggio-Emilia, we enjoyed the distraction of foosball and pool tables. Another amenity was a freezer case filled with ice cream bars—the contents of which were substantially depleted by the time we left.

The next morning, we walked fifteen miles to Modena. That afternoon, the core group gathered in a large room of a school owned by the

Capuchins. Large windows along three sides provided ample light. The warm, soothing tone of the walls calmed me. Our tired muscles sank into comfortable chairs and sofas. The stage was set for what was expected to be a successful, almost perfunctory meeting.

However, before long, our discussion stalled out as the familiar feelings and perspectives were voiced. Each pilgrim still had strong reasons for the route they favored as well as deep-seated fears against the other two. Hopes for a quick resolution evaporated. The apparent progress we had made two days before dissolved—as fear, anxiety, and mistrust swirled.

The decision couldn't be postponed any longer. Why was this so hard? Worn out and desperate, we abandoned consensus. We surrendered to a vote—whichever route got the most votes would be the way we would go. I expected that the vote would clearly indicate one route over the other two.

Someone passed out small pieces of paper. We marked the ballots. After counting the eighteen ballots (Maureen was still caring for her daughter), the vote tally was read aloud: Turkey = 6, Yugoslavia = 6, and Egypt = 6. After so many months of study and so many hours spent discussing, it was stunning to realize we were nowhere close to reaching a decision. What else could we do? We were evenly split on the three routes.

Someone proposed that we spend a half hour in silent prayer and meditation before taking another vote. Those who wished could go outside. We prayed for openness to consider each option in a new light. Perhaps if we all surrendered enough, some indication would emerge of what route we should take.

After thirty minutes, we gathered again in the large room. Someone offered a short prayer as another set of ballots was passed around. Looking around the room, I saw long faces and furrowed brows. Heavy sighs punctuated the soft rustling of paper as the marked ballots were placed in a bowl. Once again, the votes were carefully tallied. We leaned forward and hoped past hope for a clear indication of which route we would travel.

The result was announced: Turkey = 7, Yugoslavia = 6, and Egypt = 5. We all shook our heads. While several people might have voted differently, the tally was essentially unchanged. For a decision this important, there needed to be more than a one-vote margin. Shoulders drooped as it sank in—we were stuck.

Now what?! Hadn't we tried every possible approach? An exhausted silence pervaded the room. How could we continue walking if we couldn't figure out which way to go?

We were flummoxed. Minutes passed without anyone saying anything. Finally, Jack said, "Why don't we draw straws to see which way to go?"

Everyone was dumbstruck. It was sobering to contemplate that the fate of the pilgrimage, and perhaps our very lives, might be determined by casting lots. But no one could think of any reason why not. Everything else had failed.

Drawing straws seemed the only way to resolve our impasse. Slowly, one by one, each of us agreed to Jack's suggestion.

Okay, where were the straws? We searched through the kitchen. No straws. We looked through our food boxes. No straws there either.

Finally, Alice found three plastic forks and labeled each using a black marker: "Turk," "Yug," "Egypt." In order to make the fork selection as objective as possible, we asked one of our guest walkers, Catherine Peck, to hold the forks. Another guest walker, Sr. Genevieve Masuo from Japan, was asked to select one.

Hardly anyone dared to breathe. Would we be crossing the Sinai Desert, risking Turkey and Syria, or experiencing a communist country? Our fates hung in the balance.

Sr. Genevieve reached out her hand toward the three forks. Her index finger and thumb pinched one of them. She pulled and brought the fork up so she could read it. In her quiet voice, she announced, "Yugoslavia."

As I wrote to my parents the next day, "We were all relieved to have finally reached a decision. I was very content with the outcome. Although I had spent much time and energy on preparing the original walk through Turkey-Syria, I had come to the conclusion that it would have been inadvisable for us to go that route. ... the group is too tired and couldn't cope with the stress as the situation in both countries has deteriorated recently."

Even though nearly every pilgrim had strong feelings for or against each route, I never heard anyone talk about revisiting the route decision. Once it was reached, each of us supported the effort to reach Bethlehem as a unified community dedicated to peace.

Milepost: 5219 – August 1, 1983

The next morning, we walked out onto the road. The traffic was at a standstill. Had there been a bad accident? For as far as we could see, there was bumper-to-bumper traffic. The cars inched forward occasionally, but it seemed like walking was the fastest way for once. Some locals explained that today was the start of the summer holiday. I had heard that nearly everyone in Europe goes on vacation during August, but it was amazing to witness!

The next day in Bologna, we attended a huge communist-led rally marking the third anniversary of a terrorist bombing that had killed eighty-five people and injured over two hundred. More than ten thousand people filled the central plaza and its surrounding streets. During the 1970s and 1980s, fascist terrorists wreaked havoc on many western European countries by assassinating several prominent officials and kidnapping wealthy businessmen. Fences topped with barbed concertina wire, never seen in the U.S. at the time, surrounded many wealthy Italian neighborhoods. The *polizia* carried automatic weapons as they guarded the entrances of banks.

That evening, most of the pilgrims walked a few blocks to a large plaza where the London Philharmonic filled the air with exquisite music. The beauty soothed our weariness. The following morning, we left the sweltering heat of Italy's northern plain and climbed into rolling hillsides, encountering rain for the first time in a month.

Two weeks later as we neared Rome, it was my turn to drive the blue Volkswagen Vanagon, which we used as our support vehicle on the

European leg. Noticing it was low on gas, I pulled into a filling station. It was my first time gassing up the van in Italy. After stopping at a pump and turning off the engine, I got out and looked at the different grades of fuel which were all in Italian. I wasn't sure which was the right one as I had forgotten my Italian phrasebook. I found a fuel that resembled the French word for unleaded gas and began pumping. After filling the tank and paying for it, I started driving. I didn't get very far. After only one or two blocks, the van began to jerk and shudder. It acted like a bucking bronco. Then the engine died—all was quiet, except for my racing heart. "Oh," I thought, "did I just destroy the van?"

I cannot remember what happened next, but Jack wrote about it in the group journal, "...all hell broke loose with clanging and black smoke pouring out of the exhaust pipe. Anna [an Italian in her twenties who was helping with translating] went into action and lined up mechanics."

The van was towed ten miles to the next town. While the mechanics investigated the problem, we had to carry most of our gear the next day. Since so many things had already gone wrong with the van, we feared the worst: another blown engine, perhaps costing a thousand dollars or more. I was filled with dread and shame. It felt like I had let the group down.

While we waited in a cafe that afternoon, Fred drove up in the van. I blinked to make sure I wasn't seeing an apparition. The problem was easily fixed. The van hadn't needed a new engine. The mechanics discovered that I had filled the tank with diesel instead of gasoline. After flushing the fuel line, they filled it up with gas. The repair bill was only about $100. After some good humor joshing over the next few days, the pilgrims forgave my mistake.

With orchards of chestnuts, hazelnuts, and walnuts on either side of the road, we walked twenty-two miles into Rome, the Eternal City. We were scheduled to see the pope the next day, August 24. Since leaving Seattle, we had asked bishops, archbishops, and even a few cardinals to write the Vatican to support our request for a private audience with the pope. Many had responded favorably and sent us copies of their letters.

The pope seemed to be a peace pilgrim himself. In February 1981, Pope John Paul II became the first pope to visit Hiroshima and Nagasaki. While in Hiroshima, he said, "To remember Hiroshima is to commit oneself to peace." Pope John Paul met with President Reagan on June 7, 1982, just four days before the Vatican declared that nuclear deterrence was only acceptable if there was sustained progress toward the abolition of nuclear weapons.

We hoped for a private audience to impress upon the pope the need for stronger papal condemnations of nuclear weapons. Unlike other pilgrims visiting the Vatican, we had trekked 5,500 miles, perhaps the longest of any walking pilgrimage to Rome. The pope would surely want to meet us.

However, we failed to account for the Vatican's bureaucracy. In the end, we had to settle for the weekly general audience in St. Peter's Square along with fifty thousand other pilgrims.

Arriving at the Vatican at 9:00 a.m., an usher in a black three-quarter-length coat and white bow tie directed us toward a reserved seating section on the northwest corner of the huge square. In front of St. Peter's Basilica was a raised platform for the pope, about two hundred feet from our section of folding plastic chairs. As we waited for the noontime audience, a thunderstorm approached, darkening the sky. Soon it began to pour. We all rose to our feet and lifted the chairs over our heads. The chairs proved to be poor substitutes for umbrellas. Luckily, the rain abated after a short while, and our soaked clothes dried quickly in the warm August air. Forty-five minutes later, another band of thunderstorms descended on the square, drenching us a second time. We dried our chairs as best we could before sitting back down to wait.

Nearly three hours after we arrived, the crowd behind us began to cheer. We turned to see the pope riding in his white popemobile through the broad aisle between the seating sections in the huge square. Straining to see, we only glimpsed the pope above the heads of people in front of us.

The popemobile stopped before the stage, and Pope John Paul II climbed the steps to stand in front of the microphone. He led the faithful in the Angelus, the traditional noontime prayer. Next, he presented a short instruction on the role of conscience formation in Catholic theology. Finally, the pope acknowledged the dozens of pilgrim groups from various parts of the world, mentioning the groups in pairs and briefly commenting about one group in each pair. The pairs were organized according to language groups, starting with those from Francophone countries. Pope John Paul II turned next to those pilgrims from English-speaking countries. He said, "I offer a particular greeting to the Bethlehem Peace Pilgrimage from Seattle. ..." Our ears perked up. The pope continued: "And to the large group representing the International Federation of Medical Students' Associations. The cause of peace is the cause of life, and everything that wounds, weakens, or destroys life attacks peace and the destiny of humanity. May God imbue all the medical students of the world with a keen sense of service to life and responsibility for peace."

He moved on to the next pair. He made no mention of nuclear weapons. Nothing about us having walked 5,000 miles from Seattle. No acknowledgment of George Zabelka, the Catholic chaplain to the men who dropped the atomic bombs on Japan. No one in that throng had any idea what the Bethlehem Peace Pilgrimage was.

A grim realization hit me: Instead of being honored or congratulated, we had been snubbed by the pope.

After all those miles and months on pilgrimage, the papal slight was a slap in the face. It was crushing for the three priests in our group, especially George who had longed for a papal endorsement of our walk.

When the audience ended, the multitude dispersed. Several reporters from Italian television grabbed George for an impromptu news conference. George told the journalists how important it was, with the world on the precipice of nuclear war, for the pope to strongly condemn nuclear weapons. He also explained how we had hoped for a private audience with the pope. Italian television wasted no time in airing George's remarks. Later that afternoon, George, Jack, and Kevin (the three priests in our group) visited the Jesuit community in Rome. They received a rather cool reception from those scandalized by George's strong words directed at the pope.

For me, the pope's snub renewed my question about whether the long trek was worth all my time and suffering. Perhaps our efforts would prove fruitless. Yet there was little else I could do but simply abandon any desire for being seen and recognized as successful.

Conducting a courtship inside the fishbowl of our pilgrimage was not easy. Steve and Mimi's romance delighted all our hearts as the months progressed. By the time we were in England, we knew they were considering marriage. Though not as torturous a process as our experience in choosing the Mideast route, Steve and Mimi's discernment about marriage was buffeted by similar winds: the constant traveling, exhaustion, lack of privacy, and little time to relax.

The two lovers didn't settle on a date for the wedding until mid-August. The day would be September 1, when we'd be in Cassino. There was much to prepare and only a short time to do it in. Where would the wedding be? What about a wedding dress?

As with everything else on the walk, the generosity of complete strangers filled every need. Staying in Frosione two days before the wedding, the local youth group learned of Mimi's need for a wedding dress. They jumped at the chance to take Mimi shopping for one. They insisted on paying for it and later attended the wedding.

The night before the wedding, the core group split up: The men held a bachelor party for Steve in a nearby restaurant, and the women gathered with Mimi. Each party was a rather tame affair, as all pilgrims returned to our hosts by 9:30 p.m.

On the morning of the wedding, food preparations commenced. In Cassino, a community of nuns housed us for two nights and turned over their kitchen for meal preparation and a large patio area for the dinner. The weather was ideal, and the imposing historic monastery atop Montecasino provided a dramatic backdrop.

Nearby, an ancient Roman amphitheater offered the ideal setting for the ceremony. Several of us carried chairs down the steep stairs to the bottom of the amphitheater. As we were almost finished, we heard agitated voices up above. Some townspeople surrounded the gate to the amphitheater. Raising their voices and waving their arms, they urged us to come back up to the gate. After finding a translator, the village folk insisted we remove the chairs and leave immediately.

We trudged back down and began lugging up several dozen chairs. Other pilgrims searched for an alternative site for the wedding, set to begin in less than an hour.

Again, the generosity of strangers came to our rescue. The owner of a nearby restaurant welcomed us into a beautiful grotto behind his restaurant, which had a view of the amphitheater. The grotto looked as ancient as the amphitheater and had the same ambience. We hauled the chairs behind the restaurant.

Finally, all was ready.

With a freshly trimmed beard, Steve wore a white polo shirt and dark shorts. Mimi was simply beautiful. Her white dress was covered with intricately stitched three- and five-petaled flowers. Her blonde hair was drawn back in a bun encircled by a band of white hand-sewn flowers. About her waist was a wide cloth belt.

Pam began with an instrumental piece on her guitar, accompanied by Hedi Vacarro, one of our Italian organizers, on her flute. Fr. Jack officiated. Before Mimi and Steve exchanged their vows, we shared reflections on the significance of their commitment to each other. After the ceremony, we feasted on roasted chicken and potatoes. In lieu of a traditional wedding cake, we enjoyed hazelnut gelato. After a few toasts, the dancing commenced with music from an old record player lent by the local priest. Around 10:30 p.m., Dean drove the bride and groom to a hotel room—paid for by each pilgrim chipping in.

The day of the wedding was marred by the tragic news that a Soviet fighter jet had shot down a commercial airliner, a Korean Airlines 747, with 269 people aboard as it strayed off course over the Kamchatka Peninsula. Everyone perished when the plane crashed into the ocean. Cold War tensions were intensifying just as the pilgrims prepared to walk through a communist country. Even though Yugoslavia was not part of the Soviet bloc, we wondered how the escalating East-West conflict would impact our journey through the volatile Balkans.

After a rest day in Cassino, our group resumed walking toward Bari on the Adriatic. We still had three and a half months before Bethlehem. Except for our ten weeks in Italy, the six weeks in Yugoslavia would be the longest time in any one country outside the United States. Would the increasing foreignness exhaust us even more? For the rest of the way, not only would there be new languages and cultures, but we would encounter different alphabets, forms of government, and religious practices.

11 – Yugoslavia: Communism and Isolation

Bookda and Alice walking in Yugoslavia.
(Photo by Bill Cox)

Tensions from the extended route decision process had worn me out. I needed a break. Looking ahead to the remaining months, I realized that the logistics of taking time away would be much more difficult after leaving Italy. On the day after the wedding, I took a series of trains and returned to Loye and Erich in West Germany. As soon as I arrived near the Air Force base, I saw people's furrowed brows—manifestations of their anxiety about the increased East-West tensions after the Soviet downing of the Korean airliner. The increased likelihood of war weighed on everyone.

Reagan termed the Soviet attack on Korean Air Lines Flight 007 "an act of barbarism" and a "crime against humanity that must never be forgotten." As Washington castigated the Soviets for downing a civilian aircraft, Moscow was silent. Weeks later, Soviet leader Yuri Andropov issued a statement from his hospital bed (suffering from advanced diabetes and failing kidneys), accusing the United States of an "insidious provocation involving a South Korean plane engineered by U.S. special services . . . an example of extreme adventurism in politics." Subsequent investigations revealed that errors by both the Korean pilot and Soviet military units led to the Soviets mistaking the airliner for an American spy plane. The Korean pilot had erred in setting the plane's autopilot, causing it to fly hundreds of miles off course and into Soviet airspace. For its part, the U.S. withheld information that an American spy plane had flown near the area shortly before the Korean airliner.

While following the KAL 007 crisis, I devoted most of my time in West Germany to recharging my batteries. If I was to make it all the way to Bethlehem, I needed to not only rest physically, but even more so psychologically. The pilgrimage experience was pushing me to my limits. As a strong introvert, being constantly on the go and living with twenty-plus people exhausted me.

But why? Having the advantage of looking back on my pilgrim-age experience four decades later, I understand what I couldn't see then. There was a proverbial plank in my own eye that was blinding me to my emotional plight. It took energy to continue repressing my childhood trauma. I must have come across to my fellow pilgrims as emotionally stiff, rigid, even aloof. I continued with the walk, but doubts haunted me about whether I could endure all the way to Bethlehem.

After twelve days of R&R, I traveled nearly twenty-four hours by train back to Italy, rejoining the group in Bari on the Adriatic Coast. The ferry to Yugoslavia departed the next day, shortly before midnight. The nine-hour crossing began with rough seas caused by a thunderstorm. Sporadic lightning flashes turned night into day. Heaving seas made walking a challenge; I had to guess where my feet would meet the deck.

Milepost: 5769 – September 18, 1983

As the sun rose the next morning, Dubrovnik's ancient city walls emerged from the sea. After getting off the ferry and passing through the customs station, deciphering the Cyrillic street signs proved challenging. Some Catholic nuns allowed us to pitch our tents in their large backyard which was surrounded by a twelve-foot-tall stone wall. That evening we strolled atop the ancient walls of Dubrovnik as the sun set over the Adriatic.

Yugoslavia was the first country we'd entered where no one from the core group spoke its language, Serbo-Croatian. How would we com-municate? Certainly, there would be little outreach if we had no one to translate our message of peace and disarmament. In Dubrovnik, we met a man in his mid-thirties who offered to serve as our translator through Yugoslavia. Zvonko Curkic was wiry with a receding hairline, wire-rimmed glasses, and a neatly trimmed goatee. He was energetic and fit in well with our group. While we covered his expenses during the six weeks, he refused any payment for his time.

Yugoslavia was my first experience of a communist country. During a rest day in Dubrovnik, I wrote a letter to my parents to let them know I had arrived safely. From the convent, I walked 170 steps down a steep hillside to the post office in the city center. Approaching the postal attendant, I handed him the envelope addressed to my parents in Spokane. Instead of just weighing it and telling me how much the postage cost, he sliced the envelope open, took my letter out, and began reading it. Flabbergasted, I blurted out, "What do you think you're doing? That's a personal letter to my family."

He sternly replied, "This is not your country."

Exasperated, I stood in stunned silence as he read my letter. Apparently satisfied that I was not a spy, he refolded the letter, put it back in the envelope, and sealed it with tape. Then he told me the cost of the postage. This was a startling introduction to communism. For the rest of Yugoslavia, I was careful about what I wrote in my letters.

I walked back into the street, wondering if my letter would be sent. Climbing back up all those steps, my legs felt weak and wobbly. I tried to process exactly how different communism was from anything else I had experienced in my life. What other shocks awaited us over the next six weeks?

In each European country, we developed a half-page flyer that had a map of our route through that country on one side and an explanation of why we walked on the opposite. For France, Switzerland, and Italy, we had the text translated and took it to a print shop to make copies without any difficulty. In Dubrovnik, Zvonko translated the text into Serbo-Croatian. The owners at several print shops told us that we had to first obtain permission from the government authorities. The search for an authority was a classic bureaucratic runaround. We would go into a police station or city hall to make a request, only to be told that the approval could only be granted by a certain official who invariably was out of the office. When we determined when that person would be in, we would return at that time. Then, we would be told the person still wasn't available, and their colleague would suggest we return the next day. On a few occasions, we did connect with the supposed authority, only for him to say that, for this kind of request, it needed to be directed to a different official—and this person was invariably not available. At least once a day, we got another brush-off. Nobody wanted to sign off on our leaflet. It seemed that a small independent group of people walking for peace was a political hot potato.

Finally, after more than a dozen inquiries, we finally found an official who granted permission to make copies of our Yugoslavia flyer.

Because it was late September, the vacation resorts and campgrounds that dotted the Adriatic Coast were mostly empty. The weather was pleasant with little rain and mild temperatures. But one evening the wind quickly grew in force and blew over several tents. As George described it: "One helluva wind started, like the typhoon on Tinian [where George was stationed in 1945] must have been 60-70 mph wind."

As for me, the miles, the camping, and the constantly changing landscape continued sapping my energy. Even with the recent rest in West Germany, I made the following journal entry, dated September 30: "I am wishing more and more for this to be over. I'm tired, spent, and at the edge of my physical and mental endurance. ... Due to my trip to Germany, I am more aware of nuclear weapons and East/West tensions than I have been in many months. This gives meaning and purpose to my sufferings."

Except for Dubrovnik, we didn't ask church-related groups for hospitality because we didn't want to bring them under suspicion. Even the nuns who hosted us in Dubrovnik had risked reprisals by the communist authorities. Thus, we camped out nearly every night.

As we started crossing the Dolomite Mountains, the weather grew colder and wetter. We crossed three passes above 5,000 feet. Some mornings I found frost coating the bottom of my sleeping bag. Others lost sleep because they were so cold. So, we spent group funds to buy extra blankets for pilgrims whose sleeping bags were not made for subfreezing weather.

Due to the oppressive government, we didn't offer any public meetings in Yugoslavia. We missed being able to share our disarmament message with local churches and groups. When we stopped at roadside cafes, the language barrier prevented much meaningful interaction with the local people. We drew closer to each other as we had to rely almost entirely on our fellow pilgrims for social support.

Sometimes when I crested a ridge, the valley below felt so isolated that I wondered if we were the first Westerners to visit in decades. It seemed like I was walking back in time. Tiny fields, no more than an acre or two each, dotted the valley floor. We saw few tractors or other motorized vehicles. Once or twice a day, police drove by, keeping us under surveillance. The main method of transportation was horse-drawn carts. In the villages, blacksmiths pounded on their anvils. Frequently, groups of sheep or cattle blocked the road as shepherds guided the animals from one pasture to another.

Southern Yugoslavia, especially Kosovo, was the poorest region of Europe. Signs of poverty were everywhere: small dilapidated houses, coarse clothing with patches, no electricity or running water. Many houses had been abandoned during construction, often only a shell of concrete floors and a roof. We used them for shelter from the rain during our picnic lunches. Because of our pilgrim lifestyle, we felt a closeness to the local people, like we had experienced in Ireland. By our walking, simple foods, and humble accommodations, the local people could see our commitment.

In the grocery stores we entered, roughly a third of the shelf space was devoted to cheap alcohol. The alcoholic content of beer (*pivo*) was 15%, higher than most wines. The usual half-liter beer bottle sold for less than 25 cents. Another third of the shelves was filled with sugary treats: stale cookies, candy, and the like. The remaining third contained all the other foods. We bought most of our food at open-air markets.

The widespread availability of cheap alcohol resulted in a seemingly high incidence of drunk driving. Nearly every day, we would pass a wrecked car along the side of the road. Given the relatively few cars being driven, the single-car wrecks seemed to indicate the crashes were caused by inebriated drivers. As a result, we were cautious whenever a vehicle drove near us.

One town stuck out: Andrejevica, nestled in the mountains of Montenegro. It was one of the few times we decided to stay in a hotel because so many of us were sick with colds or the flu. This inn was on a corner of the town square. My room overlooked the square. Across the street to the left was a church with a bell that tolled each hour, even through the night. To the right was another church in which a wedding was held that night. The manager of our hotel was getting married.

Around dusk, several men came out into the square with guns and fired several dozen rounds into the air, apparently celebrating the wedding. To me, the noise of live gunfire in the street below my window was unsettling. I felt apprehension among such wild Montenegrins.

In the village of Murino, a police officer suggested we could stay in the police (militzia) station. Against Zvonko's advice, we accepted the invitation. During our frequent interactions with the police and government officials, Zvonko was quite direct. Sometimes his conversations became heated, and Zvonko would end up shouting at the officials. His anger and frustration were intense, and we worried that the officials would arrest him. Because the arguments were in Serbo-Croatian, we didn't understand what they were arguing about.

As Anne Galisky recorded in the group journal: "I certainly didn't think about the risk to Zvonko. We are dealing in so foreign a mentality! Janet was almost taken away for questioning—she chose a spot directly in front of the local war memorial to build a campfire to boil potatoes. Zvonko came to her rescue and convinced the authorities of her innocent intentions. ... I felt the pit of my stomach turn as Zvonko and I talked about the fire—his intense anger at the system he must put up with, his disgust at the ineptness he says there is in the bureaucracy, his lack of personal fear which, if it exists is kept well hid beneath layers of anger. 'I have spit in their faces,' he told me, jerking his head off the side to demonstrate, launching a spray of spit which sizzled on a hot pan. I hope he can keep that vehemence under control not to anger some *militzia* big shot who could lock him up."

After a few weeks in Yugoslavia, Anne—the youngest pilgrim—was running very low on energy. Most days, she could walk only a few miles. During a weekly sharing meeting, Anne said, "I do not know what is happening to my body, but it is unavoidable. I am very sick. I need to see a real doctor. I may even have to quit the walk." Her fellow pilgrims had been speculating as to what was sapping her of energy: mono, pneumonia, tonsillitis, a bad cold. Anne continued, "With the clinics I have visited recently, I'm really getting an inside view of socialized medicine. Word to the wise: don't get sick in the mountains of Montenegro."

The next day she went to the clinic in Andrejevica. She was given a shot of penicillin and a bag of antibiotics. That evening, Anne shared her experience as we ate dinner. "The medical establishment here sure is into drugs. I'm not impressed with the sanitary conditions: floors were dirty, examination tables had visible dust (no sheet covering), and I saw a hair on the tongue depressor being used by a doctor. And get this, the nurse attending to me had a cigarette in one hand. If I'm not infected with something yet, I will be soon." A week later, a doctor in Peç gave Anne a diagnosis of hepatitis. But was this any more reliable than previous doctor visits? As a precaution, Anne got a break from helping with meal preparation.

When Anne needed to get medical attention, Zvonko accompanied her to translate. He was everywhere we needed him to be—helping with grocery shopping, seeking hospitality when we needed shelter, and interacting with local people. He never seemed to tire and was always eager to be of service. During the week we walked through Kosovo where the main language was Albanian, Zvonko was assisted by Cheti, a young Kosovar we met in Peç. He had learned English while working at a movie theater that showed Hollywood films with subtitles.

Because we were not spending time offering programs, participating in prayer services, or giving press interviews, we had quite a bit of free time after walking each day's miles. Once camp was set up and dinner prepared, we would play cards, usually Hearts or Spades. For variety, Bob invented a new card game and called it Brezovica after the town where we first played it.

Bill bought a small magnetic chess set, and he and I played several times a week. Most of us were avid readers, and we would share books with each other. Along the way to Bethlehem, I remember reading a book by Tracy Kidder on the advent of personal computers, three novels by John Steinbeck, and several spiritual books, including *Letters from the Desert* by Carlo Carretto.

When staying in towns, some pilgrims enjoyed Hollywood films such as *On Golden Pond.* Others visited cafes or galleries, but I rarely had energy for sightseeing. My overloaded mental circuits couldn't take in any new information. I knew I was missing out by not learning more about the areas we were passing through, but I felt the need to conserve my energy so I could last until Bethlehem.

The natural beauty of Yugoslavia was a definite highlight of the walk. There were rocky goat paths, lush green hills, and small agricultural plots, many of which were tilled and harvested by hand. Once we camped out on a mountain pass, elevation 6,100 feet. Pam, an art major in college, shared during the morning Circle: "The dawn was so outrageous from this summit! Almost as spectacular as yesterday's sunset. I can't remember a more magnificent fall. The trees are shocking, the rocky hills a vivid violet and orange—immense walls of rock. Look at that, see how the sun plays with the ridges—it's so spectacular!" Later that day, we walked through the astounding Rugova Canyon.

One beautiful fall day, I watched a short, seemingly frail, elderly woman finish building a six-foot-tall stack of corn stalks in the middle of the dirt road. She bound the pile with some rope she pulled from her pocket. Then, squatting down with her back to the pile, she inserted her arms into the ropes. Amazingly, she managed to lift the whole pile onto her back and carried her load down the road to the shed attached to her house.

With few electric lights, the night sky teemed with stars. But even more magnificent were the diverse people of Yugoslavia. Everywhere there were large families. There were so many children that the schools had to operate in two shifts—one in the morning and the other in the afternoon. More than half the population was under the age of twenty-five. The children were especially curious about us. Sometimes it felt as if we were animals on display in a zoo. When we encountered any youth, they crowded around, eager to practice their English.

Even though the homes were quite small, only two or three rooms (not bedrooms, rooms), there would be twelve to fifteen people sharing the limited space. Most of the homes had no running water. Electricity in homes was rare. Although the people lacked material goods, they eagerly shared what little they had, whether it was a crate of apples from their orchard or a shot of *slivovitz* (plum brandy), greeting us with welcoming smiles.

As we got further into October and the mountains of Montenegro, the weather got colder and wetter. As we had experienced in England, the raw elements took a toll on our pilgrim community. In the poverty of southern Yugoslavia, there were fewer opportunities for dry shelter, and heat was even scarcer. On October 19, we reached Skopje, the capital of what is now called North Macedonia. By then, several pilgrims were in our traveling sick ward: Anne (still), Sr. Genevieve (now a member of the core group), Laurie, and Bob. We spent group funds to rent campers for the sick while the rest of us stayed in tents.

On the afternoon we arrived, I washed my dirty socks and hung them up to dry. The sun hid behind thick clouds, the temperature not getting much above forty degrees Fahrenheit. Dampness permeated the air. During the daytime, we sought refuge in libraries and cafes. As I packed to leave Skopje three days later, my socks were still damp.

Since arriving in Dubrovnik, every time we interacted with government authorities, we renewed our request to meet with Communist Party officials. These inquiries were ignored. Finally, as we neared the Greek border, a meeting was arranged in Skopje. We speculated whether the greater distance from the capital Belgrade permitted the local officials more autonomy.

As the meeting began, we wondered whether they would endorse our call for nuclear disarmament. The representatives belonged to the Yugoslavian Peace League, an officially sanctioned organization. The room was small and dingy. A glass-enclosed bookcase took up the back wall. In front of the bookcase was a large table covered with a cloth. Behind the table sat five League officials. They appeared to be of the same mold—each resting their forearms on the table and each wearing a suit and vest.

I had expected them to be more engaging than the Soviet officials had been in Geneva. Yugoslavia was not part of the Warsaw Pact and therefore not under Moscow's thumb. The late president of Yugoslavia, Josip Broz Tito, who died in 1980, had been a leader in the Non-Aligned Movement, a coalition of seventy-seven countries which were independent of both NATO and the Warsaw Pact. The Non-Aligned Movement pressed the nuclear superpowers to dismantle their dangerous stockpiles.

As the discussion in Skopje ensued, it was uncanny how many of their statements echoed the Hollywood anti-communist propaganda movies I watched growing up. One pilgrim asked why Yugoslavia didn't allow independent citizen organizations to advocate for peace. One official responded, "There is no need for that. The government is the will of the people."

The three-day stay helped many pilgrims to recover from colds, but the four sickest stayed behind, gratefully accepting hospitality at an Orthodox convent. While there, they saw how little food the nuns had available. They shared what little they had. The ailing pilgrims rejoined the group four days later.

In Yugoslavia's geographic, cultural, and linguistic isolation, we were disconnected from the wider world. One exception was my portable shortwave radio which I used to listen to news from the BBC, Radio Moscow, and the Voice of America. In Geneva, the Soviets were threatening to pull out of the nuclear reduction talks as the deployment of new U.S. missiles neared, now only a few weeks away. Additionally, Middle East tensions were increasing. On October 23, I learned of the horrendous loss of life when two truck bombs struck U.S. Marine and French barracks in Beirut, Lebanon. In all, nearly 300 soldiers were killed. We worried that such outrageous attacks might spark new fighting, making our journey even more perilous.

These ominous developments amidst the isolation of rural Yugoslavia reinforced our sense of powerlessness. We felt far removed from the easy communications in the West. Receiving mail was problematic, and one package containing dozens of letters to pilgrims was lost in Yugoslavia. This drought of letters from loved ones extended for more than six weeks.

Cooking dinner for twenty people on a small two-burner camp stove was challenging, especially as the days grew shorter. Most of the time, whoever was cooking would fix a big pot of soup. However, one evening, Janet, the group's Floridian, decided she would treat us to some of her Southern fried chicken. It took much longer to cook on the camp stove as the outside temperature fell into the forties. As the stars began to shine in the night sky, several pilgrims assisted Janet by taking turns holding a flashlight.

Just two days after the terrorist bombing in Beirut, the United States invaded the Caribbean island of Grenada. Under the guise of protecting 600 American medical students being trained on the island, the U.S. military replaced the pro-Marxist government with a caretaker one. This further escalated Cold War tensions.

On the pilgrimage, each of us submitted to that day's walk and all it had to offer, including abundant rains that sometimes left us drenched and on the edge of hypothermia. One day in late-October, a combination of wind, rain, and cold chilled me to the bone. For some reason, I had unzipped my jacket and struggled to zip it back up. My fingers acted as if they were frozen solid. My brain tried to send signals to my arms and fingers to grab the zipper and pull it up, but my fingers seemed paralyzed. As I struggled to get my fingers to move, a wave of panic enveloped me. What if I couldn't get the zipper up? I felt I was running out of time. I was all alone—the nearest pilgrim was at least a mile away. If I didn't start walking again soon, I risked losing even more body heat.

My body started shaking. This made grasping the zipper even more difficult. Why weren't my fingers responding? Why was I unable to zip up my stupid jacket?

Thankfully, determination won out, and I finally succeeded in zipping it all the way to my neck. My frozen legs slowly began to move. I lifted one leg and let gravity capture my foot. After a few plodding strides, I got back into a rhythm and managed to work up to my usual brisk pace. After several minutes, the fog of panic began to dissipate, and I thanked God for the joy of doing something for peace. It took hours to get warm again. There was no hot shower to jump into and no fire to crouch over. I prayed that my suffering was helping to turn back the specter of a nuclear conflagration.

On our last day in Yugoslavia, we stopped to have lunch a hundred yards north of the Greek border. We ate the remaining fresh fruits and vegetables because we couldn't take them across the border. We also wanted to spend all our Yugoslav dinars due to the unfavorable exchange rate in Greece.

As we sat eating lunch, we took turns thanking Zvonko for all he had done for us since leaving Dubrovnik. When Zvonko spoke, he revealed that he had been a political prisoner for four years, mostly for his writings which criticized the government. As he recounted the interrogations, ill treatment, and hardships of prison life in communist Yugoslavia, I thought of his frequent confrontations with the police over the previous six weeks. While we were enjoying hiking through the beautiful fall colors, reveling in exotic cultures, and taking pride in what we were doing for peace, here was a man who had risked his freedom, and perhaps his life, by helping us on our mission. He had given us so much more than we had suspected or imagined.

A few minutes later, we walked across the border into Greece, leaving Zvonko behind. What would happen to him? Would he be arrested after we left—when our American passports would no longer offer him any protection? Would he have to go into hiding?

12 – Greece and a Heartbreaking Farewell

Saying farewell to Bookda.

Milepost: 6215 – October 30, 1983

Crossing into Greece was a relief. The weight of being under surveillance, always needing to be careful of what we said, and being cautious on behalf of local people, especially Zvonko, was lifted. The air smelled fresher. During the six weeks we tramped through Yugoslavia, there had always been an oppressive heaviness.

This relief was accompanied by culture shock as brightly colored advertisements assaulted our eyes. Within a hundred yards of stepping into Greece, the Western cornucopia of consumer goods reappeared. Paradoxically, we also realized how relaxing Yugoslavia had been without the easy availability of so much stuff. For the past six weeks, we had enjoyed a vacation from hucksterism. The culture and language also changed as we entered Greece, as did the alphabet. By virtue of my high school science classes, I was familiar with the Greek alphabet, so deciphering the road signs over the four weeks in Greece was a bit easier.

Walking near Thessaloniki in northeast Greece, we met a group of six bicyclists. Half of them were Americans. After chatting a bit, I found out that one was from Washington State. Hearing that I was from Spokane, he said he went to high school in Chewelah, the small town where I'd grown up. I remarked, "Well, my dad taught French there. His name was Bernard Thomas." With that, his face lit up in recognition. "Oh, I remember him. He was a great teacher. Let him know that Dave Asplin says 'hi.'" A classic "small world" encounter—meeting someone my dad had taught in high school on the other side of the world!

Unlike Yugoslavia, we didn't have to search from town to town to have some government official approve our leaflet. We were in Greece, the cradle of Western civilization. Being among the local people felt easy—and so liberating to leave the oppressive police state behind.

Since more people spoke English in Greece than in Yugoslavia, we were again able to share our message of peace and disarmament. I got the impression the Greeks were a very passionate people who lived life to the fullest, and who wholeheartedly enjoyed celebrating.

Walking through eastern Greece, we came upon a string of towns whose mayors hosted us. Not content to put simply a roof over our heads (usually in a school), they treated us to dinners at their favorite restaurants, featuring live music and dancing.

One very memorable town along the Aegean Coast was Loutra Edipsos, where the air smelled of sulfur. The town straddled hot mineral springs which flowed through the town in thin rivulets, staining everything along their path with beautiful yellows, browns, and oranges.

In the surrounding countryside, farmers harvested cotton, and we began to see olive orchards. One village bestowed on us several cases of canned surplus peaches from a bumper crop the year before. This gift was accompanied by rich Greek yogurt. Combining the two became a favorite treat for us over the next several days.

Greece may have been warmer than the Yugoslav mountains, but most days were rainy and chilly. Though Anne continued to suffer, it was George who concerned us the most. The rigors of the pilgrimage seemed to have aged him more rapidly in the last few weeks. His face seemed haggard, and there was noticeable hollowing in his cheeks. His color wasn't good. After about ten days in Greece, George visited a hospital to find the cause for why he got dizzy every time he stood up. The results were inconclusive. In keeping with his disciplined nature, it was rare to hear George complain. He relished his privacy, but it was impossible to protect it in such close quarters. With alarming frequency, I noticed George pull out his small container of nitroglycerin pills and discreetly place one under his tongue. His heart must have been bothering him. Two severe heart attacks in the 1970s had forced him to retire. Now sixty-eight years old, the thousands of miles, harsh weather, and inadequate food were taking their toll on him. We worried that George might die before we reached Athens.

On the day we walked past the fabled Mount Olympus, we stayed in a youth camp that had triple bunk beds. Sleeping on a real mattress, even in my sleeping bag, was always a treat. I opted to sleep on the top bunk, which was so close to the ceiling there was barely enough room to turn over. With the lights off, I settled down, looking forward to a restful sleep. Within minutes, scurrying began in the ceiling, only inches above my head. What was the source of the noise? Only one thing could be responsible for that noise—rats. They raced from one end of the building to the other all night long. There were interludes of quiet as the rats explored distant corners, allowing me to drift off to sleep. But before long, the scurrying returned, waking me up as I worried about them gnawing a hole in the ceiling, dropping down, and biting me. I welcomed the gray light of a new day as we got ready for another stretch on the way to Bethlehem.

In Larissa, Anne visited yet another doctor. Yugoslavian clinics didn't have the resources to analyze blood samples. The Greek doctor gave her a definitive diagnosis: mononucleosis and iron deficiency. But having a name for her illness was not a cure. That week, Anne confided to us, "I do not think I am going to make it to Bethlehem. I have spent all my energy and feel I have hit a brick wall. My dizzy spells are getting worse. Sitting in a restaurant this afternoon, I thought that I was going to pass out and never wake up."

But Anne proved herself wrong. A week later, on a beach near Athens, she journaled, "I can't believe I'm in Greece in the sun by the Aegean. It's nuts. Life is profoundly ridiculous. Less than a month [to Bethlehem]. I'll make it. Hell, I'll make it."

On November 20, as we walked along the island of Euboea, ABC telecast *The Day After*. Roughly half of adult Americans tuned in to watch a depiction of Lawrence, Kansas being destroyed by a Soviet nuclear attack and its aftermath. It was a sobering portrayal of what would happen if nuclear weapons were ever used. When President Reagan had previewed the movie a month earlier, he recorded in his diary that the movie "left me greatly depressed." Three days after the ABC telecast, the first Pershing II missiles were deployed in West Germany. In response, Viktor Karpov and the rest of the Soviet negotiating team walked out of the arms control talks in Geneva.

One afternoon that week, as I walked through a small ravine without any other pilgrim in sight, I felt the safety of solitude. I was so tired from holding back my emotions, I started to cry. After resisting it for so long, I liberated years of pain. I let go the accumulated stress of living 24/7 with twenty other people in close quarters. I cried out my fear of the ever-present specter of nuclear Armageddon. My gut and chest convulsed with sobs as I walked.

In the wake of that emotional squall, a quiet calm ensued. The storm had swept away so much debris that I felt rejuvenated. I looked up at the overcast sky and thanked God for this cleansing. The dull, gray landscape was beautiful and full of life.

Toward the southern end of the Gulf of Euboea lay the town of Halkida. Someone there had offered us a large house to use for another group vacation. We were excited at the prospect of staying four nights in the same place. This was where our pilgrim family would celebrate Thanksgiving.

Members of the Shepherds' Field Pilgrimage planned to join us for the holiday feast. Two young Americans, Nancy Kiehl and Jack Jones, had been guest walkers with us in France and wanted to walk the rest of the way with us. When we declined their request so as to keep the core group limited to a manageable size, they organized their own walk. Jack and Nancy were joined by Yvette Naal (France), Bernhard (Germany), and William. Beginning in Stuttgart, West Germany at the U.S. European Command Center (one of the bases set to receive Pershing II missiles), they walked through West Germany, Austria, Hungary, Yugoslavia, Greece, Israel and the Occupied West Bank. Yvette Naal was an experienced walker, having taken part in the first Walk to Moscow (1961-1962), the same one Gerard had joined. She had asked to walk with our group, so we referred her to Jack and Nancy. Yvette belonged to the Community of the Ark in France that was founded in 1948 by Lanza del Vasto, a disciple of Gandhi's practice of nonviolence.

A few weeks before, we invited the Shepherds' Field Peace Pilgrims to celebrate Thanksgiving with us. Our local contact had assured us that the house in Halkida could comfortably accommodate thirty pilgrims, and everything would be ready when we arrived. It seemed almost too good to be true.

The day we walked into Halkida was cold and rainy. For the first hour, we walked in silence to bring to mind the West German Bundestag (parliament) during its final debate on authorizing the deployment of U.S. Pershing II missiles on German soil. Near the town of New Artaki, forty people, mostly women and children, joined us to walk the final three miles into Halkida. They infused tired pilgrims with new energy by singing songs and shouting chants.

The final stretch ran alongside the Gulf of Euboea—the water's edge just a few feet off to our right. The steady rain intensified. A strong wind swept across the gulf, driving the rain into us. Astoundingly, the wind grew even more powerful, forty or fifty miles per hour, as we walked along the seawall. Those carrying banners felt as if the gusts might carry them away. Through the torrential rain, we saw whitecaps marching toward us. With each gust, the waves broke over the seawall, flooding our shoes and drenching our legs. We were immersed in water from above and below. Surprisingly, the townspeople seemed to revel in the dramatic inundation. Their singing grew louder as they tried to drown out the storm. It was the wettest stretch of the entire walk.

Finally, we left the shoreline behind and entered Halkida. The buildings provided some protection from the wind. The downpour continued unabated. We scrapped the plans to rally in the town square. Our local host guided us through the narrow streets until we came to a large house. After being buffeted by wind-blown surf and the torrential downpour, we were very eager to get inside, hang our drenched clothes, and warm up. Upon entering the vacant house, we were stunned by what we saw.

The house was undergoing an extensive renovation. A thick layer of dust coated the seven large rooms. Construction tools and materials were scattered everywhere. There was no furniture except for a few folding chairs and wood benches. The kitchen was all torn up. Plastic covered the chandelier. There was no hot water, a few broken windows, and one space heater. Disappointment multiplied our exhaustion. A few pilgrims opted to go to a hotel.

Someone broke the spell by picking up a broom and dustpan. This house was a gift, and we soon chose to be grateful—it was Thanksgiving after all. As road-hardened pilgrims, we could make it work. Another broom and a mop were found. We dug out the wash basin and rags from the van. By bedtime, it looked hopeful. As for tomorrow's Thanksgiving feast, we left that challenge for the morning.

At breakfast, we discussed a strategy for preparing dinner. We didn't know whether Greece had anything like our American Thanksgiving tradition, but we were certain it wouldn't fall on the fourth Thursday in November. Bill and I volunteered to look for a turkey and someplace to cook it. Several others took charge of shopping for the trimmings. Other pilgrims accepted the challenge of arranging a way for all thirty of us to have dinner at the same time.

Bill and I began our quest for a turkey. There were several shops offering pork and beef but no turkey. Finally, we found a place that had enough roasted chickens to feed thirty people. Other pilgrims scoured Halkida in pursuit of the other items. It was like a scavenger hunt.

Back at the house, the largest room was cleaned more thoroughly. Several doors were laid down on sawhorses to make a dining table. Potatoes were boiled on the camp stove. Two salads—one fruit, the other green—were prepared. When all thirty of us sat down late that afternoon, we discovered that our body heat made the room comfortable, even without the space heater. The love we shared warmed the room as we gave thanks.

As we neared Athens, the birthplace of democracy, we felt the warmer temperatures of the Mediterranean climate. George rallied. A stubborn old bird he was. Undoubtedly, he sensed how close we were getting to the Holy Land, and he got a second wind. Our attention shifted to the uncertainty about whether Bookda would be able to continue to Israel and under what conditions.

Bookda Gheisar was the second-youngest member of the core group and the only non-Christian. She was a citizen of Iran at a time when Iranians were widely seen by Americans as terrorists, the 444-day ordeal of the fifty-two U.S. hostages in Tehran still fresh in people's minds. For Bookda, crossing international borders was challenging at best, and danger always lurked. The farther we traveled in Europe, the more visa problems Bookda experienced.

During our stay in Skopje, Yugoslavia, Bookda tried on two consecutive days to obtain a visa for Greece. On the second attempt, a local Orthodox priest went with her to assist. Both efforts failed. Then, accompanied by Kevin, Bookda traveled from Titov Veles to Belgrade to obtain a visa for Greece. While the trip succeeded, Bookda's Greek visa would expire ten days after crossing the border. We would need a month to walk to Athens. Luckily, Bookda was able to extend her visa.

Her final hurdle was an Israeli visa. Knowing this would be difficult, we had been making inquiries since January. Some officials said it would be possible. A visa could be granted if Bookda had a minimum amount of money to spend while inside the country and an airline ticket out of Israel. But would the Israelis agree to have the visa stamped on a small white card which would be removed upon leaving the country? Such courtesy was routinely extended to all Americans so there would be no record of ever having been in Israel.

The significance of this was that all Muslim countries refused to allow entrance to any person whose passport had an Israeli visa stamp in it. If a person from a Muslim country had an Israeli visa stamp in their passport, then not only would the person be denied admission into the country, but they would be unable to renew their passport. In many respects, they would cease to be a citizen of any country. If Bookda allowed an Israeli visa to be stamped in her passport, she would be effectively ceding her Iranian citizenship.

As Athens drew nearer, the pressure on Bookda grew more acute. What conditions would Israel finally stipulate for entry? Given those, what would Bookda decide? On the morning of November 27, two days before we walked into Athens, Bookda complained of sharp pains in her heart. She saw a doctor who advised rest. The following morning, Bookda phoned the Israeli embassy. She could enter Israel, but the visa would have to be stamped directly in her passport. When we gathered for lunch, Bookda told us, "This is very hard for me. If this was six months ago, I would have risked it. Then I had the strength to fight it when I got back to the U.S. But at this time, I am so exhausted, I don't feel my heart can take what I [would] have to go through after I leave Israel."

Bookda spent the rest of the day pondering her dilemma: continue all the way to Bethlehem and risk being stateless or abandon the pilgrimage so close to the end. The next morning, Bookda joined the group in walking thirteen miles into Athens, still undecided.

When we arrived in historic Syntagma Square, photographers and reporters surrounded our group as we sang "We Shall Overcome" and "Down by the Riverside." Scores of peace activists then escorted us to the dinner they had prepared.

As we waited for the food to be set out, Bookda told us, "In the midst of all this madness, I have made my decision. I cannot risk my citizenship. I do not have the energy to get a new passport at the Iranian embassy in Washington, D.C. I will finish this walk by spirit … in Grand Champ [Switzerland] with the beautiful sisters." We all took turns hugging Bookda, expressing our hope for a world without borders.

On December 1, we walked the last seven miles on the continent of Europe, from Athens to the ferry dock in Piraeus. Hovering overhead was a thick layer of brown smog. In 1983, the Athens metro area had some of the worst air pollution in the world. Acid rain had so disfigured the statues at the Parthenon that the ancient treasures had to be transferred to a museum. The extensive flaking of the sculptures reminded me of the movie *The Wizard of Oz* when the Wicked Witch of the East screams, "I'm melting!" The air stank, and it felt like particulates were scratching my face. Every quarter-mile or so, there was a factory whose smokestack belched putrid emissions, thickening the smog layer. I covered my nose and mouth with my handkerchief. I knew that such a measure was probably useless.

As we prepared to board the *Sol Olympia* ferry to Haifa, we said goodbye to Bookda. Mary Jude recorded this entry in the group journal: "We prayed with her. Dean gave her a bouquet of flowers and sang her favorite song, 'Today while the blossoms still cling to the vine.' We took turns hugging and exchanging our last words with her. Many of us were in tears, and so was Bookda. But she looked peaceful and light of heart as we waved to her from the boat."

To ease Bookda's sorrow, Anne Galisky and Mary Frazel stayed with her for a few days before Bookda flew to Switzerland and Anne and Mary took a plane to Israel. This gave Anne a chance for more rest. Mary Jude observed, "It was good to see the three of them laughing together on the shore."

13 – Setting Foot in the Holy Land

Walking in the Old City of Jerusalem.
(Photo by Bill Cox)

Milepost: 6552 – December 1, 1983

The four-deck Greek ferry sailed calm waters on its three-day voyage across the Mediterranean Sea. It stopped at the islands of Rhodes and Cyprus for five or six hours each. We took these opportunities to stretch our legs. During the crossing, we discussed how we would speak about the complex political and religious situation in Israel and the Occupied West Bank. The Israeli military controlled the West Bank, the part of Jordan captured by Israel in the 1967 war. The population was Palestinian. While most were Muslim, about ten percent were Christian—some of whom spoke Aramaic, the language Jesus had spoken 2,000 years before.

On Sunday morning, December 4, the ferry docked in Haifa—exactly three weeks until Christmas. We were in the Holy Land! When I first heard about the walk in 1981, I never thought I would be here. The end of our long trek was near. We hoisted our packs and took our place in the long line for Israeli customs. When my turn came, the security guard thoroughly searched my pack and pawed through the nylon stuff sack containing my sleeping bag. Finding nothing suspicious, the guard waved me on to the next station. I handed over my passport. The customs official examined the other visas stamped in my passport and then grabbed a small white card from a tall stack. He lifted his visa stamp, pressed it against the ink pad, and then thud, stamped the white card. I was authorized to be in Israel. Just that simple. The card was then placed inside my passport.

I thought of Bookda being left behind in Greece and the harsh injustice of official papers. Had I betrayed Bookda? I felt soiled—very much like the titular ugly American in Burdick and Lederer's 1958 novel. The small white card was evidence of the special relationship between the U.S. and Israel. The Israeli government depended on billions of dollars in U.S. foreign and military assistance. Some U.S. Jewish groups lavished additional billions on Israel. In my passport, there is no proof I was ever in Israel—the white card was removed when I left. My four weeks there and on the Occupied West Bank never officially happened.

That was the way Israel and the U.S. wanted it—that I was never there. They turned a blind eye to what I saw, heard, smelled, tasted, and felt. Then as now, two governments disavowed the reality of Palestinians being kept prisoners in their own homeland. They pretended that I didn't see the wreckage after Israeli soldiers bulldozed a Palestinian home and orchard. They wanted me to forget what I heard from boys who limped beside me on the Occupied West Bank—limping because Israeli soldiers had maimed them by smashing their knees with nightsticks during a raid on their school. They wished I did not see the terrible fear in the eyes of the children surrounding me on street corners when they saw an Israeli army jeep barreling down the road. They disregarded the warnings I heard to watch for tripwires on the gates of the Jerusalem church that housed us—Jewish extremists had been booby-trapping Christian churches prior to Christmas. They hoped I would forget that Jewish reporter storming out of our press conference after we criticized Israeli policies against Palestinians.

The Palestinians have been abused by others, too. In 1917, Great Britain issued the Balfour Declaration that supported "the establishment in Palestine of a national home for the Jewish people." The British governed Palestine under a colonial mandate until 1948 when Israel declared its statehood. In the wake of the ensuing war, Jordan claimed the West Bank, and Egypt the Gaza Strip. Generations of Palestinians have been relegated to refugee camps ever since.

Two days after leaving Haifa, we entered Nazareth, the hometown of Jesus. Dominating the town was the Basilica of the Annunciation. I had no energy to visit it, though; I was too exhausted. Even though key sites of Jesus' time on earth (the Sea of Galilee and the Mount of the

Beatitudes) were only a short drive away, I did not have any motivation to get into any vehicle and do more traveling. My brain was fried. I couldn't absorb any new sights, sounds, people, or information.

I conserved whatever determination I had left for walking the last miles to Bethlehem. Just doing that would be a challenge. So, on the rest day we had in Nazareth, when other pilgrims went this way and that, I simply hung back and rested.

In December 1983, Israel waged two wars: one in Lebanon and the other against the Palestinians. Each day we walked for peace in northern Israel, we saw evidence of the war being fought less than fifty miles north of our route. Military flatbed trucks hauled mangled tanks away from the front lines. Jet fighters screamed overhead, heading north for attacks. In the faces of young Israeli soldiers, we saw the strain as they awaited orders that would send them north to provide reinforcements.

In response to an assassination attempt on the Israeli ambassador to the UK, Israel invaded Lebanon on June 6, 1982. Casualty estimates for the Lebanon War put the death toll at more than 20,000 people. The largest loss of life was the massacre in the Sabra and Shatila refugee camps in mid-September 1982. The perpetrators were armed militants supported by the Israeli Defense Forces. Thousands were killed. While most of the fighting ended in the fall of 1982, sporadic violence continued for years. Israel didn't completely withdraw from Lebanon until 2000.

On the road from Nazareth to Afula, Alice and Mary Jude spoke with an Israeli soldier who had just gotten off a bus. As Mary Jude described their encounter, "His English was very good, and he was more than willing to talk. In fact, he poured out his heart. He had been in Lebanon and saw his best friend killed by a man. He had Arab friends whose brothers murdered Palestinians for talking to a Jew. He said those people were mad, and what he said was not out of bigotry, but out of pain. He wanted to be a soldier, but as he left us, he also said he was glad we were doing what we were doing, and he took our leaflet and kissed it. Then, gun in hand, he ran off."

The next day, we headed toward Hadera. En route, we walked across the Plain of Megiddo (also called Esdraelon)—the purported site where the final battle of good and evil will be waged (Revelation 16:14). With Israeli military jets thundering overhead, I wondered how close the world was to a nuclear Armageddon.

Milepost: 6632 – December 13, 1983

The entire West Bank, an area west of the Jordan River and about the size of Delaware, was occupied by Israel from 1967 until 2000, when a patchwork of areas came under the control of the Palestinian Authority. The total territory under Palestinian control amounts to only 18% of the West Bank. Twenty-two percent is under joint Israeli and Palestinian control. Israel retains control over 60% of the West Bank which includes over 200 settlements connected by a series of protected roads. Under international law, all the Jewish settlements on the West Bank are illegal.

As we crossed from Israel into the Occupied West Bank, we immediately noted the sharp contrast. Israel was like California's Imperial Valley with its lush, irrigated fields and orange groves. The Palestinian farms were strewn with rocks and struggling, parched crops. Israel diverted most of the flow of the Jordan River on its way south. By the time the Jordan reached the Occupied West Bank, its trickle was nowhere close to making the Palestinian desert bloom.

Military vehicles frequently passed us on the road as we walked. In Palestinian towns, we encountered Israeli troops on foot patrol, with their Uzis usually slung over one shoulder or the other. The Israeli military barred Palestinians from any public gathering larger than five people. We routinely attracted more people on street corners, driven by the oddity of a group of Americans walking. During these impromptu gatherings, everyone watched for the approach of army patrols.

Israel blocked any significant economic development in the West Bank. The Palestinian roads were not maintained by Israel—locals had to make repairs by hand. Israel barred Palestinians from building any factories and imposed frequent blockades on supplies from other countries. Houses appeared dilapidated. Moreover, the wages paid to Palestinians were only about one-fifth of those paid to the Jewish workers doing the same job.

In Tulkarm, we encountered our first refugee camp. Since the establishment of Israel in 1948, over one million Palestinians have been confined to squalid camps. Built on just sixty-five acres, the Tulkarm camp was one of the most densely populated refugee camps in the Occupied West Bank (estimates range from 150 to 330 people per acre). In addition to the nineteen Palestinian refugee camps in the West Bank, there are thirty-nine other camps for Palestinian refugees throughout the Middle East (Lebanon, Jordan, Syria, and the Gaza Strip) with services provided by the United Nations. For more than seventy years, generations of Palestinian refugees have lived and died within the confines of the camps. In addition, more than four million Palestinian refugees live near the camps and are eligible to receive services through them.

It occurred to me that the Israeli oppression of Palestinians resembled the United States' conquest of indigenous American Indians. The U.S. relegated the first peoples to parcels without any apparent economic potential. The Israelis pushed the Palestinians to the wastelands that the Jews didn't want. As in the U.S., with its network of forts and military outposts, Israel continues to develop its own system of fortified Jewish settlements proliferating across the West Bank.

On December 15, we walked four miles from Beit Iba to Nablus, the second-largest city in the West Bank. As we entered the dusty streets around mid-afternoon, it was eerie how quiet the town was. I saw only a few people. But there was something else, a physical sensation I'd never experienced before, or since. It was as if there was a thick, invisible fog clogging the streets, almost as if it was a type of force field. My skin began to crawl.

After venturing into the town center, I realized the entire town was seething with heartbreak, anger, and hatred. A few days before, I had heard a news broadcast about a Jewish settler having fired several shots in the central plaza. One of the bullets killed a ten-year-old Palestinian girl in a shop lining the square. The settler was not arrested.

I looked around and saw a group of buildings atop a hill looming over the town. It was a Jewish settlement. I wondered whether the settler who shot the girl lived there. Even before sunset, the security lights shone brightly, ringing the hilltop fortification. The West Bank was dotted with such strategically placed settlements, each one an obstacle to a two-state solution.

One night on the Occupied West Bank, I was hosted by a Palestinian family. In my pilgrimage experience, Palestinians were very generous in offering hospitality, second only to the Irish. After dinner at the local community center, the father of one of the families drove me along a curving road to his home. The squat house blended in with the arid and barren landscape. After showing me where to put my backpack, he ushered me into the living room. He introduced me to his wife and children who then quietly made their way to other parts of the house. The father invited me to have a seat on the sofa. I sat on one end, and he on the other.

The room's beautiful splashes of color made the humble home feel full of life. The father was in his mid-thirties and of medium build. His face was animated and bright, telegraphing his excitement at having the opportunity to converse with a visitor from the United States.

I thanked him again for his kind hospitality. He replied, "It is my pleasure. Please let me know if there is anything you need. As you can see, my family does not have much, but we are glad to share what we have. Permit me to ask you a question."

"Sure, go ahead."

"Now that you have had a chance to walk in both Israel and the West Bank, what is your impression of our situation? How does it differ from your previous understanding—before your trek?"

I answered honestly. "I think the biggest surprise for me is how harsh the Israeli soldiers treat the Palestinians. I was shocked to learn how Israel diverts water from the Jordan River to irrigate its own agricultural enterprises while providing only a trickle to Arab farmers. I have spoken with several Palestinian youths in recent days. They told me of the frequent visits of soldiers to their school to harass them. One boy who was about twelve years old walked with a limp and said that several months ago, soldiers came and hustled all the students out onto the nearby soccer pitch. One soldier struck him with his nightstick and fractured his kneecap."

I continued, "Probably the worst thing I saw was the ruins of a house that had been bulldozed by the army the day before because a youth in the family was suspected of throwing stones at a security patrol. Not only had the Israelis bulldozed the family's home, but they also uprooted their grove of olive trees. It is appalling the number of human rights abuses that Israel commits with impunity. None of this is ever reported on American television. Seeing all of this, it seems to me that you are prisoners in your own land. I can't help but think of how similar it is with World War II."

"What do you mean?" my host asked.

"The situation seems eerily like Nazi Germany and how Hitler killed six million Jews and five million other people whom he considered to be subhuman. I do not understand why the Jewish Israelis cannot see the parallels to the Holocaust. They are trying to subjugate Palestinians in the hopes they will leave."

My host's jaw tightened. Leaning forward, he raised his right hand and shook his index finger at me. Looking directly into my eyes, he sternly said, "You are mistaken, my friend. What the Nazis did to the Jews was not as bad as the Jewish propaganda imagines. Perhaps a few hundred Jews were killed, but certainly not millions."

I couldn't believe my ears. A Palestinian home on the West Bank was the last place I expected to encounter someone who discounted the Holocaust. I was speechless. I didn't want to get into an argument with him, but I couldn't help saying, "What about all the film footage and photographs and records? How can you say the mass killing of Jews and other Europeans didn't happen or that it wasn't horrible?"

"Again," he replied, "that is just what the Jewish propaganda machine wants the world to believe. Most of it is manufactured."

Arguing with him was pointless. I can't remember if I tried to change the subject or just made a comment about how late it was getting. Whatever words I used, I tried to politely say that it was time for me to go to sleep.

As I climbed into my sleeping bag, I pondered his failure to acknowledge the full horror of the Holocaust. How was it possible he couldn't accept the Nazi crimes against humanity? How could one subjugated people not understand the horrendous suffering of another, especially one so well-documented? Could his hatred of Israeli Jews be so intense as to blind him to historical facts? Here was an example of how truth is the first casualty in war. Somehow my mind quieted down, and I drifted off to sleep.

The next morning, I woke to bright sunshine. I heard people moving in the rest of the house. As I dressed and stuffed my sleeping bag into its sack, I tried to make sense of my conversation the night before. But there was no sense to it. I decided there was no point in me getting him to acknowledge historical facts. Any such attempt would only frustrate both of us.

When I walked into the living room, the mother of the family was setting out food for breakfast. At the far end of the room, she placed bowls of hummus, olives, and feta cheese in the center of a dark red Turkish rug. She invited me to sit down on the rug. I was soon joined by several children all dressed for school. The mother sat down and placed a large bowl of dough beside her. She took some in her hands and started working it to make a flat circle. She placed it in the bottom of a nearby pan to cook. When it was slightly brown on each side, she handed the pita bread to me and motioned for me to load some of the food from the bowls and start eating.

The children looked at me with curious expressions—as if to say to each other, "This should be interesting." As the mother quickly prepared more of the thin bread and gave it to her children, I struggled to figure out a way to hold the bread so it could serve as a plate while I ate. The children were well-mannered and began to load up their own pieces of bread with the toppings. The father entered and sat beside me. We greeted each other warmly enough. I was grateful for this family welcoming me into their home, giving me a place to sleep, and feeding me. Like so many of my experiences since setting off from Seattle, I better understood the complexities of making peace in the world.

Two days later in Ramallah, the West Bank's largest city, about ten other pilgrims and I experienced a moment of terror as we drove to Jerusalem to attend the opening ceremony of a new peace academy at the Tantur Ecumenical Institute. Tantur is a program of the University of Notre Dame and strives to foster deeper understanding among Christian churches and build relationships with people of other faiths, especially Judaism and Islam.

As our van passed a school, the students were leaving the campus. Immediately, they picked up stones and pieces of metal and began pelting the van.

Dozens of thuds and dings hit the van. We saw the students' faces fill with hatred as they hurled more and more objects against the van. Why was this happening?

Suddenly, the rear window of the van shattered as a large rock burst through. The van sped up, and our attackers ended their barrage.

Inside the van, everybody began breathing again. We checked with each other. No one had been injured, though hundreds of bits of broken glass now littered the van's floor. For the rest of the trip into Jerusalem, we replayed that explosion of violence and tried to make sense of it. Why had the students attacked us?

As we pieced the incident together, we concluded the students mistook us for Jewish settlers—both due to our light complexions and the color of the van's license plates. In the Occupied West Bank, Palestinian license plates were blue, while Israeli plates were yellow. Since we bought the van in the Netherlands, the license plates were light-orange, nearly the same color as Israeli plates. We hypothesized that the students had vented their hatred of Jews for relegating Palestinians to an oppressed and persecuted caste. The stone-throwing had been an automatic reflex. See enemy—hurt enemy.

After walking through the Occupied West Bank, I was able to see how the hatred of each side toward the other hindered progress toward a peaceful resolution. American dollars, both U.S. foreign assistance and private donations from Christian Evangelicals and Jewish Americans, enabled the construction and operation of the settlements.

Milepost: 6692 – December 20, 1983

A few days later, we walked into Jerusalem. Christmas and Bethlehem were now close. The long journey from the Trident base outside of Seattle was nearly complete. I had stuck it out—I could hardly believe it. The little town of Bethlehem was only a few miles away. I had remained faithful to my calling and overcome my fears, self-doubts, and temptations to quit. My mind and body ached with exhaustion.

Our host church in Jerusalem was St. Peter in Galicantu, built to mark the Gospel account of St. Peter hearing the cock crow and fulfilling Jesus' prediction that Peter would deny Jesus three times. Beneath the church, archeologists had discovered an old dungeon which may have been where Jesus was held the night before his crucifixion.

In contrast to the ornately decorated sacred sites I visited (e.g., the Church of the Holy Sepulcher and the Church of the Nativity), this simple stone site was unadorned. The dungeon had been hewn out of solid rock with only a circular, two-foot hole at the top through which the prisoner was lowered down or hoisted up by rope. Around the rim of the hole were four crosses that had been chiseled centuries before. The hole extended down two or three feet through solid rock before opening into the dungeon. The chamber was about ten feet wide. There were no other markings or decorations. The only thing changed from the first century was a stairway for pilgrims to use. On the afternoon I visited, I sat alone on a stone bench.

After a short while, I felt a presence. In ways I cannot explain, I understood this presence was Jesus, sitting to my left, almost shoulder to shoulder. I had never experienced anything like this before. While I knew that saints had had mystical experiences, I never imagined that I would have one. I was skeptical of the Bible's miracle accounts. This took me by surprise.

My encounter with Jesus was intimate and silent. I didn't hear Jesus speak. His silence invited me to ponder all the suffering Jesus had borne and experienced through the centuries—for I believe that Jesus experiences the suffering caused by wars and the pain of people caused by spending money on weapons instead of human needs.

I cannot remember how long I sat there or when other pilgrims entered, bringing an end to the silence. That time and space was blessed—I came away feeling a profound reassurance—Jesus lives within each of us.

On the day before Christmas Eve, we were given a guided tour of Yad Vashem—the World Holocaust Remembrance Center in Jerusalem. The center is dedicated to preserving the memory of the six million Jews and five million others (Roma, gays, Catholics) exterminated during the Holocaust. Inside on a wall, a huge map of Europe lists the number of Jews who lived in each country before the Final Solution, the number deported to concentration camps, and the number who died there. What was most surprising to me was that Denmark was the only country from which relatively few Jews had been sent to the extermination camps. I wanted to know why Denmark was different—how had they resisted the Nazi madness? After the pilgrimage, I found the answer: The Danish had organized themselves to resist the Nazis through mostly nonviolent means and prevented the mass deportation of Jews.

Laurie Hasbrook described her experience at Yad Vashem in this excerpt from our pilgrimage newsletter: "Walking the grounds, I found that silence pervaded all. Few of the many visitors spoke as they looked at the displays. I noticed a young woman with tears streaming down her face pass me, and on a bench sat a man with his head in his hands. The director emphasized that one cannot understand the present state of Israel or the Jewish people without understanding the effects of the Holocaust. Never before had an entire people been targeted for elimination. The concern for security which dominates Israeli society is a result of an abandonment experience during the Holocaust.

"My own desire to witness for peace results, in a large part, from the impact of knowing that the majority of Christians remained silent as the Jews were persecuted in World War II. How could people remain silent when such evil occurred? … When will the cycle of violence end? This cycle of violence which daily destroys life in this land where Jesus once walked. The cycle of violence which permits America, Russia, and others to prepare for the final war, a total Holocaust.

"Leaving Yad Vashem, I walked a road bordered by trees planted in memory of gentiles who risked and sometimes lost their lives aiding the Jews in World War II. May each of us dare to shatter the silence as they did. May the memory of the martyrs of the Nazi concentration camps compel us to cry out against all injustice and take those risks which will ensure that the trees of remembrance at Yad Vashem will blossom for centuries to come."

That evening, several Jewish families in the Jerusalem area welcomed us into their homes to share in the Shabbat dinner. I went to the home of Rabbi Jeremy and Hillary Milgrom. Both were born in the United States but had emigrated to Israel. Rabbi Milgrom became a conscientious objector while serving in the Israeli military and advocated against the violations of human rights in Gaza and the West Bank.

The next day, Christmas Eve, around 200 of our supporters joined us for an afternoon reception in a long hallway at the Pontifical Institute Notre Dame de Jerusalem Center, located just outside the Christian Quarter of the Old City. Guest walkers came from many countries including the U.S., Ireland, Great Britain, France, Italy, Netherlands, Germany, Australia, and Japan. Because the final walk would be during the dinner hour, we fortified ourselves with sandwiches and hot chocolate. At 4:00 p.m., we gathered outside in the large courtyard, forming several concentric circles. As the sun set, the evening chill started to wick away heat from our bodies.

We listened closely to details about the evening's route, security precautions, and other logistics. For those supporters who were unable to travel to Bethlehem, we took turns reading aloud messages that they had sent, pledging to join us in prayer from their home countries at the same time as our last segment. The most touching note came from Switzerland where the Grand Champ sisters were keeping vigil with Bookda. After a final prayer of thanksgiving, we set out in silence on the final eight-mile stretch of our twenty-month journey.

Twilight surrendered to night as we walked through the Kidron Valley with the Mount of Olives to our left. We skirted the City of David (an ancient community on the southeastern edge of the Old City) and walked along a heavily trafficked road. After several miles, wanting to avoid the large crowds heading to Bethlehem, we turned onto a less traveled road and soon found ourselves in a surprisingly eerie setting. The air was smoky. Various odors wafted from the darkness ahead. Our eyes began to adjust to the near-total darkness as the nearly full moon had yet to rise. Was this really the way? Had we taken a wrong turn? Would the road be a dead end? Would we be attacked by terrorists in this desolate area?

Numerous small fires dotted either side of the road, stretching for perhaps a hundred yards or more. Without any streetlights, it was difficult to see. The haunting silence was punctuated by the forlorn barking of dogs.

We were walking through a garbage dump! A bit further on, we caught glimpses of stray dogs silhouetted against the flickering flames, scavenging among the trash piles.

The whole scene was surreal. None of us ever imagined that the final leg of our long trek would be through a dark, smoldering garbage dump. From a few feet behind me, I heard Pam remark in a low voice, "It feels like hell itself."

Milepost: 6700 – December 24, 1983

Wanting to avoid the throngs of tourists in Manger Square and the Church of the Nativity, we held our closing celebration at Shepherds' Field in Beit Sahur, on the eastern outskirts of Bethlehem. Dim electric lights around the stone grotto allowed our candles to shine.

Singing "Silent Night," we processed in and sat on the concrete floor, leaning our backs against the wall. The older pilgrims sat on a small ledge at the far end of the grotto.

In offering a reflection to the assembled, Benoit Charlemagne, the French Capuchin priest, shouted in his heavily accented English, "We are here. WE ARE HERE! It was a crazy idea. It was a CRAZY idea. Some day we will have peace by taking lots of little steps and we'll find ourselves saying, 'Here we are.'"

Pam then came forward with the four colorful bags of soil and healing herbs that Steve Old Coyote entrusted to us at the grave of Chief Seattle on the second day of the walk. She opened the small bags and carefully mixed the dirt and herbs into the soil at Shepherds' Field. When the bags were empty, she walked a few feet away and scooped up some of Bethlehem's soil to take back to the Suquamish Tribe.

Next, we took turns reciting the names of all the nearly 400 towns we stayed in: "St. Andrew's Mission ... Holbrook ... Steamboat Springs ... Norcatur ... Lone Jack ... Salt Fork State Park ... Cumberland ... Trim ... Belfast ... Edinburgh ... Milton Keynes ... Taizé ... Nyon ... Modena ... Brezovica ... Halkida ... Tulkaram. ..."

Maureen Casey, the retired nurse from Georgia, recalled as she listened to the hundreds of towns being read out, "All those people in all those towns had somehow been affected ... there was an awesomeness about just reading the litany of those towns. It was, wow, these ... people have traveled all that way! They've been through it all and they've stuck it out."

How did I feel as I sat there on the cold, hard ground? My tiredness enveloped me like a fog. Exhaustion mingled with deep satisfaction—we had reached our geographical goal. I was sobered by knowing that our ultimate goal—abolishing nuclear weapons—was still far off.

The ceremony ended with everyone singing "Joy to the World." We thanked those who had walked this final stretch. As they dispersed, we and the Shepherds' Field pilgrims walked into Bethlehem. Due to the influx of Christmas tourists, we hadn't been able to find a place to spend that night—no room in the inn. After walking a mile or so, we arrived at the Bethlehem Bible College, and our host led us up a set of stairs. After ascending several flights, we passed through a doorway and into the chilly air. We were on the roof. To our right was a pile of sleeping bags and backpacks. For the final night of our journey, we slept under the stars.

It was hard for me to settle down to sleep. Yes, I was bone-tired. But my mind buzzed with the wonderment that we had made it. After eighteen months of organizing and twenty months of nearly constant traveling, it was over. By persisting, I forged lifelong bonds with nineteen amazing people. Together we had made a powerful statement for nuclear disarmament—ordinary citizens can tackle global threats in effective and creative ways that instill hope.

As dawn brightened, we climbed out of our sleeping bags. The rooftop provided a 360° view of Bethlehem. We posed for group photos with the town in the background. After grabbing some breakfast, we walked to Manger Square. Because we got there early, the square was empty. At the Church of the Nativity, we learned the doorway had been built to be intentionally short, forcing people to bow their heads when entering the church that two millennia of pilgrims have honored as the birthplace of Jesus Christ, the Prince of Peace.

We spent the next two days reflecting on our achievement and staged our own awards ceremony, sharing many humorous anecdotes from the walk. Before we departed to go our separate ways, we held our final sharing meeting. The most recent pilgrim to join the core group, Sr. Genevieve began, "It was a gift of grace that I could reach Bethlehem. I marvel at how we have been supported by the tremendous numbers of good-willed people we met along the way and who walked with us in spirit. We are still confronted by the most dangerous and fatal age in which we possess nuclear weapons. But who's to blame? I know that I, myself, have that evil within. I should not forget as a Japanese that I have responsibility for the numerous lives which Japan took in past wars. For me, on the pilgrimage, I have been called to do something for peace with my whole being."

As the first one inspired to walk to Bethlehem, Jack recalled, "I saw God over and over again in Ireland's tons of beautiful children, in the grit of Yugoslavia and Palestine, in the haunting look of so many Europeans who knew war all too well and looked upon us with hope for a better world. Above all, God was present in our little band of pilgrims—determined, forgiving, generous, prayerful, and honest. We fell in love with that great round world that is God's. Above all, I learned, or relearned, the meaning of dependence on others: for food, lodging, interpreting foreign tongues and pointing the way. I relearned that God is more present to us than we are to ourselves, that God is incredibly faithful to those who are of goodwill, lean upon God's mercy, and search the way of peace."

For myself, I shared, "The pilgrimage has given me a visceral sense of the interrelatedness of all people and all creation. I feel this connectedness in my marrow and sinews and blood. Through being exposed to hours of all kinds of weather each day, I feel in sync with the cycle of the seasons. By meeting so many people, by receiving abundant hospitality from so many, I have not only an intellectual appreciation for the rich diversity of the human family but a vibrating resonance throughout my body, mind, heart, and spirit of being intimately connected with every other human person. The pining for peace is universal."

Over all those miles and months, I also gained a robust sense of self-confidence. If you can help organize and endure a walk spanning three continents and nearly two years, you come away with a feeling that you can do almost anything. During the long flights back home to Spokane, I began to ponder what next—what would I do for an encore after walking halfway across the world? What else could I do to turn back the world's mad rush toward nuclear conflagration? How could I continue my quest for peace?

Trail Two

Pursuing the Truth about Hanford

14 – The Plutonium Factory in My Backyard

Hanford's Redox plant.

After so many months on the road, it was disorienting to stay in the same place for more than a few nights, especially when that place was the basement of my parents' house. I had not lived there for five years. I was the most tired I had ever been. Now, this quiet, cozy, familiar room offered me a restful sanctuary until I could figure out what I wanted to do next.

The arms race proceeded apace. In the January 1984 issue of the *Bulletin of the Atomic Scientists*, the editors moved the minute hand of the "doomsday clock" from four to three minutes to midnight. The editors observed, "The accelerating nuclear arms race and the almost complete breakdown of communication between the superpowers have combined to create a situation of extreme and immediate danger." Only once before, in 1953 when the first hydrogen bomb was exploded, had the doomsday clock been any closer to midnight.

With my pilgrimage experience, could I get a job advocating for disarmament? I checked with several peace groups in Spokane and Seattle, but there were no openings, and none were likely to become available. Many nonprofits were experiencing funding shortfalls, as donors shifted their contributions to candidates for the 1984 presidential race. As I regained my energy, I mailed out the last newsletter, closed the bank account, and filed the necessary forms to dissolve the Bethlehem Peace Pilgrimage as a nonprofit organization. I searched for a new avenue for my disarmament efforts. I had been back from Bethlehem for six weeks when the answer landed on the front porch one morning.

The Spokesman-Review's banner headline on February 11 read "Soviets Mourn Death of Leader." The caption under a photo of Yuri Andropov noted that his time as the top Soviet leader was the briefest in history. His demise raised questions about the stability of the Soviet Union.

At the bottom of the page was another story related to the arms race: "Hanford defends 'non-problem' emission." The Hanford Nuclear Reservation, about 110 miles southwest of Spokane, sprawled over 570 square miles of desert—roughly half the size of Rhode Island. The "non-problem" in question was a radioactive release that had come from the Plutonium Uranium Extraction facility—known by its acronym PUREX. Its product was not bleach but plutonium—the material at the core of every nuclear weapon in the U.S. arsenal. Established in 1943 as part of the Manhattan Project, Hanford's original plants produced the plutonium in the atomic bomb that obliterated Nagasaki. Built in the mid-1950s, PUREX was mothballed in 1972 and had only resumed operations in November 1983 while I was walking through Greece. Its purpose was to produce plutonium for the Reagan Administration's nuclear weapons buildup.

Around the same time, I saw the newly released movie *Silkwood,* starring Meryl Streep and Cher. Streep portrayed Karen Silkwood who worked at a plutonium plant in Oklahoma that used plutonium from Hanford and configured it for use in Hanford's newest reactor, the Fast Flux Test Facility (FFTF). Silkwood died in 1974 when her car crashed on her way to meet a *New York Times* reporter with documentation of falsified safety records concerning the welds of fuel elements destined for Hanford. Her documents disappeared from her mangled Honda Civic.

The brief reference to Hanford in the *Silkwood* movie piqued my curiosity. My high school physics class had visited Hanford on a field trip in 1973, touring the Fast Flux Test Facility, then under construction. That Hanford was the largest producer of plutonium for the U.S. nuclear arsenal drove me to devote the next several weeks searching for information about Hanford and the Silkwood case. Because the internet was still in its infancy, I scoured the public library's card catalog for books on Hanford and found only one: Paul Loeb's *Nuclear Culture*. It mostly focused on the workers at Hanford and their attitudes toward their jobs.

There were few details about the plutonium factories and little mention of its operating history.

At the downtown B. Dalton bookstore, I bought *The Killing of Karen Silkwood* by Richard Rashke. It was a chilling account about Silkwood who, in the weeks leading up to her death, had been contaminated with enough plutonium that very likely would have caused a serious cancer. The Silkwood book described how workers at her plutonium plant were being pressured to alter safety documentation to meet production schedules. I wondered if workers at Hanford's PUREX might be subjected to similar pressures, especially as President Reagan seemed determined to acquire more nuclear warheads as quickly as possible.

Silkwood's family sued the plant operator, Kerr-McGee. Investigators for the family's attorneys determined that her car had been forced off the road. They searched for the documents that had been in Karen's car—evidence of doctored quality assurance reports and the secret diversion of plutonium from the plant. According to Rashke's book, the trail led to several federal agencies that were apparently covering up anything connected to Silkwood's death, including the FBI, CIA, and the National Security Agency (NSA). At least two key witnesses died under mysterious circumstances shortly before their depositions by attorneys for Karen's family. There was also an attempt to kill the plant's personnel director. Because of the Hanford connection, I wondered about what I might encounter if I investigated Hanford.

I called a physics professor at Gonzaga University, my alma mater. What did he know about Hanford and its radiation releases? He made it clear that he didn't consider radiation exposure to be a serious concern and said I was wasting my time asking about any hazard from Hanford. Several of his former students worked there, and he assured me that everything was under control. I asked about Three Mile Island, the partial meltdown of a Pennsylvania commercial power reactor in 1979. He scoffed at that, telling me that the news media had been alarmist and blown things way out of proportion.

In May 1984, Spokane's Unitarian pastor Bill Houff delivered a galvanizing sermon to his congregation, titled "A Silent Holocaust: A Trail of Ignorance, Deceit and Tears." He recounted the history of human suffering caused by exposure to ionizing radiation. "It would be bad enough if the present and future legacy of the atomic era were simply the result of ignorance. What makes it ever so much more tragic is that it is a story rife with deceit." Throughout, he raised many questions about Hanford as a radiation hazard. Houff concluded his hour-long sermon by exhorting his congregation to find the answers. "We must become a great deal better-informed personally and an enormous amount more hard-nosed in confronting our politicians, bureaucrats, and technicians who offer us platitudes and lies while inexorably killing us and our unborn children."

Responding to his challenge, about fifteen Unitarians started a study group to seek answers. A few weeks later, I saw a notice in the local social justice newsletter about the group's weekly meetings. I joined their next one.

Throughout that summer, we shared the fruits of our research about Hanford and radiation. Led by several members who were physicians, we learned about how radiation damages human health. In addition to its nuclear weapons role, Hanford and two other sites were being studied as the repository of the nation's high-level nuclear waste. If Hanford was chosen, nearly all the country's highly radioactive waste would be transported through the center of Spokane on its way to Hanford.

We also learned that Hanford's weapons-grade plutonium was shipped to the Rocky Flats facility near Denver. Following refinement there, the plutonium went to the Pantex plant outside Amarillo, Texas, where it was assembled with other nuclear weapon components. From Pantex, the weapons were deployed to U.S. military bases, including the Trident base near Seattle—by a train painted white, ostensibly to keep the cars' nuclear warheads cooler during transit.

On Tuesday, July 24, I got a call from Jim Douglass, a peace activist whose house sat beside the train tracks as they entered the Trident base. "The white train with its load of nearly 200 nuclear warheads left Pantex a few hours ago. I'm estimating that the train could pass through Spokane in two or three days. Could you help me monitor the movement of the train when it nears Spokane?" I told Jim that I would do whatever I could to help. On its way from Texas, the train would pass through Oklahoma, Kansas, Colorado, Wyoming, Montana, and the northern tip of Idaho. Jim had enlisted my help so protests could be planned along the route as the train passed.

The next day, Jim called me back to give me an update on the train's progress. "I expect the white train to pass through Spokane on Thursday night." With guidance from Jim, I scouted various locations in Spokane for a local protest. There was a vacant lot just west of downtown that provided an ideal location for a group of people to gather near the elevated rail line. It also provided a view of the junction where trains could either go right (west toward Seattle) or turn left onto tracks that led south and west toward Portland.

Early on Thursday evening, protesters in Sandpoint, Idaho called Jim shortly after the train passed through there. Jim then asked me to be at the vacant lot in Spokane by 10:30 p.m.

When I arrived, there were already a hundred people milling around and conversing. It was a warm summer night. Some people had been there for hours, keeping vigil and letting others know about the approach of the white train and its purpose. They held candles or carried signs.

The white train was unique in more than its color. The custom-designed cars were unlike any of the rolling stock that crisscrossed the country every day. The white train had nine cars that were significantly lower in height than normal freight cars. These held the warheads. In front, behind, and in the middle of the weapon cars were three security cars that carried armed guards and special communications equipment. Because the train would roll through Spokane at night, I was unsure how much I would be able to see. Would the train be traveling fast or slow?

I looked down at my watch. A few minutes past eleven o'clock and still no sign of the train. My fellow protesters and I kept our eyes focused eastward. How much longer would it be? By now, the crowd had swelled to around 150 people, and several camera crews broadcast live for the nightly news. As one of the demonstration's organizers, I was very pleased with the turnout.

Around 11:15 p.m., a Spokane police car parked at the far end of the vacant lot. A few minutes later, another car pulled alongside it. On its door was the logo for the Burlington Northern Railroad, the company that owned and maintained the tracks. Their arrival indicated the train was approaching.

Even at night, there was considerable traffic noise from nearby arterials, and Interstate 90 was only a block and a half south of the tracks. Streetlights illuminated the vacant lot and the rail line looming about ten feet above our heads. Then I saw three men scramble up the steep embankment and stand on the tracks. Two of them unrolled a large banner that read, "Halt! This train is under arrest for breaking international law and the law of the heart." Several police officers clambered up the embankment and arrested them.

As I turned my attention back east down the tracks, I saw the powerful headlight of the locomotive. It was moving much slower than the freight trains that trundled through downtown a dozen or more times every day.

When the train was a block away, I could see white cars behind two engines. As the train crawled closer, the crowd of protesters turned silent. I tried to fathom the potential destructive force of the nuclear weapons rolling past less than fifty feet from where I stood. The train bore the explosive equivalent of thousands of Hiroshima bombs.

To provide Jim Douglass with the information he wanted, I watched closely as the train started across the bridge spanning Latah Creek, 175 feet below. I strained to see the fork in the rail line.

The train angled south. I dashed to the payphone outside the Rosauer's grocery store, a block due west. I punched in my calling card number, code, and Jim's phone number.

"Jim, the train went south a few minutes ago."

He thanked me for the information and said, "Can you do me one more favor? Would you drive down to Washtucna? It's a small farming town, ninety miles south of Spokane."

"Yes, I know where it is," I responded.

"I know it's a ways, but getting another sighting of the train will help me better estimate the train's arrival time at other protests, especially

Portland. Just east of Washtucna, the tracks pass under state Highway 26. I think it will be a good location for you to view the train."

"I'll try my best, Jim." I hung up and hurried to where I had parked my car.

On my way, I saw my friend Al Mangan, a retired postal worker. Al organized weekly early-morning vigils at the main gate of Fairchild Air Force Base to remind the workers entering the base of the danger posed by nuclear weapons. Since it would be the middle of the night by the time I reached Washtucna, I was leery of being alone in such a remote place. Al readily agreed to keep me company.

We headed southwest on I-90 before turning south at Ritzville and onto State Highway 261. Shortly before 2:00 a.m., we arrived in Washtucna and found where the highway crossed above the tracks.

Since I didn't know if anyone would be guarding the overpass to provide extra security for the train's ultra-destructive cargo, I parked my car about 100 feet from the overpass. Al and I walked slowly up the overpass. We didn't see any security. Would any townspeople phone the sheriff and report us?

To the northeast, about a block away along the tracks, was a grain elevator. A few lights shone, pinpricks in the surrounding darkness. The small town was sleeping, the summer air calm and still. Had the train already passed through and we missed it? We waited. Enveloped in darkness, the quiet stillness seemed to have slowed time down. Another five (or was it ten?) minutes ticked by and still no train.

I asked Al, "How much longer do you think we should wait?"

Al, being retired, was in no rush. He assured me, "Be patient. The train will come."

After a few more minutes, there was a bright light coming down the tracks, about a quarter mile away. The light grew brighter as the train slithered along the tracks. It was not a speeding locomotive. It had a methodical, consistent pace. No one wanted a train carrying scores of nuclear warheads to derail. There was enough megatonnage coming at us to wipe much of Eastern Washington off the map. The residual radiation would render some of the most fertile land on the planet a toxic wasteland for centuries.

As the train neared, the eerie silence continued. I was expecting to hear the usual squeaks, creaks, and groans of train cars rolling on the rails. But a robust suspension system rendered the white train almost totally silent. As Al and I stood on the overpass, I wondered if the guards on the train were wearing night vision goggles and could see us. Were they pointing guns at us? Would the train stop and disperse guards to arrest us?

Nothing happened as the train glided underneath the overpass and continued on its way through rural Eastern Washington. As the white train disappeared back into the darkness, I wondered how many Germans during World War II had watched trains bound for the concentration camps. Had they known the evil purpose? I remembered how Yad Vashem paid tribute to the six million Jews and five million other people the Nazis murdered.

Al and I returned to my car in silent reflection. Preparations for World War III were continuing apace. At the payphone at Washtucna's lone gas station, I called Jim to report the train's passing. Now it was up to the protesters down the tracks.

Two weeks later, on August 11, 1984, as President Reagan was doing the soundcheck for his weekly radio address, he quipped, "My fellow Americans, I'm pleased to tell you today that I've signed legislation that will outlaw Russia forever. We begin bombing in five minutes." While it was not broadcast live, the comment was widely reported in the following days. How could the president be so cavalier about the peril of nuclear war?

Growing up in Eastern Washington, I knew how staunchly conservative it was. Spokane's annual festival, the Lilac Parade, was held on Armed Forces Day. Especially in those several months after returning home, challenging nuclear weapons often felt like a lonely, futile effort. But what if I and others could show that Hanford was unsafe? Would citizens support nuclear disarmament if they knew that producing nuclear weapons threatened their health and that of their children?

By the time September rolled around, the Hanford study group that Bill Houff's sermon had sparked decided to form a nonprofit. Spokane was the largest city downwind from Hanford. If Hanford was chosen for the nation's nuclear dump, then most of the nation's high-level nuclear waste would travel through Spokane's central business district by rail or truck.

It was exciting to be one of the founders of a new organization. We named our group the Hanford Education Action League (HEAL). That same month, I was hired by the Catholic Diocese of Spokane to a half-time position coordinating peace and social justice ministry. I volunteered the other half of my time for HEAL and joined its steering committee.

Politically and culturally, HEAL was well aware of the challenges we faced. Plenty of Americans, especially in Spokane, would resist a group formed to scrutinize a facility that many believed was vital to America's national security. The Cold War was at one of its most intense junctures. Spokane was an anti-communist bastion, just as stalwart as when my parents took me to that campaign rally for Barry Goldwater two decades earlier. In asking any probing questions about Hanford, we would be perceived as unpatriotic or even worse, Soviet puppets.

HEAL set out to hold Hanford accountable to health and safety laws. We took great pains to establish and maintain our credibility by being a reliable source of information. We did not want to be easily dismissed.

I remember one bright, sunny morning sometime in 1985. My office in the Diocese of Spokane's Chancery looked out over Riverside Avenue—across the street was the ornate Spokane Club and the Chamber of Commerce. Beyond, I could see dark basalt outcroppings, the result of centuries of erosion as the Spokane River carved its channel ever deeper. Ron Gerton, the director of environmental safety and health for the U.S. DOE at Hanford, was on the phone, returning my call from earlier that morning.

I wanted to know if he had the authority to shut down PUREX if it could not meet health and safety standards. Almost immediately Gerton got defensive. I had asked a simple question: Did he have the authority to protect worker safety and public health? I was hoping for a simple yes or no answer.

Gerton sounded agitated, as if my question had struck a raw nerve. Did he not want to admit that he lacked the authority to shut down a plant for safety reasons? He seemed to be hiding what everyone guessed—the production of plutonium for nuclear weapons was paramount.

Why did he seem so afraid to answer my question? Could the situation at Hanford be similar to the Karen Silkwood case?

My dad suffered his second heart attack in the summer of 1985 (his first had been in 1974 when I was a freshman in college). As he recovered from this second attack, he was noticeably weaker and spent more time around the house. I did not like being in the house when he was there. This made my living situation so uncomfortable that I moved out a few months later. I found a bright apartment overlooking Latah Creek on the western edge of Spokane's historic Browne's Addition neighborhood, within easy walking distance of my office. While I enjoyed the quiet of living alone, my solitary existence did not last long.

On the first Sunday in December, the Chancery held an open house. One of the visitors was Jan Perry, an assistant youth minister at the cathedral. She asked if I might be interested in a meeting of her young adult group that evening. After arriving at the meeting, I found Jan to thank her for letting me know about the group.

Soon, she asked, "How did you get involved with peace and justice?"

I responded, "I walked to Bethlehem for nuclear disarmament."

While her friends milled about, we found a quiet corner, and for the next hour she posed one question after another about the pilgrimage. Jan's curiosity probed beyond the physical adventure—she sought to understand the spiritual aspects of the journey and its impact on me.

She wore simple clothes and no makeup—a clear sign to me that she was comfortable with being herself. I found this very attractive. After college, she had spent several years living in a convent, discerning whether she was called to religious life. When I was twenty years old, I had spent four months in the Jesuit novitiate in Portland, Oregon, doing the same thing. Independently, each of us had decided that religious life was not our calling, but our relationship with God was central to who we were.

The morning after the young adult meeting, I invited Jan to a benefit performance for the Spokane Peace and Justice Center on the following Sunday. The Interplayers Ensemble was doing *Master Harold and the Boys* by Athol Fugard about South Africa under apartheid. Jan immediately accepted and offered to bring dinner to my apartment before the play.

Jan arrived at my door with a large grocery sack and a crockpot that steamed in the winter air. She set the crockpot on the kitchen counter and plugged it in to reheat the hearty soup which she rounded out with salad and bread.

The weather that December was cold and snowy. Since the theater was only a mile from my apartment, we walked there. It was more trudging than walking as the sidewalks were covered with compact snow and ice and the temperature hovered in the teens.

While the play was thought-provoking and entertaining, I was preoccupied with my new friend sitting beside me. When we got back to my apartment, Jan collected her crockpot and told me how much she enjoyed the evening. As she stood by the door, she stepped toward me and gently kissed me. What a surprise! And how wonderful!

Following that night, we got together at least once a week. In February, I took her to meet Jack Morris, Fred Mercy, and several of the other Bethlehem pilgrims living in Western Washington. Within weeks, we were engaged, and in August 1986, we married. Naturally, several pilgrims were involved in the wedding: Fr. Jack presided, Bob Patten was my best man, and Bill served as the wedding photographer. In all, about a dozen pilgrims attended, including Maureen all the way from Atlanta. My life felt complete. Jan's calm faith in God and in me acted as an anchor. Jan was more than my better half. She called forth my better self.

In January 1986, the Environmental Policy Institute, the Hanford Education Action League (HEAL), and other citizen groups filed a massive Freedom of Information Act (FOIA) request seeking access to documents on Hanford's operational history. Before 1986, the public knew hardly anything about what had happened at the Hanford Nuclear Reservation, as it was then called. Even many of the people who worked at Hanford didn't know much. Since the super-secret days of the Manhattan Project during World War II, each worker was told only the minimum needed to do their job. Nothing more. All information was strictly controlled and shared on a need-to-know basis. The place was so secretive during the war, even the amount of beer and ice cream consumed by workers was classified. We wondered how long we'd have to wait for the documents.

15 – Documents Reveal Citizens Exposed to Invisible Radiation

PUREX control room, 1971.

Within the span of two months, my involvement in Hanford issues increased substantially. On the morning of February 26, 1986, I flew to Yakima for a meeting with Bishop William Skylstad whose diocese encompassed most of the Hanford site. The Yakima diocese was one of the poorest in the country, and most of the Catholics there were migrant farm workers. The Washington State bishops were developing a statement about radioactive wastes and the applicable ethical principles. Bishop Skylstad shared a draft of the statement with two Hanford officials: Mike Lawrence, head of the US Department of Energy's Hanford office, and Paul Lorenzini, president of Rockwell Hanford, DOE's lead contractor at Hanford. They expressed concern over the draft. In response, Bishop Skylstad invited them to his office to discuss the matter. Because I was the principal author of the paper, Bishop Skylstad asked me to be there.

The four of us sat around a small white circular table at one end of Bishop Skylstad's office. The bishop wore all black except for his white Roman collar. The two executives were impressive in their finely tailored suits and shiny shoes. My off-the-rack suit from JCPenney was no match. The two executives had spent their careers in the nuclear field. I felt massively intimidated. It had only been two years since I started looking into Hanford. Now I was in a private meeting with Hanford's top two managers.

Bishop Skylstad began with brief introductions. I learned that Lawrence was a Catholic and belonged to Christ the King Parish in Richland. Lorenzini was Episcopalian and active in his local church. I felt even more vulnerable. Not only was my paper critical of their management of Hanford, but the paper's faith perspective probably challenged their views about religion's role in public policy. How much of a hornet's nest had I stirred up?

Over the previous year and a half, I had faced three challenges in drafting the statement: (1) There wasn't much public information about Hanford and its impact on the environment; (2) Catholic theology on the environment was only then emerging; and (3) I had never written a policy statement for bishops. The first papal statement on environmental concerns would not come until 1990 when Pope John Paul II started raising moral concerns about global warming. While a physics professor from Seattle University had guided me through the various drafts of the statement, he was not in this meeting. I was definitely out of my comfort zone. I wondered if the two Hanford managers could see how nervous I was.

The two executives wasted no time in spelling out their concerns. Lawrence charged that the paper was inaccurate without citing any specifics. Lorenzini was offended by the negative tone directed toward both the Department of Energy and Rockwell. He insisted that his company had been asked to do a difficult job by the federal government—one that was crucial to ensuring the country's national security. Both acknowledged that contamination had occurred during the four decades of plutonium production, but Hanford's workers were doing everything necessary to control the spread of pollution. Lawrence also gave an overview of Hanford's new openness initiative that sought to combat recent criticisms.

I responded that everything in the statement was well-documented. I stressed that each of the drafts had been reviewed by scientists and Catholic theologians. Bishop Skylstad guided the discussion away from an adversarial debate by restating the bishops' purpose for the paper. This process was to educate themselves about an important regional issue. The bishops and their staff would continue to study the issue of radioactive waste and Hanford's role in it. Bishop Skylstad expressed his appreciation for their pledges for greater openness.

I was relieved when the meeting was over and everyone shook hands. As I made my way back to the airport, I thought I had done okay. I had a list of changes for the next draft. But when the board of the Washington State Catholic Conference met the following week, the bishops suspended any further work on the paper. Instead, they sought opportunities to continue the dialogue. Six months later, the bishops organized a panel presentation that included a theologian from Seattle University, Mike Lawrence, and me. A few days before the panel met, banner headlines across the Northwest reported new safety concerns about Hanford operations, stemming from recent safety audits. While I thought this information bolstered the need for the bishops to issue a statement, they had a different interpretation: The issue was too technical. The WSCC board voted to end any further consideration of the paper about Hanford and its nuclear waste. I was partly consoled that the bishops and key Hanford managers had at least read my paper and had an opportunity to consider the moral aspects of radioactive waste.

Also in February 1986, the U.S. Department of Energy announced its first public involvement group, the Northwest Citizens Forum on Defense Wastes. I was chosen to represent HEAL as one of two dozen members. Others included Washington and Oregon state legislators or represented tribal governments and environmental groups. The chair was Fr. Bernard Coughlin, SJ, president of Gonzaga University. Our purpose was to augment public outreach on a major environmental impact statement concerning Hanford's environmental legacy of plutonium production. A huge volume of radioactive and toxic waste had accumulated since 1944, including tens of millions of gallons of high-level nuclear waste stored in 177 large underground storage tanks.

The day after the meeting in Bishop Skylstad's office, Lawrence released a five-foot-high stack of environmental monitoring reports spanning Hanford's first forty years of operation. The release of 19,000 pages of declassified records was unprecedented. Now the public could find out what happened during the operation of the world's first industrial-scale nuclear plant. News organizations, tribal and state governments, and citizen groups including HEAL had all been clamoring for an accounting of Hanford operations. The 19,000 pages comprised many of the documents being sought through FOIA. In announcing the document release, Hanford manager Mike Lawrence assured the Northwest "there should be no observable health effects from Hanford operations."

Karen Dorn Steele of *The Spokesman-Review* and other journalists filed stories about the tall stack of documents. However, with so many other Hanford issues to cover, reporters didn't have time to read all but a few of the 19,000 pages.

Before the release of documents, citizen activists such as myself expected the documents would reveal a few serious accidents, like the 1979 Three Mile Island reactor accident in Pennsylvania. What we discovered shocked even the pessimistic among us: Hanford's bomb-making had spewed extensive radioactive pollution into both the air and the Columbia River since 1944. Even more jarring: The contamination was no accident. The releases resulted from regular factory operations, just as designed. The chief culprit was Hanford's plutonium processing plants, which operated for the first three years without any stack filters. There had been numerous accidents and equipment failures, but the contamination released during routine operations dwarfed the accidental releases. People living downwind of Hanford desperately wanted to know whether their exposure to radiation had impacted their health. Within two weeks, the U.S. Department of Energy placed sets of the 19,000 pages in public libraries around the Northwest, including Spokane.

At a meeting of the HEAL steering committee on March 13, we learned that many of the documents had paragraphs or whole pages blacked out because the information was still classified, even after more than forty years. While a cursory review of the oldest documents had generated some headlines, were there other surprises in the rest of the five-foot-high stack? Since I was working only part-time, I volunteered to take up a challenge and read all 19,000 pages.

The next morning, I grabbed a spiral notebook and headed to the Spokane Public Library, which was housed in a classic Art Deco building. HEAL's first staff person, Tim Connor, had done a preliminary review of the earliest records. At the library, Tim briefed me on how the documents were organized—chronologically in two dozen magazine boxes.

Tim grabbed the first box containing several hundred pages, and we sat down at a nearby table. He selected a report dated December 5, 1946 (document number HW-7-5463). On page three, it reported that Hanford had released 470,000 curies of iodine-131 during the first two years of operation. Tim and I could hardly believe our eyes. That amount of radiation was more than 20,000 times the amount released from the partial meltdown at the Three Mile Island reactor in 1979. During that accident, the governor of Pennsylvania advised parents to keep their children more than five miles away from the damaged and unstable reactor—as he and other officials pondered an evacuation order.

I felt sobered by my memories of working at a Spokane television station during those tense days in 1979 when the buildup of hydrogen gas threatened to blow the damaged reactor wide open. Would I find similar events in the Hanford documents? Tim left me alone with the documents—his main assignment then was scrutinizing the safety record of Hanford's N reactor.

I reached for the next document and began turning more pages. My persistence in walking all those miles to Bethlehem had prepared me well for this painstaking excavation of Hanford's history. Now I was forging a new trail—pursuing the truth about Hanford's secret history.

In the 1980s, Hanford was a vital part of U.S. national security. It had also escaped scrutiny for over forty years. Because Hanford was a key component in the nuclear weapons complex, everyone who worked at Hanford had to have a security clearance, even the janitors. Employees were admonished not to talk about their work at home. I have interviewed people who grew up in Richland because their dad worked at Hanford. But they didn't know what their dad did or even which building he worked in. Nobody said anything about their occupations, and residents quickly learned not to ask any questions.

At the start, I struggled to decipher the documents. What should I be looking for? The reported measurements used arcane units. Which ones were significant? While I took two years of chemistry and a year of physics in high school, I had no real qualifications at the outset. I learned though, as I reviewed box after box of documents. Over the next several weeks, a clearer picture emerged.

Numerous pages were filled with scientific tables and graphs. Entire reports were blotchy photocopies of carbon copies that had been transferred to microfilm, deteriorating over time. Sometimes it was impossible to make out the text. Fortunately, nearly all the documents had been typed on typewriters using the same font. By the time I reviewed half the documents, I became adept at distinguishing a blotchy letter "i" from a "t."

The documents revealed the spread of Hanford's radiation through the environment. I found a brief mention of something called the "Green Run," which turned out to be an intentional release of radiation in December 1949. A more detailed report was listed as a reference, but it was not included in the 19,000 pages. At 4,000 curies of iodine-131, the Green Run was the largest single release of radiation into the air from Hanford. A subsequent detailed analysis by Maurice Robkin of the Technical Steering Panel calculated the total release to be more than 11,000 curies of iodine-131.

While continuing my peace and justice work for the Catholic Diocese of Spokane, I grabbed every chance I could to go back to the library and read more documents. As I neared the end of all those pages, I had many more questions than when I began. During my reading, I had compiled a list of all the reports referenced in the 19,000 pages, hoping they would provide more answers. Six weeks after I began, I finished reading the last of the 19,000 pages on April 25, 1986. The next day, on the other side of the world, reactor #4 at Chernobyl exploded. The clouds of radioactive explosion encircled the earth, some of it raining down on Spokane in early May.

About a month later, I got to see what I had been reading about—I toured the Hanford site with the other members of the Northwest Citizens Forum on Defense Wastes. On a spring morning, the Forum members milled around the hotel lobby of Richland's Hanford House until the tour bus pulled up to the entrance. Several Department of Energy and contractor personnel handed each of us a security badge that included a radiation dosimeter. The dosimeter would measure how much radiation we received during the tour. While the risk of exposure was low, the tour would take us inside buildings where radioactive contamination was present. As the bus driver closed the door and headed north onto George Washington Way, one of the guides took a microphone and began to present an overview of the sprawling Hanford site. Spread out over 570 square miles, the Hanford site is half the size of Rhode Island. Sagebrush and other drought-tolerant vegetation cover most of the arid landscape.

The guide described the alarms we might encounter while in or near the nuclear plants. An "ah-oo-gah" howler meant that a criticality (an uncontrolled nuclear chain reaction) had occurred, and we should run. If a flashing red light was accompanied by an alarm bell, it meant that dangerous levels of airborne contamination were present, and we should immediately hold our breath and evacuate the building.

Hearing these sobering details gave me pause. What danger was I facing by stepping inside these nuclear weapons production facilities? Though the risk was hopefully low, I accepted it as I had embraced the risks on the pilgrimage.

In a few minutes, the bus slowed as we approached the first security gate. When the bus door swung open, two uniformed security guards boarded and started walking down the aisle. One had an M16 rifle slung over his shoulder. We were told to take out our photo IDs. The guards went slowly down the aisle, checking each person's ID against the list of the Forum members and staff. The guards cautioned us that no cameras or tape recorders were permitted. The whole procedure took about ten minutes. After the guards exited, they motioned for the driver to continue the tour. The guide resumed his narration of the site's history and an overview of the two main areas we would see on the tour: the nuclear reactors that produced plutonium by irradiating uranium fuel and the processing plants that chemically separated plutonium from uranium and the other radioactive materials.

The vast scope of Hanford can be intimidating. Clumps of buildings are separated by miles of desert—designed to prevent a catastrophic accident at one plant from damaging the others. The expanse makes it hard to gauge perspective; huge buildings seem diminutive. It takes nearly an hour to drive to the B reactor, the farthest of the nine plutonium production reactors from Richland. The processing buildings are mammoth. The largest is longer than three football fields—it rises seven stories above ground and descends three stories below ground.

For a few short weeks in the spring, the desert flora turns green. The sagebrush blooms and a wonderful perfume fills the air. Such was the landscape that rolled past as the bus sped along a series of paved roads. Strung out along the Hanford Reach, the last free-flowing stretch of the Columbia River in the U.S., were nine nuclear reactors.

The bus stopped at the N reactor—N for new. Completed in 1963, it was the only one of the nine still operating. The others were closed between 1964 and 1971. As we got off the bus, the guide handed each of us a hard hat before entering the large box-like building. After passing offices and meeting rooms, we went through a doorway plastered with radiation warning signs. This room was cavernous. Before us was the front face of the reactor. This was where workers loaded uranium fuel into the reactor. Big red flashing lights warned that the reactor was operating.

Standing this close to a nuclear reactor, less than three weeks after the Chernobyl disaster, unsettled me. The N reactor shared the same basic graphite-moderated design as the destroyed Chernobyl reactor. We heard the hiss of cooling water rushing through the pipes embedded within the core of the reactor. It was scary to think of the intense radiation inside that core, less than seventy feet from where I stood. The large graphite block and biological shield protected people in this room from the intense radiation inside the reactor. When enough plutonium was generated, some of the fuel elements would be pushed out through the rear face of the reactor. The irradiated fuel elements would be so radioactive and thermally hot that they needed to be cooled in a huge pool of water before being transferred into railcars. Once loaded, the railcars transported the fuel elements to the chemical processing areas atop Hanford's central plateau, our next destination ten miles away.

Workers at the processing plants built during World War II dubbed them "Queen Marys" because they were roughly the same size as the ocean liner that sailed across the Atlantic. During the war, the *Queen Mary* was pressed into service as a troop transport, ferrying as many as 15,000 soldiers in one trip.

The bus stopped at the PUREX plant. Having been built in the mid-1950s, it was the newest processing plant. The acronym stood for "Plutonium Uranium Extraction." It was a mammoth building—even bigger than the "Queen Marys." The light gray exterior of the concrete building was blinding under the desert sun.

The area surrounding the plant was flat and barren, devoid of vegetation. Areas around Hanford's plants had to be kept clear of any vegetation to prevent the spread of radiation, as the roots of sagebrush could tap into contamination as deep as thirty feet underground and bring it to the surface.

Pointing to several nearby fenced areas, our guide told us these were underground tank farms, used for storing high-level radioactive waste. To shield workers from the waste's intense radiation, the tanks are buried underneath six to ten feet of soil. Numerous pipes rise above the defoliated areas, enabling workers to retrieve samples from inside the tanks. Most of the tanks are seventy-five feet in diameter, thirty-five feet tall, and capable of holding one million gallons. At least a third of the 177 tanks have leaked over the decades.

After entering PUREX, my eyes strained to adjust to the relative darkness inside. Regularly spaced bare fluorescent tubes provided just enough light to walk through the corridor which stretched for more than three football fields.

In response to questions, the guide explained that overhead were some of the more than 2,000 miles of piping inside PUREX, connecting eleven processing cells, each another step in extracting plutonium. Highly radioactive elements like cesium and strontium were discharged into the underground tanks. Huge volumes of processed liquids that were less radioactive were dumped directly into the soil. By the 1980s, these discharges had created a 200-square-mile contaminated lake beneath Hanford that eventually flowed into the Columbia River.

Because of the intense radioactivity in the process cells, the concrete walls were six feet thick. All the work in the cells had to be done remotely. Even maintenance had to be done without any direct human contact. The cells were accessed by an overhead crane. To see what they were doing, the operators used closed circuit television cameras.

After walking several hundred feet, we came to a doorway that led to the control room. This was 1986, seventeen years after the U.S. had landed people on the moon. Since I grew up watching the launches of the Mercury, Gemini, and Apollo programs, I expected the PUREX control room to be similarly equipped with the same "Right Stuff" vibe.

Looking around the forty-by-fifteen-foot control room, illuminated by more fluorescent fixtures, I was immediately underwhelmed. Stunned would be a better word. Far from being cutting-edge technology, nearly all of what I saw appeared to be original equipment from when PUREX was built thirty years before. From floor to ceiling, hundreds of analog gauges, dials, and valve handles plastered the four walls. Several workers stood along the walls, attending to the controls. I saw only one small computer.

Our guide described how PUREX operated. The controls directed the flow of liquids through the miles of pipes. Several members posed questions about the chemical separation process. Meanwhile, I took a closer look at the assortment of dials, gauges, and valves. Many were tagged or had notecards taped alongside the controls. The notes warned that a gauge was not properly calibrated, or a valve was out of order. Operators were directed to use a different control as a work-around.

As I grasped the significance of the tags and cards, I examined the rest of the controls. The notes were quite plentiful—as many as a third of the controls had some cautionary message associated with them. Instead of being the state-of-the-art national security facility I had expected, PUREX was an old industrial dinosaur, a decrepit factory with many patches. Later that day, I recorded in my notebook, "astounding/appalling [the] number of instruments and valves that were broken." The control room's shocking state of deterioration helped me understand why operators struggled to meet their production quotas. As one federal safety expert testified in 1990 about his inspection of PUREX, it's "not difficult to find five or six areas that inspectors would just have a cardiac arrest over." Like the N reactor, which was seven years newer than PUREX, the Reagan nuclear weapons buildup at Hanford was an accident waiting to happen.

When we exited the control room, we walked down the long corridor. There were two prominent sounds: 1) the clip-clop of our shoes on the bare concrete floor, and 2) the scratching sound of the toxic liquids coursing through the pipes. The dingy concrete, the asbestos-wrapped pipes, the bare light bulbs all said one word: industrial.

Passing through the exit door, my eyes recoiled from the blinding sun. It was a painful contrast from the half-darkness inside. Replacing the industrial din were the high-pitched chirps of swallows as they swooped and twirled above in the blue sky.

Over the summer of 1986, I typed up the document titles referenced in the 19,000 pages and filed my first request under the Freedom of Information Act (FOIA) on behalf of HEAL. The following April, the Department of Energy shipped a batch of 20,000 pages of declassified historical documents to HEAL. At a table in the HEAL office, I sat down to review my second batch of Hanford records.

I was disappointed that this set of documents didn't reveal much more about Hanford's history. What's more, the April 1987 batch didn't include all the records I sought in the FOIA request. Chief among the missing was the Green Run report, which was subjected to a special review because it concerned intelligence gathering. As I waited, I compiled another FOIA request for the most interesting reports listed as references in the 20,000 pages.

In May 1987, my position at the diocese was among those being eliminated in a round of budget cuts. By the end of June, I would be unemployed. Instead of looking for work, I decided to complete my master's degree in theology that I had begun in 1985. In my scripture classes, I learned hermeneutics—the careful interpretation of documents within their historical context. This technique greatly aided my research on Hanford documents. Despite my graduate coursework, nuclear weapons remained my focus. Since nuclear deterrence remained the backbone of U.S. national security policy, my thesis examined whether it was ethical to threaten the mass killing of human beings to prevent war. I argued that it was immoral. To me, the mere possession of nuclear weapons was incompatible with Jesus' call to love our enemies.

Dad never fully recovered from his 1985 heart attack. By early 1987, he was suffering from congestive heart failure. When his weakened heart couldn't pump enough blood to his brain, he became confused.

One night in late May, he didn't come home. His silver Volkswagen pickup truck was missing. Mom worried that something had happened to him. Was he in an accident or just lost? Should she file a missing person's report?

The next morning, Mom got a call from a gas station. Dad was there and seemed very confused. He didn't have a credit card. My sister Mary went to the gas station. He couldn't remember anything about where he had been during the night. Mary talked Dad into going to the hospital for additional tests, which turned out to be inconclusive.

After Dad was released from the hospital, Mom and I talked with him about surrendering the keys to his pickup. In the dining room, Dad sat across from me, not in his usual chair at the head of the table. He still wore the same clothes from the day before. Dad was defensive and accused me of being irresponsible. His thinking was muddled and disjointed. He seemed on the verge of becoming belligerent. Mom and I backed off and prayed he wouldn't get back in his truck again.

Within days, Dad was readmitted to Sacred Heart Hospital. His vital signs were erratic. His doctor told me that in all his years as a cardiologist, he'd never seen such irregular heart rhythms in a person who remained alive.

On a Friday afternoon, the hospital asked us to come immediately—Dad was nearing the end. Entering his room, I was taken aback by his sunken cheeks. His breathing was shallow and labored. Above his bed, a monitor traced his erratic heartbeats. We started saying the

Rosary—calling on the strength of our faith and hopefully giving Dad some solace. With each recitation of the "Hail Mary" prayer, we intoned "pray for us sinners, now and at the hour of our death." Was this Dad's hour to die? Over the next few hours, though, he mysteriously rallied. I drove Mom back home. Dad was stable over that weekend and into Monday.

On Tuesday, the cardiologist asked Mom and me to meet him at the hospital that afternoon. The doctor admitted, "I do not understand how he is still alive. I don't see any hope for recovery. He could die at any time." After a brief pause, the doctor continued, "There is nothing more we can do for him here, so tomorrow we plan to transfer him to a nursing home. I think it would be best if you informed him of the move."

As Mom and I walked down the corridor to Dad's room, Mom asked me to be the one to tell Dad.

The head of his hospital bed was elevated about a foot, and there was a pillow behind his head. Overhead, the fluorescent light cast a sickly cold light throughout the room. I walked up to the right side of his bed. Mom stood a bit behind me.

Haltingly, I began. "Hi, Dad. Mom and I are here. We have something we want to talk with you about."

Dad's eyes were open, but he gave no indication that he heard me or was even aware of our presence.

I decided to continue and get it over with. "We've just spoken with the doctor. He says there is nothing more they can do for you here in the hospital. Tomorrow, they'll transfer you to Saint Joseph's nursing home."

Again, Dad's face didn't move. Could Dad hear what I was saying? Did he understand what would happen the next day?

Mom was restless and wanted to go home. Still not knowing whether my message had registered with Dad, we walked down to the parking garage.

Mom's house was only a fifteen-minute drive from the hospital. As she unlocked her back door, I heard the phone ringing. I ran to answer it. It was the hospital. They asked to speak with Mom. I handed her the receiver. Mom nodded her head several times and then thanked the person for the call. Mom relayed the news to me. Dad had just died.

Perhaps Dad had heard me after all about the impending transfer. From visiting my paternal grandmother in a nursing home with Dad when I was a teenager, I knew he would have hated being in a nursing home. I imagined that Dad simply let go of life and slipped away.

I felt relief that I would never again have to interact with my dad. I relaxed and breathed deeply. Simultaneously, I felt guilty—that it was wrong for me to feel this way. For much of my life, Dad had haunted me—all those times when he pulled my hair or had angry outbursts. The wounded little boy inside me did not need to fear him anymore. A great weight had seemingly been lifted from me. I thought I was now free of those painful emotions from childhood trauma.

In a little more than three years, though, tragedy would strike and prove how mistaken I was. I still bore my childhood emotional scars.

16 – Dismantling Hanford's Iron Curtain of Secrecy

Photo of Judith Jurji.

Two weeks before I completed my master's, I found out that HEAL was hiring. I enthusiastically applied. After four years as a volunteer, I became an employee for the organization I helped found. Now I could devote myself full-time to ending plutonium processing for nuclear weapons and pursuing the truth about Hanford's history.

Several weeks later, Keith Schneider of *The New York Times* visited the HEAL office. As he entered, he apologized by saying, "Sorry—I'm two years late." He was inferring that his newspaper should have sent a reporter in 1986 when the 19,000 pages were released. Keith's report was the lead article in *The New York Times* on Monday, October 17, 1988. For the next three days, phone calls from journalists across the country (*48 Hours*, Fox, *Newsweek*, CBS, *USA Today*, CBC Radio, and *TIME*) inundated the HEAL office. Since Keith's story focused on the historical releases and possible health effects, it was like the 19,000 pages had been released all over again. Except now it was national news. One of the callers was a producer for *Good Morning America* who wanted me to appear on the show with House Majority Leader Tom Foley, who represented Eastern Washington in Congress. Joan Lunden interviewed us on October 20.

The appearance on national television caught the attention of a congressional committee that oversaw the nuclear weapons production complex. I was invited to testify about the radiation releases from Hanford. I would be part of a panel that included three others: June Stark Casey and Millie Smith, two Hanford downwinders, and Herbert Kelly, who worked for twenty-seven years at the Fernald plant near Cincinnati. The Fernald plant reclaimed Hanford's uranium and sent it back as fuel for Hanford's reactors.

The committee flew us to Washington, D.C., and we met with a committee staffer at a restaurant for dinner. We were all nervous about the hearing the next morning and wanted to know what kind of questions the committee members might ask.

The next morning, we took a cab to the U.S. Capitol. The committee hearing was in the Rayburn House Office Building, south of the Capitol. After passing through security, we walked down a long corridor, our shoes echoing through the marble hallway.

There were four panels of people testifying that day, and ours was slated to be third. When it was my turn to testify, I summarized the huge radiation releases revealed in the historical documents and then remarked: "[T]he most dramatic atmospheric release happened during the so-called Green Run of December 2 and 3, 1949. ... The exact details of what was released and where it went remain classified in a secret government report which the Department of Energy has repeatedly refused to make public."

Sitting to my left was Millie Smith. In her testimony, she put a human face on the abstract environmental data I gleaned from the documents. Millie was a downwinder, one of the people whose milk and other foods had been contaminated by Hanford's radioactive fallout:

"I was born and raised in Pasco, WA, several miles downstream from the Hanford plant, residing there from 1947 to 1967 and one of the 20,000 children that the Centers for Disease Control believe have been exposed to the secret radioactive releases from Hanford.

"Not only did the government fail to warn us and take safety precautions, but the releases were kept secret for forty years. If the releases hadn't been made public when they were in 1986 through the Freedom of Information Act, I likely wouldn't be alive today. After years of weakness and poor health, I was finally checked for and discovered to have metastasized thyroid cancer. On Christmas Eve 1986, I was told I had less than two years to live and immediate surgery was my only hope. One month later, the five-hour surgery revealed extensive cancer throughout my neck, jugular vein, trachea, between my lungs, and throughout my upper-right chest. I have to take thyroid medication the rest of my life.

"Due to my health problems, I've lived in poverty most of my life. There have been times when all I had to eat was rice or popcorn for months. There were many winters of having to go without heat. There were times I was homeless. I remember two close friends and two other classmates who died of cancer while still in high school.

"We are as abused children, victims of our own country. ... As Hanford downwinders we want an apology from our government. We want to know the full truth of what happened to us. We want the Department of Energy to be accountable for their actions. We want justice for all downwinders. Two years ago, I was fighting for my life. Today I'm fighting for the life of all of us."

When irradiated uranium fuel was dissolved to extract plutonium, a radioactive isotope of iodine (iodine-131) escaped as a gas and went up the stack, was carried by the wind, and fell out onto farmland, sometimes hundreds of miles downwind. The primary way people were exposed to radioactive iodine was by drinking milk from cows grazing on contaminated pasture. In the 1940s and 1950s, milk was a key part of a healthy diet. I wondered how early Hanford scientists realized the danger to human health from drinking radioactive milk.

In the publicly available reports, there is no mention of the hazard of consuming iodine-131 through drinking milk for the first ten years of Hanford operations. Then in a declassified 1955 memo, Hanford's health protection chief Herbert Parker wrote, "Since the first year of Hanford operation, we have known that ... the real hazard arises from [the] drinking of milk from cows on contaminated pasture ..."

After years of researching the cow-milk-iodine pathway, I found that the Manhattan Project's thyroid expert Joseph Hamilton knew of the pathway's significance before 1942. While there's no documentation of Hamilton informing Parker of the pathway, the two began collaborating in 1943 under Robert Stone, the Manhattan Project's medical director.

Instead of sharing their knowledge with the scientific community, Hanford never published articles to warn about radioactive iodine in milk. But two doctors from the University of Tennessee College of Medicine did publish an article in 1952 to warn against treating nursing mothers with radioactive iodine therapy because the infant's thyroid gland may take up enough radioactivity from the milk to damage the gland. If Hanford scientists had published a similar warning in a national journal, much suffering could have been avoided.

There is no evidence that Hanford managers tried to lessen the huge iodine releases in 1945, even after Japan surrendered. In fact, the opposite happened—the releases rose dramatically in the second half of 1945. But Hanford officials still didn't warn the public about the radioactively contaminated milk. In 1951, the U.S. began atmospheric nuclear weapons tests in Nevada. Throughout the 1950s, those tests released an estimated total of 150 million curies of iodine-131 (200 times more than Hanford released). Still, Hanford management and the Atomic Energy Commission kept silent. Hanford officials chose not to alert the public about drinking contaminated milk. In 1997, the National Cancer Institute estimated there were between 11,300 and 212,000 "excess cases of thyroid cancer resulting from the Nevada weapons tests." How many Millie Smiths suffered for decades because of Hanford's failure to issue public health warnings?

In the late 1980s, Hanford was frequently in the national and regional news. Many former residents and workers began to share their stories with HEAL. Through them, I learned details about Hanford that were never mentioned in official documents. In the 1940s and 1950s, all Hanford managers had to do was to yank a meddlesome worker's security clearance, and they disappeared. Without the proper clearance, workers could not hold their job. Without a job at Hanford, they could no longer live in Richland. Over the years, I had former workers, their spouses, or their children tell me about waking up one morning to discover that their next-door neighbor's house was empty—the family had disappeared under the cover of darkness. Those who remained kept their mouths shut.

One man who grew up in Richland told me about FBI agents who would visit the neighborhoods, asking questions about how much they knew. One day, agents asked him about the man across the street and whether he knew where the man worked. At the time, he was only about ten years old, yet he knew what the right answer was: He was not supposed to know what the man did. This was the answer that was expected, and so he said it. It was the answer that would not lead to complications.

In fact, the boy knew exactly what job the man had at Hanford. He saw him nearly every morning driving the bus that took his dad and other workers in the neighborhood out to their jobs at Hanford. How secure is a society that instills fear and dishonesty in children when they are questioned by law enforcement personnel?

I frequently visited the Tri-Cities of Richland, Kennewick, and Pasco while I worked for HEAL, usually two or three trips a month. On the surface, everything seemed as normal as in every other prosperous city across America. But then I met people who had experienced something starkly at odds with the Tri-Cities' all-American façade.

My first encounter was of a woman researching old school records that might be used in a study about Hanford's radiation releases. Meeting at a local restaurant, the researcher told me how unnerved she was after finding a message in her child's homework assignment. On an otherwise blank sheet of paper, someone had written, "We're watching you." Any suggestion that operations were harmful threatened the Hanford establishment.

Later, I visited the home of a woman who had blown the whistle about explosion hazards in Hanford's underground waste tanks. After welcoming me into her humble one-story house, she led me to the kitchen and offered me a glass of water. In a matter-of-fact tone, she recalled that a few weeks earlier she had come home after work and, pointing to her microwave oven, told me how the display had read "HELLO." While she was at her job, someone had broken into her house and reprogrammed the microwave oven readout. After checking every room, she determined that nothing else was out of place. Only the oven display. A message had been delivered. She was under surveillance. Someone could access her house at any time, for any purpose. As long as she persisted in rocking Hanford's boat, she was vulnerable.

In May 1989, I met Judith Jurji at the second Downwinder Gathering that HEAL sponsored in the hopes of bringing together those who had been impacted. Many downwinders had moved out of the exposure area in the intervening years and were struggling to organize due to their geographic dislocation and health problems. HEAL didn't see itself as a downwinder organization. We were a watchdog group that was trying to close PUREX, secure a cleanup agreement, and uncover more about Hanford's operational history. Still, our aims often intersected with the downwinder communities.

Judith's life may have been much different had she found out earlier about her exposure to Hanford's radioactive iodine. Judith was born in 1945 in California, but her family moved to Pasco, Washington in 1949 so her father could take a job at Hanford.

It was an ill-fated move. Although Judith wouldn't find out until four decades later, she was irradiated by the largest single atmospheric release of radiation in Hanford history. Because radiation cannot be detected by any of our five senses, Judith and the thousands of other people who lived downwind from Hanford had no way to tell that their food was contaminated. And because Hanford officials kept the radiation releases secret until 1986, they prevented Judith and others from seeking early treatment of their cancers and other diseases.

On May 1, 1989, the 130-page Green Run report was finally made public, exactly thirty-nine years after it was written. After years of persistence, advocacy, and organizing, we finally had the report we'd sought.

Conducted on December 2 and 3, 1949, the Green Run was an intentional release of radioactive iodine-131. It was called green because the fuel being dissolved was only cooled for sixteen days rather than the standard 1949 practice of ninety days ("green" as in not yet ripe). The stack filters were disconnected to further increase the amount of radiation released.

The experiment was a collaboration between Hanford operators and the U.S. Air Force which was developing airborne radiation detectors for top-secret flights near the Soviet Union to gather intelligence about atomic bomb plants there. The Green Run was meant to see which of three types of detectors worked best.

The declassified document revealed that the Green Run encountered a host of problems including malfunctioning equipment, changing weather, and severe contamination of the laboratory used to analyze the radiation samples. Problems also plagued the Air Force's specially equipped plane. Nearly everything that could have gone wrong did. The radioactive plume blanketed thousands of square miles in Eastern Washington, Northeast Oregon, and North Idaho.

For four decades, the people exposed were unaware of Hanford's invisible radiation releases, and many suffered various ailments connected to the thyroid gland—part of the endocrine system. A properly functioning thyroid is essential to regulating the body's metabolism. Radioactive iodine concentrates in the thyroid and bombards the gland.

As a little girl, Judith drank lots of fresh milk. One of her father's coworkers at Hanford had his own cow and always had more milk than he could use. Unbeknownst to Judith and her parents, the milk was contaminated with iodine-131.

Years later, Judith recalled that "even in my twenties I was fatigued a great deal, which got worse and worse. As a college student I got so sick of people constantly saying, 'Oh, you look tired, you must have pulled an all-nighter last night.' When in fact I got to bed at nine o'clock and had twelve hours of sleep."

Judith married in her twenties and "was trying to have a baby [but] realized I was infertile. ... my insurance didn't cover infertility. Which is tragic because if I'd been able to go to an infertility clinic, one of the first things they check is for your thyroid function. Because if your thyroid's not functioning properly, it can interfere with ovulation. I would probably have been put on thyroid medications quite early ... I still had my late twenties and thirties to get pregnant, and I would have had children, and I probably would have had a very, very different life."

It was not until Judith was in her early-forties that she found out about Hanford's radiation releases and the potential for thyroid damage. In 1987, Judith landed her first teaching job in art design and art history at Bellevue Community College. Toward the end of the first quarter, one of her students approached her with a question about a class assignment. Judith had been noticing this student all quarter because of her sickly, ashen appearance. The student said she had recently had surgery for thyroid cancer. She was about Judith's age and had also grown up in Pasco. Several months prior, the student learned of Hanford's radioactive iodine releases and the risk of thyroid cancer. Her doctor checked her thyroid. It was cancerous. This revelation hit Judith hard. She recalled in a 1999 interview, "I literally felt faint … I was just shattered. … Oh, my God, that is what's wrong with me."

Judith went to see her doctor, but he was reluctant to check her thyroid. He thought all she needed to do was to exercise more and lose some weight. Dragging herself through life since she was in college, she knew that something was wrong. Now Judith was frightened she might have cancer—just like her sickly student.

Judith insisted that her doctor check her thyroid hormone levels and examine her thyroid with an ultrasound scan. Reluctantly, he complied.

After the results came back, her doctor called to apologize for doubting her. The tests revealed her thyroid was barely functioning. The ultrasound revealed that her thyroid was shriveled and covered with abnormal growths. He immediately prescribed a thyroid hormone supplement, saying she should start feeling better in four to six weeks. He told her to get annual check-ups so he could monitor her nodules and take quick action if any turned cancerous.

Seemingly like a miracle, Judith started to feel better. Her thinking became clearer. She was not tired or cold all the time. Her sleep improved and she started to have dreams again. She began to realize that for more than twenty years, she had been only partially alive—almost like a zombie. For the first time as an adult, she was able to enjoy life.

But she couldn't rest. Judith knew she had to act. How many others had been exposed and didn't yet know about Hanford's releases? Like her, were they stumbling through life, half-dead? She had to find out how the government had allowed this to happen and why it had kept the releases secret for four decades. Soon, Judith formed the Hanford Downwinders Coalition and reached out to other downwinders.

I have pursued a full accounting for those responsible for the Green Run. Since it became known, the U.S. Air Force has repeatedly refused to declassify the name of whoever authorized the Green Run, claiming that the release of this name could damage the nation's security. I believe downwinders and their descendants have a right to know the name and why they were kept in the dark for so many decades. In my years of research since 1986, I have scoured document archives in person and online, conducted scores of interviews, and filed numerous FOIA requests—all to glean information about who was responsible. From declassified documents, I have identified two men who were involved in authorizing the Green Run: Maj. Gen. Morris R. Nelson and William D. Urry.

Beginning in August 1949, General Nelson was the Chief of the Air Force Office for Atomic Energy (AFOAT-1). That November, he authored two letters that coordinated the preparations for the Green Run. He died in 1985 at the age of eighty-four.

William (Bill) Urry, Chairman of the Technical Working Committee for AFOAT-1 visited Hanford on at least three occasions during 1949 prior to the Green Run: January, April, and October. During his visit in late-October, he participated in detailed planning for the Green Run. Urry died of a heart attack in December 1959.

Given Urry's multiple trips to Hanford in 1949, he was likely the Air Force supervisor in charge of the Green Run. Meanwhile, given General Nelson's rank and position, it seems logical that Nelson approved the secret intentional release.

17 – The Case of the Two Autopsies

Ernest Johnson
"had never been
sick and he had
never complained
of a heart
condition,"
according to his
wife.

A clipping from Karen Dorn Steele's
Spokesman-Review article, September 9, 1990.

I should not have seen his name. All personal identifying information is usually deleted (i.e., redacted) from government records before being released, in accordance with the federal Freedom of Information Act and Privacy Act. But there it was: "Ernest E. Johnson." I couldn't believe my luck. It was May 10, 1989. I marveled at this surprising find as I sat in HEAL's sparse, one-story office. Adjacent to the office was a dual set of railroad tracks with frequent trains rumbling past, just west of downtown Spokane. I was poring over a thick computer printout—the kind from old IBM mainframes with perforated holes along both sides of greenish pages. It listed the Hanford-related holdings at the Nuclear Testing Archive in Las Vegas.

Not only was Johnson's name listed, but the rest of the document title marked it as a significant find: "Claim Filed by Widow of Ernest E. Johnson, Alleging that the Death was Attributed to Radiation." Immediately, I requested the document. Several weeks later, I received a blotchy photocopy of a three-page teletype message from Hanford's manager to U.S. Atomic Energy Commission headquarters, dated November 17, 1952. Ernest Johnson died suddenly in June 1952, and his body was subjected to not one, but two autopsies. The widow's pension claim was filed with the Washington State Department of Labor and Industries (L&I), and it alleged that Ernest Johnson's death was "attributable to special hazard [i.e., radiation] injury."

I realized this could be a rare opportunity for a human-interest story about Hanford's secret past. It had to be handled with expert care. I didn't know how to find or interview Ernest's widow, so I turned to Karen Dorn Steele, a journalist who covered Hanford for Spokane's *Spokesman-Review* newspaper. Since 1986, Steele and I had collaborated several times on researching Hanford's historical documents. I gave her a copy of the 1952 teletype. Several months later, Karen called me to say that she had spoken to the widow, Marie Johnson. Karen told me the case was "a complete cover-up." A week later, Karen phoned to say that she'd found a coworker of Johnson. The next day, Karen tracked down one of the physicians present at the first autopsy. Karen also obtained the claim file from the Washington State Department of Labor and Industries. Karen's articles were published in *The Spokesman-Review* on September 9, 1990.

Ernest Emanuel Johnson had thick, reddish-brown hair. He packed 218 pounds onto his nearly six-foot frame. In April 1944, he began working at Hanford when the site contractor was DuPont. As a member of the Richland Lutheran Church, he served as a deacon and was on the building committee. He was a past president of his church's men's club. After General Electric replaced DuPont as the site contractor in 1946, Ernest stayed on as a general maintenance foreman, in charge of scheduling repair work on the nuclear reactors.

The morning of Monday, June 9, 1952 was sunny, and the desert air was warming fast. Ernest rode his usual bus to the northernmost region of the vast Hanford Nuclear Reservation. He began work at one of the nuclear reactors strung along the Columbia River.

Around 9:30 a.m., Ernest became suddenly ill and went to the nearest first aid station, complaining of a very sore throat. After a while, he decided to return to his office. Not long after, he went back to the first aid station, but nothing seemed to offer any relief. Once again, Ernest made his way back to his office.

At midday, his supervisor telephoned Ernest's wife, Marie, to say that Ernest was being driven to Kadlec Hospital in Richland by another employee. The supervisor also called Dr. William E. Russell, a General Electric physician—Ernest had experienced an attack of some sort at work. Because of the remoteness of the reactor areas, it took most of an hour to reach Richland. The car was stifling as the afternoon temperature rose above ninety degrees.

At the hospital, Ernest was seen by the ear, nose and throat specialist for GE. Ernest complained of a burning sensation and a sore throat. The doctor diagnosed a slight infection of the tonsils while assuring Ernest that his tonsils didn't have to come out. Ernest's workmate drove him the short one-and-a-half miles to his home. Arriving there around 4:40 p.m., Marie noticed her husband was "very warm and sweating profusely." He lay on the couch complaining of "pain and sinking attacks." Each time she offered him food, he refused it, except for a little chicken broth, which he sipped very slowly. Later, a friend came to visit. Sometime around 6:30 p.m., as the visitor was talking, Ernest suddenly slumped over. "Oh my God!" Marie cried, and then immediately called a doctor—but it was too late. When Dr. Russell arrived twenty minutes later, he couldn't feel a pulse and pronounced Ernest dead. He was forty-eight years old.

The local undertaker took Ernest's body to his mortuary. Later, the undertaker phoned Marie to ask about burn marks on Ernest's back and arm. He suggested those marks should be examined by a pathologist. The next morning, the undertaker asked GE's Dr. Russell to examine the marks. Because Russell thought the marks might be work-related, he called Dr. Philip Fuqua, head of GE's Industrial Medicine.

Arriving at the funeral home that afternoon, the two GE physicians examined the marks on Ernest's back and right arm. Fuqua reported, "Since the cause of these marks was not clear and in view of the suddenness of death, we recommended that an autopsy be done." While GE had a pathologist in Richland, Dr. Russell "felt it most fair to have a different pathologist" conduct the autopsy, someone not directly tied to Hanford. So, he brought in Dr. Frederic Davis, the pathologist from Walla Walla, sixty miles to the east. Davis was a young doctor, having arrived in Walla Walla with his wife and three children only three years before to begin his practice. Davis referred to himself as a bushwhacker pathologist because of his extensive travel to small towns throughout the region.

Davis arrived at the funeral home and began the autopsy at 10:30 p.m., in order to fit in with Marie's plans to take her husband's body back to Chicago the following day. Before coming to Hanford, Ernest and Marie had lived in Chicago. Despite having a non-GE doctor conduct the postmortem examination, three General Electric doctors witnessed it. The autopsy report noted two marks on the back. The biggest mark began several inches below his right shoulder blade and extended halfway down the buttock, "dark in color and appeared most like a healing burn mark." The report concluded that the burn marks were "Non specific dermatitis ..." and concluded that Johnson's death resulted from a ruptured aortic aneurysm, fluid on the heart, and kidney disease.

During her 1990 interview with Steele, Marie recalled that shortly after her husband's death, his fellow workers told her that Ernest "was in a radiation area when he was supposed to be timed [but] wasn't ... From what these men said, they let him get irradiated." Workers in a contaminated area were supposed to be timed to limit their radiation exposure.

After Ernest's death, Marie noticed Hanford agents "following [her] all over the Tri-Cities"—when she went to the funeral home and when she picked up Ernest's last paycheck—causing her to become more suspicious.

Back in Chicago, Marie arranged for Dr. Thomas Carter to conduct another autopsy at the funeral home. Even on the fourth day after Ernest's death, Carter described the mark as "red to brown and of intense nature." Carter concluded that Ernest's death was caused by a ruptured aorta, heart and kidney disease, and "radiation contacts." In his one-page report to Marie, Carter wrote, "I am positive his death was due to exposure to radiation, and that you will have no trouble in proving your claim for insurance or compensation."

Armed with Carter's report, Marie filed a workers' compensation claim with Washington State Labor & Industries (L&I), alleging that her husband's death was due to his occupational exposure to radiation.

With two conflicting autopsy reports, the state Labor and Industries had a dilemma. General Electric wanted a favorable determination and proposed that "physicians familiar with radiation injuries and with Hanford Works operation would be best qualified to give an unbiased opinion..."

Three weeks later, the AEC Manager of Hanford sent a teletype to AEC headquarters (the document I obtained in 1989), proposing that a GE doctor go to Chicago to meet "as soon as possible" with Dr. Carter. The purpose "would be to see whether [Carter's] conclusions can be altered."

On December 1, 1952, Philip Fuqua, head of GE's Industrial Medicine, met Carter in Chicago. Fuqua was accompanied by a GE attorney. A few days after the meeting, Fuqua wrote Carter urging him to "write without delay" to R. McLean, Washington State's Labor & Industries Supervisor of Claims. Fuqua wanted Carter to restate "what you told me …[that] the mark was not the result of a burn … [and] this mark could not have been produced by radiation as you originally believed. …." Fuqua added that if Carter changed his opinion, then "I believe we can avoid unnecessary litigation."

On December 23, Washington State's McLean wrote to General Electric (GE) about a letter that Marie Johnson had sent to him, seeking his advice. Carter told Marie that GE was pressuring him to change his diagnosis. Marie continued, "They have never been able to explain the unusual marks on my late husband's body … or how or where or when he received them. Would you please advise me what to do? I realize the cost of court and attorneys to fight the case for me will not leave much left for me after it is all over. Any assistance you can give me … will be greatly appreciated."

Marie's letter caused GE great concern. A few days after Christmas, GE wrote McLean and asked him to disregard Marie's statement about GE pressuring Carter, declaring, "It is not our policy to apply pressure to anyone. …" The next day, New Year's Eve, Fuqua sent his own letter to McLean and declared that "absolutely no pressure was incurred."

On January 6, 1953, McLean wrote to Carter and asked if he had changed his diagnosis. Receiving no response from Carter, McLean sent another letter to him on February 2. Finally, on February 9, Carter replied: "My report must stand as is." He added, "I think from what Mrs. Johnson has told me, you might get further information from some of Mr. Johnson's fellow workers at the time of his last illness." The state's L&I file on the Johnson case, however, contains no evidence that Mr. Johnson's coworkers were ever interviewed.

Having failed to get Carter to change his opinion, McLean turned to Dr. Simeon Cantril to provide a third opinion. Cantril was director of Seattle's Swedish Hospital Tumor Clinic and had worked at Hanford during the Manhattan Project. After the war, he continued as a consultant to General Electric at Hanford.

Cantril wrote to McLean about how he was already familiar with the Johnson case, having been briefed about the first and second autopsies. Cantril concluded that Carter's opinion about Johnson's death being caused by radiation was "without substantiation," and he declared that L&I "in no instance ... should assume any responsibility for or make compensation for the death of the deceased." On March 11, 1953, L&I rejected Marie Johnson's claim.

Marie had moved back to Chicago the previous fall. GE paid Marie $10,500 from Ernest's life insurance policy. Marie thought she also qualified for a payment through the GE Employee Benefits Fund which offered "$10,000 to any employee who has died ... as a result of special hazards connected with the project." Throughout Hanford workplaces, GE even displayed posters promoting the fund. She considered filing a lawsuit after Ernest's workers' compensation claim was denied, but her brother-in-law, a Chicago attorney, discouraged her.

What Marie Johnson didn't know was that the State of Washington was required to consult with GE and the AEC on any claims involving Hanford workers. This agreement remained secret until 1990, when Steele's investigation forced the state to release it. The agreement gave the AEC and GE the right to approve who the state hired to process Hanford workers' compensation claims. In addition, the state was required to accept "the Contractor's description of any accident, even though full details may not be given."

With the secret agreement, the AEC and GE had complete control over how Hanford worker claims were handled. Marie Johnson never had a chance. When Steele told Marie about the lengths to which Hanford officials went to reject her claim, she said, "The men who did this are just like criminals. They weren't honest people." This "bothered me for a long time ... Ernest was a good person, and to treat his family that way was wrong. It's a very sad story, and I probably wasn't the only one." Marie died three months later.

In its annual report to the Atomic Energy Commission (AEC) for 1951, General Electric wrote, "Radiological safety of employees continued to receive utmost emphasis throughout 1951. At year's end Hanford's slate was still clean. As far as discernable, there has never been an injury from radiation at Hanford Works." In April 1953 (a month after Johnson's claim was denied), General Electric reported to the AEC, "Through [regular] medical examinations and prompt treatment of injuries … [we] help keep Hanford Works people in good health." In 1955, GE wrote, "No lost time has resulted from radiation over-exposure."

18 – Cold War Ends and Family Tragedy Strikes

The Berlin Wall, November 1989.

November 9, 1989: I could hardly believe my eyes as I watched the evening news. People on both sides of the Berlin Wall were tearing it down. The wall was the paramount symbol of the Cold War. I never thought I would live to see the day. The defining element of the only world order I had ever known was collapsing. That communism was disintegrating in so many countries simultaneously was surreal. And without any large-scale violence.

From 1989 through 1990, I coordinated a coalition of national and regional organizations to end U.S. processing of plutonium for nuclear weapons by closing PUREX. In 1988, my HEAL colleague Tim Connor led a similar coalition that closed the N reactor by highlighting safety issues. When Energy Secretary John Herrington announced the N reactor's demise, he declared that the country was "awash in plutonium." That admission, coupled with the developments in Eastern Europe, eliminated any national security rationale for operating PUREX. Moreover, PUREX was plagued with equipment malfunctions. The hulking 1950s factory frequently failed to meet safety and environmental requirements.

While I was immersed in my HEAL work, a family tragedy struck. On September 30, 1990, around 4:00 p.m., my mom was walking across Mission Avenue in Spokane on her way to her sister's house for Sunday dinner. Mom had bought some ice cream for dessert at the neighborhood Safeway. It was a beautiful autumn afternoon with clear blue skies. As Mom stepped into the eastbound lanes, a 1965 green GMC pickup truck slammed into her. An eyewitness told police that he heard tires "screeching" and "a loud thump." The force of the impact launched my mother's body into the air—hurling it eighty-five feet, according to the police report.

The police found skid marks and calculated the truck had been going nearly forty miles per hour when it hit my mother. The driver, Anthony Ray Bumgardner, stopped and looked back, but didn't move. Occupying the passenger seat was his brother Tim who quickly got out. Anthony panicked, stepped on the gas, and sped away. Tim owned the pickup and explained to police that Anthony had been driving because he, Tim, was too drunk to drive. Both had been drinking with some friends at a lake and were heading home.

At some point, Anthony turned around and drove back to the scene of his crime. He parked his pickup on a residential street about a block from where he'd hit my mom. What Bumgardner did not know, though, is that he'd parked the pickup across the street from my aunt's house, the one my mom was going to visit. By then, my aunt was not home. She had already called me about the accident before rushing to Sacred Heart Hospital, promising to meet me there. My aunt's neighbors saw Anthony get out of the truck and cross several lawns before hiding in some bushes in front of the last house on the block. Next, he walked six blocks to his house where police arrested him.

When my wife Jan and I arrived at the hospital, doctors in the emergency room were trying to save my mom's life. We joined my Aunt Jo in the waiting room. She was grief-stricken—her eyes already bloodshot from crying. She couldn't tell us much—she had not been allowed in the ER. She'd been told that Mom had spoken briefly with the medics in the ambulance. That seemed like a hopeful sign.

Hour after hour, we waited. By not being allowed in the ER, the lack of information weighed on me. How could this be happening? Only the night before, Mom had fixed a fried chicken dinner for Jan and me. We'd played a game of Scrabble. Now she was at death's door. The enormity of it all pulverized me, but there was nothing we could do but wait. Some friends who'd heard the news brought us a pizza, so at least we had some food. The hospital chaplain and then our parish priest came to the waiting room. As evening turned to night, a nurse told us that Mom had been transferred to the ICU. But we were still not allowed to see her.

As the medical team struggled to control the internal bleeding from her extensive injuries, Mom lapsed into a coma.

Total exhaustion hit me sometime after midnight—I laid down on the hard floor and got some fitful sleep. At one point, I saw a nurse nearby and rose to ask her about my mom's condition. She paused as she opened the door to a stairway. In a quiet, caring voice, she confided, "I don't think you're going to get a mom out of this."

Morning dawned on the first day of October—but nothing had changed. Doctors and nurses continued their efforts to save Mom's life. We were still not allowed to see her. We could only wait. A doctor came to us that afternoon. His somber expression telegraphed bad news. He reported that Mom's condition had not improved. They were still struggling to keep her blood pressure stable. He asked the family to meet with him and the hospital's ethicist at 4:00 p.m. to discuss the situation.

The doctor escorted Aunt Jo, my sister Mary, Jan, and me into a conference room. He thought it was very unlikely that my mom, at seventy-five, would ever fully recover. She'd been on life support since arriving at the hospital. At the very least, she would need months of rehabilitation and, even with that, probably wouldn't be able to fully care for herself.

He would allow us to see her but cautioned, "Before you do, please understand that her body has swelled extensively as a result of our attempts to stabilize her blood pressure and stop the internal bleeding. She is unconscious, but she may be able to hear what you say. I think you need to consider disconnecting her from the ventilator. I can't give you any hope that your mom will live without life support." He added, "I will give you some time alone to discuss this."

We had accompanied Mom through Dad's dying days. We knew how much she valued her independence. She wouldn't want to suffer indefinitely in some type of half-life. Imagining the force of the pickup's impact, we suspected that the doctors and nurses had not told us everything. Even my Aunt Jo acknowledged that her sister wouldn't want to be kept alive in such a tenuous condition. We acknowledged the inevitable.

With a quiet knock, the doctor came back in. We gave him permission to remove Mom from life support.

Entering the ICU room, we saw Mom's bloated body. The machines hissed and sighed with each respiration. The monitors blinked and chirped, all under a veil of sadness. It was hard for me to grasp that this was happening. The nurse encouraged us to talk to Mom, assuring us that the sense of hearing was often active even though the person couldn't respond. My sister Mary was much better at talking to Mom than I was. Perhaps all my repressed pain prevented me from caring for my mother in the hour of her death.

The nurse told us she was there to turn off the machines. She didn't know whether my mom was able to breathe on her own for any length of time. When she flipped a switch, the room quieted. No more hissing or sighing. The green trace lines continued to march across the monitor.

After about a half-hour (or was it closer to an hour?), Mom breathed her last. The nurse turned off the monitors. After all the violence of the accident and the intense medical response of the last twenty-seven hours, Mom could now be at peace.

When I drove my aunt back to her house, the shock and grief intensified when we saw the lethal pickup across the street—a menacing reminder of the disaster that had struck. Concerned neighbors had been calling the police, pleading for the pickup to be towed away. Every time my grief-stricken aunt looked out her front window, there sat that truck. It took several agonizing days before it was taken away.

The shock of Mom's violent death paralyzed me. I went through the motions of making funeral arrangements, but most of me was someplace else. Where? I didn't know. In the days and weeks following, I would come to my senses and find myself standing in the middle of my living room. I had no idea how long I had been standing there. I couldn't recall what I had been doing before. I couldn't figure out what I had planned to do next. I was frightened. What was happening to me? It was obviously connected to the tragedy. Getting back to work helped a bit, but even there, I was nowhere near my normal self.

I went to see a good friend who urged me to give up alcohol. I had never drunk much, usually only one beer a week; but he advised me to give it up so that alcohol wouldn't become a problem in my emotional state.

My friend also encouraged me to see a grief counselor. Soon I began meeting weekly with a counselor. It was hard at first, especially as he asked me to talk about my relationship with my parents. Something in my gut resisted. As on the pilgrimage, I didn't see the need to revisit my childhood pain. Must I? Wasn't Mom's horrendous death enough? What would be gained by dredging it all up?

But then there were more episodes of me blanking out at home or the office. Something powerful was welling up inside me. It was pushing to come out. I had to face it—whether I wanted to or not. The counselor helped me understand that the shock of Mom's death had burst the dam holding back my childhood trauma. Processing my painful childhood memories was the key to dealing with my grief. On the pilgrimage, I had shunned Jack and Fred's invitations. After Dad's death, I passed up another opportunity. If I didn't go through this process now, those negative emotions would continue to haunt me. They also threatened to infect my happy marriage with Jan.

Two weeks after Mom died, in the fog of my grief, I learned that U.S. Energy Secretary James Watkins had announced he was closing PUREX permanently. Its days of processing plutonium for nuclear weapons were over. Our coalition had succeeded in halting a key element of the arms race. I didn't feel like celebrating.

I sensed that the weekly counseling sessions were helping—but Christmas was coming. Mom had loved celebrating holidays and birthdays. Christmas was her over-the-top favorite, and the joy she infused in Christmas was remarkable: the decorations, her faithfulness to the family traditions (like her five-pound batch of homemade fudge), and her thoughtfulness in giving gifts. This would be my first Christmas without her exuberance. Without her light, it was the darkest Christmas of my life.

Along with the counseling, I sought healing by hiking the five-mile loop trail at the Turnbull National Wildlife Refuge southwest of Spokane. During Lent in 1991, my outings were weekly. The cold gray of the refuge in winter meant there were few if any other people around. The silent solitude of nature provided me a place where I could cry out my grief. As a child, I was taught that men and boys weren't supposed to cry. In being conditioned not to cry, I had dammed up sorrow, grief, and pain.

I imagine my experience is not unique, and that our society would be less angry and violent if we encouraged boys and men to cry. Otherwise, they bottle their sorrow and pain inside. We should not be surprised when those imprisoned emotions explode with anger and violence. As Fr. Richard Rohr wrote, "Pain that is not transformed is transferred." Giving men and boys permission to cry would make for more peace in our families and world.

The counseling and inner work were life-giving. Grieving Mom's death liberated me from my long-repressed fear, hurt, and shame. All those years of pretending I didn't need to deal with those painful memories had robbed me of fully enjoying life. When uncomfortable emotions are strangled, joyful ones are diminished. Since that year of counseling, I have been more fully alive.

The experience of mourning Mom's death also helped my work with Hanford downwinders by listening to their suffering and anger with greater empathy.

The sentencing hearing for Anthony Bumgardner occurred on February 13, 1991. He had pled guilty to vehicular homicide, acknowledging his responsibility. My sister and I were relieved that we didn't have to endure a trial. Weeks before, the court asked if I wanted to make a statement at the hearing. Was I strong enough emotionally? My counseling was going well. But was I up to facing Mom's killer?

The hearing was the first time I had ever been in a courtroom other than as a tourist at the U.S. Supreme Court. It was a cold, overcast morning. The walls inside the courtroom of Judge Kathleen O'Connor in the Superior Court of Spokane County were cold slabs of marble. Stark, unfriendly, alienating. The room was filled with years of shame, pain, and tragedy. Even four and a half months after Mom's death, my emotions were still raw.

At the appointed time, the bailiff announced the case. A door to the right opened, and the defendant entered and sat next to his lawyer.

He was thirty years old, just a few years younger than I was. We lived in the same city. But here, we were on opposite ends of the courtroom. Judge O'Connor sat on her bench—perhaps 100 feet away. Several times I glanced over at Bumgardner—the man who had killed my mother.

The charge was read out. The thin gray light from the winter outside reinforced the chill of the courtroom. I wondered what Bumgardner was feeling on the verge of being sent to prison. Judge Kathleen O'Connor asked if anyone wanted to make a statement before she passed sentence. I rose from my seat. I took out my prepared statement from inside my suit jacket. My whole body felt as if it would burst from the strong emotions. There was also a wave of numbness—the kind that had been sweeping my body since that awful Sunday at the end of September.

I began reading. "Nothing that will be done here today will ever bring back my mom. According to the sentencing guidelines, Mr. Bumgardner will only have to serve two to three years for killing her. It does not feel just to me. By driving drunk, he robbed my mom of many years of life.

"The day Mr. Bumgardner's pickup crashed into my mom, his blood-alcohol level was over three times the legal limit. He was driving with a suspended license for driving drunk only five months previously. His first DUI offense was when he was only seventeen years old. And now he has killed someone."

With a short pause, I looked directly at Bumgardner.

"But I am aware of the harsh conditions of prisons. They break people down rather than provide support in reforming their lives and realizing their full potential when released.

"Mr. Bumgardner, I beg you to never again get behind a steering wheel if you've been drinking. I will pray for you while you are in prison. Please use your time behind bars to get treatment." I could see remorse in his eyes. But there was something else. I sensed a note of surprise in his face. I hoped my words had sunk in.

Of his entire sentence of 1034 days, Bumgardner served 670 days, getting out early for good behavior. Even after three decades, I still consider such a short sentence unjust. For killing someone, even though not technically murder, ten to fifteen years would have been justified. While in prison, he earned his GED. In doing research for this book, I didn't find any other DUI offenses for Bumgardner since 1990.

Five months after the sentencing hearing, Jan and I received the happy news that she was pregnant, and on March 2, 1992, after thirteen hours of labor, our daughter Katie was born. When it came time for Jan and Katie to go home, I was determined to carry Katie out of the hospital. In the five years before Katie was born, both my parents, an aunt, and a cousin had all died in that hospital. From that hospital of loss, I carried forth my newborn daughter.

19 – First Visit to Hiroshima and Nagasaki

Memorial Cenotaph, Hiroshima Memorial Peace Park, March 1993.

On March 4, 1993, I stood in front of the red brick exterior of the Urakami Cathedral in Nagasaki, Japan. Its twin towers were simple and humble—not grandiose like Notre Dame in Paris or the Duomo in Milan or Saint Peter's in Rome. For centuries before the Second World War, Nagasaki had been the Christian center for not only Japan, but for most of East Asia. For Japanese Catholics, Urakami Cathedral symbolized their faithfulness after experiencing centuries of persecution.

On August 9, 1945, at 11:02 in the morning, Urakami Cathedral was only 500 yards from the hypocenter, the point over which the atomic bomb exploded. An intense heat, millions of degrees, incinerated thousands of people instantly, and the radioactivity poisoned tens of thousands of others—relegating them to weeks of agony before they succumbed.

I felt a rightness in standing before the rebuilt cathedral, paying my respects to all who suffered from atomic and nuclear weapons. My fellow Bethlehem pilgrim, Father George Zabelka had walked among the ruins of the cathedral only weeks after the atomic bombing. Eight months after reaching Bethlehem, George returned to the cathedral in August 1984. Nine years later still, in 1993, I stood in the same place. Studying the reconstructed landscape, thinking of its devastated past, I tried to imagine what George must have felt upon his return—himself being so transformed since his first visit to Nagasaki as part of an occupying army.

With each step on the way to Bethlehem, George sought to atone for his role in the atomic bombings. Now that I was standing where he'd stood in 1945 and 1984, I wondered what must have been cascading through his body, mind, and heart. Throughout our time together on the pilgrimage, I'd gotten to know George's grief and guilt at his role in that atomic destruction, having blessed those men before and after their bombing missions.

Since George had died less than a year before my trip to Nagasaki, I felt his presence in a special way. I imagined George looking down on me with deep appreciation for my Hanford work. I had stood inside the buildings that produced the plutonium that destroyed Nagasaki. I had discovered many secrets Hanford managers had concealed for decades. I had toured other sites in the U.S. nuclear weapons complex.

Hanford's destructive power was not limited to one Japanese city. Its radiation releases blanketed large swaths of four states and part of Canada. In the decades following 1945, hundreds of U.S. nuclear weapons tests at the Nevada Test Site, the Marshall Islands, and other sites wafted Hanford's plutonium across America and around the globe, harming human health and the environment. Over the past decade, I helped end plutonium processing and forced the release of thousands of once-secret documents. I had shared that knowledge with millions of others around the world. Now I was bringing that information to Japan. Standing before Urakami Cathedral, I could almost hear George say, "I'm proud of you, Jim."

Four days before my visit to Nagasaki, I spoke at a conference in Shizuoka focused on the risks of Japan's plan to build a plutonium processing plant. Conference presenters detailed the environmental and public health costs that resulted from the atomic bombing in Japan and nuclear testing in the Pacific. For my part, I recounted the massive contamination of air, water, and soil that Hanford's processing of plutonium caused, exposing two million people to harmful radiation. Instead of warning the public about ways to reduce their exposure, Hanford officials offered reassurances that no one would be harmed. Two weeks after Hanford's plutonium destroyed Nagasaki, Hanford's top health protection officials stated that plutonium is "safely confined behind walls or barriers in the plant. What little of him [sic] as does escape is not going to relegate anyone to purgatory."

After the one-day conference, the organizers arranged for me to visit Hiroshima and Nagasaki. I traveled with my guide and interpreter,

Masa Takubo, via the Shinkansen (the bullet train). It was a marvelous way to travel: swift, clean, and quiet. I was fascinated by all the sights along the way: eel farms, bamboo forests, and, on the return trip from Nagasaki, stunning views of Mount Fuji. Food carts on the train offered an assortment of bento boxes and, by the third day, I got pretty good with chopsticks.

Emerging from the train station in Hiroshima, we walked past several long rows of bicycles. Across a wide plaza was a small hotel where we stayed the night. After an American-style breakfast, Masa hailed a cab out front. Riding through the busy traffic, my gaze shifted from side to side, trying to soak in as much of the cityscape as I could. The taxi delivered us to the Hiroshima Memorial Peace Park.

As Masa and I toured the park, I was struck by the solemn atmosphere. This was where on August 6, 1945, at 8:15 in the morning, the first atomic bomb vaporized thousands of human beings in an instant. The heat of the fireball ignited so many fires a conflagration ensued, fanned by hurricane-force winds induced by the firestorm. The museum's photographs depicted the horrible burns of the A-bomb survivors.

In the center of the Peace Park, Masa and I came to the Memorial Cenotaph, dedicated to all who perished. The large gray arch frames the Atomic Bomb Dome in the distance. Under the cenotaph is a stone chest containing the names of all who are known to have been killed by the atomic bomb. On the front of the chest is an inscription in Japanese that is translated, "Let all the souls here rest in peace, for we shall not repeat the evil."

Standing before the cenotaph was a slight man with a fringe of white hair. He stood very erect and slightly to the right of the center of the archway. He wore a black suit with a white shirt and tie. He was totally still. Perhaps he was marking the anniversary of his wife's death from cancer, or maybe his parents' deaths from the atomic bombing. Out of respect, we stood silently ten feet behind him and made no attempt to intrude on his solitude.

In the afternoon, Masa and I took another train south to Nagasaki. The following morning, Masa and I toured the Nagasaki Atomic Bomb

Museum, the nearby peace park, and Urakami Cathedral. Next, we went to the city hall for a press conference. In my remarks, I tried to make sense of all the horrific injuries and deaths that are memorialized at the museum. "It is very hard for me to see the things which happened on August 9th, for which my government is responsible. The people of Nagasaki learned from the experience and dedicated themselves to peace. But the U.S. has not learned this lesson."

Over lunch, I met with a dozen hibakusha—people who survived the atomic bombings. The room had bright, yellow walls adorned with plaques, photos, and mementos. They were all older men, dressed in dark suits. Immediately, they started asking me questions about Hanford. They wanted to know about the experience of Americans who grew up around the plutonium factory and had been exposed to its radiation. One of the men wanted to know how many people living downwind of Hanford were suffering and with what diseases. Another asked about when the downwinders had found out about their exposures. One balding man commented that they knew of their radiation exposures shortly after the atomic bomb exploded, but Hanford downwinders only learned of their exposures in 1986—more than four decades later. They discussed this information with great sensitivity—exemplifying solidarity with other radiation victims.

After the meeting ended, they enthusiastically thanked me: "Arigato, Jim-esan" [thank you, Mr. Jim]. In my interactions with the aging hibakusha, I learned much about their efforts for peace and disarmament so that other human beings would never have to suffer their pain.

My visit felt deeply personal. By closing the circle between Hanford and Nagasaki, I paid tribute to George and all I had absorbed from him while we walked to Bethlehem. It wasn't only his connection to the men who dropped the bomb on Nagasaki or the fact that he had walked through the radioactive ruins of Urakami Cathedral and visited the hospitals where the many injured writhed in agony. I was giving thanks to George for the tenacity he showed every mile on the road to Bethlehem and for his unwavering dedication to peace every step of the way.

If it had not been for my pilgrimage experience, it is unlikely that I would have had the stamina to devote most of my life to delving into

Hanford's legacy of secrecy. Because the federal government and its contractors had many layers to their deception, it took me decades to figure out what Hanford managers understood of the danger and when they knew it.

It was George's tenacity that I took with me into every library and archive and meeting room in my quest for the truth about Hanford. As I turned page after page of yellowing documents, I sensed important details were missing, and perhaps had never been committed to paper. I often imagined George looking down on me from heaven—his face glowing with his soft smile and intense eyes: "There is more to this story. Go ahead, Jim, keep digging. Take courage and keep searching. We need to know the truth."

20 – The Pervasiveness of Atomic Deception

Shannon Rhodes, February 1944.

In late 1993, I moved to Seattle to work for the Hanford Health Information Network (HHIN), a project by the state health departments of Washington, Oregon, and Idaho and nine Native American tribes. HHIN provided information to healthcare providers and downwinders about Hanford's releases and radiation health effects. In April 1997, I accepted an offer to work at the law firm of Short Cressman & Burgess on the Hanford downwinder litigation.

A few months later, I was in my thirtieth-floor office one beautiful summer morning. My office had floor-to-ceiling windows that provided a magnificent view of Mount Rainier. That morning, *The New York Times* ran a story headlined, "U.S. Atomic Tests in 50's Exposed Millions to Risk." A National Cancer Institute (NCI) study had estimated radiation exposures from iodine-131 to Americans during the atmospheric testing of nuclear weapons at the Nevada Test Site. Nearly all 150 million Americans living in the continental United States in the 1950s had been exposed to the fallout.

But the radioactivity was not evenly distributed. Certain areas were hot spots, places in which the iodine-131 deposition was significantly higher. The hot spots were caused by thunderstorms intersecting the radioactive plume. The rain flushed iodine-131 from the atmosphere, depositing it on pasture where cows grazed.

The 1997 report revealed that children living in certain counties were exposed to contamination levels that rivaled those downwind of Hanford and Chernobyl. Of all the counties in the United States, Meagher County in central Montana had the highest iodine concentration. In 1954, I was born in Cascade County which bordered Meagher County on the north. After working on Hanford downwinder issues for thirteen years,

I was shocked to learn that I too was a downwinder. Whereas I appear to not have suffered from my exposure, my sister Mary has suffered from thyroid problems most of her life. She had to have part of her thyroid surgically removed and must take thyroid hormone supplements for the rest of her life. Due to her malfunctioning thyroid, she suffered two miscarriages. Like many Hanford downwinders, if she and others with thyroid disease had known about their exposures earlier, they could have received medical treatment earlier, thus reducing their suffering.

The government knew in the 1950s which areas had the heaviest contamination. The National Weather Service collaborated with the Atomic Energy Commission (AEC) in identifying where rain intersected with the radioactive plumes across the country. While the federal government issued no public warnings, it knew about the significance of the milk pathway. It knew young children were at highest risk, especially those whose milk came from a backyard cow.

In Paul Loeb's *Nuclear Culture*, he reported that a Hanford worker warned his wife not to go out riding her horse one day in 1953 because fallout from a Nevada test was expected to pass over the Hanford area. Around the same time, the Atomic Energy Commission began sharing information with the Kodak film company about when the nuclear tests would occur, enabling Kodak to protect its film stocks from being fogged by radioactive fallout. But no one told the millions of parents across America that the milk their children drank was poisoned with radioactive fallout. They were kept in the dark. People with access to classified information were able to protect their film and loved ones. Meanwhile, the government denied parents any opportunity to protect their children.

Secrecy is a form of power, one that has been used to a much greater extent in the U.S. since the end of World War II. With the National Security Act and the Atomic Energy Act, the United States built and maintains a fortress of secrecy. Behind this edifice, the bureaucracy fears what the public might demand if citizens knew the truth.

One of the plaintiffs in the Hanford downwinder litigation, Patricia Zumwalt, called me on May 11, 2000. She was sixty years old and had been released from the hospital after thirty-six days. She was being treated for stage four kidney cancer that had metastasized. While weakened by the cancer treatments, her voice shook with anger. She wanted to know why her own government betrayed her. "They lied to us and kept it all hidden," she lamented.

Pat was born in January 1940. When she was six, her family moved to Kennewick. After spending the following year in nearby Connell, her family moved again in 1948 to Finley (five miles southeast of Kennewick). The frequent moves were caused by her dad's struggles to find a job. They stayed in Finley until 1956 when they moved back to Kennewick.

Due to their meager resources, the family grew much of their own produce. One of her dad's co-workers had a backyard cow and several times a week supplied Pat's family with fresh milk. Her dad loved to fish in the Columbia River, furnishing several meals each week. He also was successful with hunting ducks and pheasant.

During our May 2000 phone call, she told me her sister worked at Hanford for twenty years, and Pat's own daughter was now working there. She asked me to tell the attorneys to hurry with the case because she wasn't sure how long she had to live. Within weeks, the attorneys petitioned the court to add Patricia Zumwalt to the downwinder plaintiffs.

During World War II, the Manhattan Project built three reactors along the Columbia River, the first full-scale nuclear reactors in the world. While Hanford's reactors began contaminating the Columbia in 1944, the largest releases of radioactivity to the river were between 1955 and 1965. During those years, as many as nine plutonium production reactors turned the mighty Columbia into the most radioactively contaminated waterway outside of the Soviet Union.

Through my research, I discovered that in 1959, Hanford scientists accidentally discovered that Hanford's radioactive effluent had reached as far as the Pacific Ocean. A routine screening of a Hanford worker determined he had elevated levels of radioactive zinc. After searching the worker's house, the radiation source was some oyster stew he had eaten the previous day. The oysters had been harvested from Willapa Bay on Washington's Pacific Coast.

In a 1954 classified report, Herbert Parker, Hanford's radiation safety manager, considered imposing a ban on public fishing "between Priest Rapids and McNary Dam. The public relations impact would be severe." Priest Rapids was upstream from Hanford and McNary Dam was along the Washington-Oregon border. The proposed ban on fishing would have covered more than a 100-mile stretch of the Columbia, including the Kennewick-Finley area where Pat's dad hunted and fished.

When forwarding Parker's report to AEC headquarters, Hanford's manager assured his superiors, "The public relations problems have been with us always. We expect to handle them adequately in the future, as we have in the past." According to my review of Hanford environmental monitoring reports, radiation levels in the Columbia River exceeded the proposed fishing ban limit for six years: 1957, 1958, 1960, 1961, 1963, and 1964. No ban was ever imposed. An unsuspecting public kept fishing.

I also found a 1961 memo addressed to General Electric executives advising that, because the radiation levels in the Columbia River were ten to 100 times above most other surface waters, "It is extremely difficult ... to lead the public to the point where the Columbia River is viewed as a relatively clean river." The memo also pointed out General Electric's desire "to avoid significant risk of the corporate image in the eyes of the public."

In addition to fish, Hanford's radiation heavily contaminated waterfowl. Eating a half pound of one duck in 1969 would have resulted in a radiation dose more than 300% above the standard exposure limit. Another duck sampled in 1970 was contaminated four times above the applicable standard. Hanford managers issued no warnings to hunters.

Art Zumwalt, Pat's husband, phoned me in July 2001, fourteen months after Pat first called. He said that Pat had died two weeks earlier, at the age of sixty-one.

I have a small, black-and-white snapshot of Shannon Rhodes when she was about three years old. She called me in June 2003 to find out how she could join the Hanford downwinder litigation. In the photo, Shannon is sitting in a highchair—a diffuse shaft of sunlight casts her shadow onto the refrigerator in her Aunt Loretta's kitchen. She is wearing long pants and a T-shirt, her wavy hair parted in the middle and pinned back, drifting over her shoulders. Her small hands hold a quart milk bottle as she drinks. Her eyes peer toward the camera. Along the bottom border of the snapshot, someone noted, "Dinking 'Mow' Feb. 1944."

Pure, wholesome, and nutritious. Milk was a standard component of a healthy diet in the 1940s, especially if you grew up on a farm and had your own cows. The milk Shannon drank that day in early 1944 was still wholesome and pure. But on the day after Christmas that year, the Manhattan Project's race for the atomic bomb began poisoning milk downwind of Hanford with an invisible, tasteless contaminant: radioactive iodine. A 1946 Hanford document stated, "The most hazardous poison present in any large concentration is the iodine which deposits in the thyroid glands of animals and bombards the surrounding tissue with beta particles."

By the time Shannon Rhodes became aware of her Hanford radiation exposure, the iodine had already infected her thyroid with cancer. Usually, thyroid cancer is easily treated if detected early and has low fatality rates. But Shannon didn't learn of her childhood exposure until after Hanford was forced to reveal its secrets. By the time she found out, she not only had thyroid cancer, but it had already metastasized to her lungs.

Shannon was born on August 5, 1941, to Clarence and Doris Caldwell. They lived in a small, two-bedroom house on the south end of Colfax, next to the railroad tracks. A small farm town and Whitman County seat, Colfax lies about 100 miles east of Hanford. Clarence worked as an electrician and, for a while, was one of the 50,000 construction workers helping to build the Hanford atomic complex during 1943 and 1944. Shannon was an only child who grew up playing with cousins on the family homestead seventeen miles west of town. She spent summers and holidays at the farm. In 1948, Shannon and her parents moved into their own house on the homestead which had been settled by Shannon's great-grandparents who emigrated from Ireland.

Shannon's Aunt Loretta and Uncle Sam lived only a quarter-mile away, and her Aunt Rachel and Uncle Dick were a couple of miles up the road. Like many of the other farms on the fertile soil of the Palouse, the three farms grew wheat and barley and raised some animals, including milk cows.

Her second husband Ken described Shannon as "just an outstanding person. She stands out in a crowd, like sunshine. She was intelligent, articulate, had a great sense of humor, and found a great deal of wonder in life."

When she was thirty-six years old, during a three-hour surgery, doctors removed a huge tumor, along with the left half of her thyroid gland. In 2000, Shannon had surgery to remove her parathyroid gland. Follow-up tests led her medical team to suspect lung cancer.

After operating on her lung, her doctor delivered the bad news. "I am sorry, Shannon. You have thyroid cancer that has metastasized to the lung." In shock, Shannon asked, "How can I have lung cancer? I don't smoke—why would I have that?" The doctor reported that the cancer was also in her blood and lymph glands. "I also suspect that you have been living with cancer for more than twenty years."

Devastated, Shannon thought, "My life is being taken away from me. I have always been healthy. I eat correctly, I exercise, I try to do everything that is good. And then this terrible thing comes upon me that I had nothing to do with. I am so afraid. I am not afraid of death, but of the dying. It is the pain and running out of air, the suffocation. I know it is going to be a miserable death." Shannon died in 2011, aged sixty-nine.

In May 1943, Robert Stone, MD, Director of the Health Division, Metallurgical Laboratory (Met Lab), wrote to the manager of Oak Ridge where Hanford's pilot plant was located. "You are well aware of the Iodine problem," he began. "A minor help in this problem would be to have only iodized salt sold at the [Oak Ridge] stores so that everyone gets a certain amount of iodine each day. This will prevent the thyroid from taking up as much iodine as an unsaturated gland would take. ... it might be well to see that only iodized salt was sold." Later, Hanford's medical director Dr. Norwood wrote that the "prophylactic administration of [potassium iodide] in a daily dose of 100 mg. will adequately protect the thyroid against deposition of radioactive [iodine]."

In 1945, two Hanford scientists wrote, "If one wished to promote an adequate iodine intake, … the simplest method would be to either educate the public to use iodized salt, or make iodized salt only available for sale." One week after the atomic bombing of Nagasaki, Japan, the *Richland Villager* ran a story by the Hanford medical department that recommended people use only iodized salt, but it didn't mention anything about the huge releases of iodine-131 or that using iodized salt would have reduced people's exposure to the radioactive iodine. There is no indication there were any further articles in the Richland paper or that other news outlets were asked to promote iodized salt.

Why did Hanford officials not act to limit people's exposure to its radioactive pollution? That 1945 memo provides a clue: "The security aspect of [potassium] iodine feeding to groups not acquainted with the problem [of radiation] was considerable."

In August 1945, two weeks after the atomic bombings of Japan, Herbert M. Parker, Hanford's radiation protection manager, wrote, "The amounts [of iodine-131 in the Hanford area] are entirely innocuous and approach the levels of natural radioactivity found in the atmosphere at any location in the country." While the 1979 Three Mile Island reactor accident released an estimated 24 curies of iodine-131, Hanford's plutonium plants belched more than 555,000 curies in 1945 alone. Hardly innocuous.

From the 1940s until 1986, Hanford was shrouded in secrecy. Because the radioactive emissions were invisible and tasteless, people in a four-state area were exposed to harmful levels without the public's knowledge or consent. Hanford management kept the public in the dark until citizens demanded an accounting. By withholding information, Shannon, Judith, Millie, and thousands of other downwinders suffered needlessly. Hanford's secrecy about the iodine-milk pathway caused suffering for tens of thousands more exposed to fallout from the atmospheric testing of nuclear weapons.

21 – Emotional Return to Hiroshima and Nagasaki

The author in front of Atomic Bomb Dome.
(Photo by Helen McClenahan)

I felt my body sway. It seemed so heavy—as if my blood had turned to liquid lead. I moved on to the next exhibit. I read yet another horrific account of a child remembering what she saw and felt on the morning of August 6, 1945, when an atomic bomb exploded above Hiroshima.

I felt dizzy among the somber exhibits in the dimly lit atomic bomb museum in Hiroshima. I leaned back against a wall to steady myself. I realized this wasn't jet lag nor the hot summer heat, but emotional overload. It was the burden of all I knew about the evils of nuclear weapons: all the deception I'd uncovered, all the suffering of radiation victims I'd known, and all the silence of officials who knew about the secret releases but chose to remain silent—all the people who could have blown the whistle but lacked the courage.

In August 2023, thirty years after my first visit, I again traveled to Japan. Now I carried the knowledge from scrutinizing thousands of additional classified documents. I bore the pain from listening to thousands of downwinders sharing their suffering from cancers and other diseases. My mind held the haunting questions for which I've not yet found answers. Unlike my 1993 trip, I now knew that I too had been exposed as a young child to radioactive fallout. I knew my sister's exposure had seriously damaged her thyroid. In the intervening thirty years, I had worked out that Hanford officials knew by 1945 that iodine-131 was significantly contaminating the milk throughout Eastern Washington, Oregon, and Idaho. But they feared telling the public. The United States had the world's most powerful nuclear arsenal, but it did not trust its own citizens with the truth.

In 2023, I was a member of the Pilgrimage of Peace led by two American archbishops. Archbishop John Wester of Santa Fe had been wrestling with the immorality of nuclear deterrence for years, as thousands of people in his archdiocese worked at the Los Alamos and Sandia national labs developing new nuclear warheads. Since Russia's 2022 invasion of Ukraine, Seattle Archbishop Paul Etienne was increasingly concerned about the risk of nuclear war. In his role as a moral leader, he felt a particular responsibility since his office was only twenty miles from the Kitsap-Bangor Naval Base. The Trident submarines based there have over 1,000 warheads aboard—the largest concentration of deployed U.S. nuclear weapons. Archbishop Etienne asked me to come to Japan because of my expertise on nuclear disarmament matters.

The purpose of the pilgrimage was to meet with three Japanese bishops: Archbishop Nakamura of Nagasaki, Bishop Shirahama of Hiroshima, and Archbishop Emeritus Takami of Nagasaki. Archbishop Emeritus Takami is a hibakusha, having been exposed in utero on August 9, 1945.

The pilgrimage delegation met with several hibakusha, including Setsuko Thurlow. We had an hour-long meeting with her at the offices of the Diocese of Hiroshima on the morning of August 5. Ms. Thurlow, along with Beatrice Fihn, accepted the 2017 Nobel Peace Prize for the International Campaign to Abolish Nuclear Weapons (ICAN). In her Nobel lecture, Thurlow recounted, "I was just thirteen years old when the United States dropped the first atomic bomb, on my city Hiroshima. ... At 8:15, I saw a blinding bluish-white flash from the window. I remember having the sensation of floating in the air. As I regained consciousness in the silence and darkness, I found myself pinned by the collapsed building. ... As I crawled out, the ruins were on fire. Most of my classmates in that building were burned to death alive. I saw all around me utter, unimaginable devastation.

"Processions of ghostly figures shuffled by. Grotesquely wounded people, they were bleeding, burnt, blackened and swollen. Parts of their bodies were missing. Flesh and skin hung from their bones. ... The foul stench of burnt human flesh filled the air."

After our meeting ended with Ms. Thurlow, I approached her saying, "I am very honored to meet you." I added that I had walked to Bethlehem with Fr. George Zabelka. At the sound of his name, her eyes lit up and she exclaimed, "He stayed overnight at my house! Oh, the past experiences," she remarked as she interwove her fingers together. "We invited him to Toronto as a speaker."

The next day, August 6, we left the hotel early to return to the Peace Park for the commemoration ceremony marking the seventy-eighth anniversary of the atomic bombing of Hiroshima. As I found a seat in the section reserved for international attendees, I greeted three young men, all in their twenties, who sat behind me. One came from Brazil, another from Virginia, and the third from Sweden. The adjoining section was for officials representing more than 100 countries. Near the front, I could see Setsuko Thurlow. A large choir sang a song, and several people delivered short speeches. As the clock neared the time when the atomic bomb erupted seventy-eight years earlier, the large crowd grew quiet.

Then, at precisely 8:15 a.m., a single large bell on the stage was struck. The bell was struck again, and again, about every five seconds. The tolling reverberated deep in my heart. Tears welled up in my eyes as I thought, "I am here in Hiroshima, mourning the tens of thousands of people who suffered such agonizing deaths. I also weep for the millions of downwinders in the United States, the Marshall Islands, the former Soviet Union, and throughout the world."

I remembered George's voice from our many presentations on the road to Bethlehem when he described how the people of Hiroshima were busy going about their normal lives to school or to work at 8:15 in the morning and were vaporized by the intense heat or condemned to die excruciating deaths from severe burns or radiation sickness.

The next day, our delegation traveled to Nagasaki in a mini-bus along with the three Japanese bishops. In addition to touring Nagasaki's atomic bomb museum and peace park, we celebrated Mass inside Urakami Cathedral to mark the exact time (11:02 a.m. on August 9) when the second atomic bomb (whose plutonium core was produced at Hanford) destroyed Nagasaki. Later that day, the five Japanese and

American bishops announced they had formed a Partnership for a World Without Nuclear Weapons—an interfaith effort to pray, educate, and advocate for nuclear disarmament.

Epilogue

*The Doomsday Clock, set to 89 seconds to midnight,
January 28, 2025.
(Photo from Bulletin of the Atomic Scientists press release)*

Daniel Ellsberg, the person who leaked the Pentagon Papers, confided in a March 2023 interview, "President Biden is right when he says that this is the most dangerous time, with respect to nuclear war, since the Cuban missile crisis. That's not the world I hoped to see in 2023." After all my efforts to delegitimize nuclear weapons since 1981, I certainly had hoped to see a much more peaceful world by now. In 1993 when I first visited Hiroshima and Nagasaki, a peaceful world seemed attainable: the Soviet Union had collapsed, both East and West were dismantling thousands of nuclear weapons each year, and Congress was discussing a peace dividend—using reductions in military spending to fund social programs.

The historical record establishes that Hanford officials knowingly took chances with people's lives—exposing the public to levels of radiation they knew to be harmful. The secrecy enveloping the production and testing of nuclear weapons enabled deception that continues even now. The U.S. government has yet to acknowledge its complicity, nor has it offered any apologies.

More Hanford secrets wait to be exhumed. The massive cleanup of Hanford's millions of gallons of toxic and radioactive waste is far from complete. Cost estimates top half a trillion dollars. Even then, a total restoration of the environment is impossible. How many more downwinders will suffer during the next 250,000 years—the time required for the radioactive contaminants to decay, a period as long as *homo sapiens* has walked the Earth.

Most of this book has been devoted to the Bethlehem Peace Pilgrimage, and you might wonder whether walking all those miles was worth it. The pilgrimage failed in our call for a global gathering of religious leaders to condemn war. The nuclear powers did not disarm. In fact, there were more nuclear weapons deployed at the end of the walk than when we began.

But we did succeed in many ways. We gave people hope. We discovered how most people are generous to strangers—even those who appear to be vagabonds. When we walked into Bethlehem, all thirteen who walked the first six miles twenty months earlier were there. By walking thousands of miles, I learned persistence that enabled me to unravel the U.S. government's secrets surrounding Hanford's huge radiation releases.

Russia's invasion of Ukraine placed the threat of nuclear war back in the headlines. This is not where I wanted the world to be four decades after the Bethlehem Peace Pilgrimage. While there were sharp reductions in the numbers of nuclear weapons during the 1990s, progress on nuclear disarmament has stalled. During his visit to Japan in November 2019, Pope Francis unequivocally declared that nuclear deterrence and even the possession of nuclear weapons is immoral.

The prospect of millions of people dying in a nuclear conflagration is at least as high now as during the first Cold War. The United States is modernizing its nuclear weapons and delivery systems with a price tag approaching two trillion dollars. Russia is expanding its nuclear arsenal that includes a nuclear-powered missile. China, though long-content with a minimal deterrent force of about 300 warheads, is expected to grow its stockpile to a thousand nuclear weapons within a decade. The other six nuclear-armed countries are also expanding and modernizing.

The weight of all this pressed down on me as I sat amongst the thousands of people from all over the world gathered for the commemoration ceremony in Hiroshima on August 6, 2023. The United Nations Secretary-General's message—delivered by Ms. Izumi Nakamitsu, Under-Secretary-General and High Representative for Disarmament Affairs—acknowledged that "the drums of nuclear war are beating once again. Mistrust and division are on the rise. The nuclear shadow that loomed over the Cold War has re-emerged. ... The only way to eliminate the nuclear risk is to eliminate nuclear weapons. ... Disarmament is not some utopian dream. Disarmament is the only pathway to a safer and more secure world for all."

My 2023 visit to Japan gave me a new sense of urgency. Over the past eighty years, there have been hundreds of accidents involving nuclear weapons and numerous false alerts. Luckily, none of these have resulted in catastrophe since the incineration of Nagasaki. There are now two existential threats confronting the planet: the climate crisis and the nuclear peril. Humanity does not have the luxury of focusing on only one of these.

Abolishing nuclear weapons will not happen because of a treaty. Nor will a well-honed policy argument do the trick. The nuclear weapons complex is entrenched, much like the Jim Crow laws before the Civil Rights Movement. I believe that only collective action by concerned citizens will rid the planet of nuclear weapons.

Do I know what this will look like or how we will get there? No. But I'm confident that we can figure it out. When I took those first steps toward Bethlehem, I had no idea what lay ahead. When I embarked on unraveling Hanford's secrets, I didn't know how or what I'd find. But in each instance, I joined with other citizens whose dogged determination proved that ordinary people can make an important difference for the future of our planet.

What Happened to the Other Bethlehem Peace Pilgrims (listed alphabetically)

Maureen Casey – Initially Maureen helped her daughter Lisa's family. Lisa died in 1994. Maureen became a certified drug and alcohol addiction counselor in Georgia. She's retired and living with her son and his family.

Bill Cox – Returning to the Puget Sound area, Bill worked as a graphic artist and taught computer graphics. Some years after Bethlehem, Bill walked with Fr. Benoit Charlemagne across France, Spain, and Morocco. After he and Pam divorced, Bill remarried and has a son.

Mary Frazel – Mary walked with the Women on the Line, following the route of the White Train. She worked as a manager for Burnside Loaves & Fishes, serving low-income people in Portland. Later she completed studies at Bastyr University to become a naturopath. She's married with a daughter.

Anne Galisky – Anne needed several years to regain her health after getting sick in Yugoslavia. She finished her BA degree and earned a master's degree. She has continued to work for social justice and is a documentary filmmaker based in Portland, Oregon, with her partner of twenty-eight years, Rebecca Shine.

Bookda Gheisar – After completing a degree in sociology, Bookda spent a year with the Jesuit Volunteer Corps. The mother of twin daughters, she served as the executive director of several nonprofit organizations and is now the Senior Director of the Office of Equity, Diversity, and Inclusion for the Port of Seattle.

Laurie Hasbrook – At the start of 1984, Laurie spent six weeks in East Jerusalem and the West Bank. This began Laurie's lifelong advocacy for Palestinian liberation—working with human rights organizations, including Kathy Kelly and Voices in the Wilderness. Married with three sons, Laurie is active with the Chicago chapter of Jewish Voice for Peace.

Rev. Janet Horman – Janet completed her studies at Garrett-Evangelical Theological Seminary and was ordained in the United Methodist Church. She went on to law school in Atlanta, Georgia. She served in both pastoral roles as well as in immigration law. Janet adopted two boys and a girl. She retired in 2023.

Pam Ingalls – After Bethlehem, Pam pursued a career as an oil painter. Her paintings have won numerous awards, and she gives workshops in the United States and Europe. After her divorce from Bill, she remarried and still enjoys traveling.

Fr. Kevin Lafey, O.Carm. – Initially, Kevin volunteered in a Jerusalem hospital for terminal cancer patients. After several years serving as a pastor of a parish in Idaho, he went to Peru in 1989 as a missionary high up (13,000 feet) in the Andes. Returning to the United States in 2009, he continues to help in parish ministry.

Sr. Genevieve Masuo, SV – Genevieve worked at her provincial headquarters in Japan and accompanied George during his 1984 trip to Japan. In San Francisco, she studied to be a hospital chaplain and then helped train others in the U.S. and Japan. Genevieve died in Kamakura, Japan, in 2012.

Dean McFalls – Dean continued walking in 1984 with the World Peace Walk in Europe and coordinated the European Peace Pilgrimage in Washington, D.C. After finishing theological studies, he served as a missionary before being ordained for the Catholic Diocese of Stockton in 1995. In 2015, he married. Dean helps raise his son and teaches in the public schools.

Alice McGarey-Martin – Along with Mary Jude, Alice spent four months in silence at Grand Champs in Switzerland. In 1985, Alice married Paddy Martin whom she met when he was one of our guest walkers in Greece. They worked at a farm that helps people with mental health and substance use challenges. Paddy and Alice have two sons and one grandchild.

Mimi and Steve McKindley-Ward – Mimi and Steve remained in the West Bank/Jerusalem for six additional months—traveling, volunteering, and learning more about Palestinian-Israeli history and the ongoing conflict. Returning to the U.S., they settled in the D.C. area, raising three boys in Mount Rainier, MD. Mimi worked as a public school ESOL teacher and continues to teach ceramics on the side. Steve worked for a series of environmental organizations and capped it off as an arborist for the D.C. government. Currently, Mimi has found a home with Threshold Singers DC and Steve with the native plant community.

Br. Fred Mercy, S.J. – Fred was involved in a variety of ministries after the walk, including helping alcoholics and supporting the Jesuit Volunteer Corps. He also spent time with the Jesuit Refugee Services in Uganda. Fred died in Los Gatos, California in 2025.

Fr. Jack Morris, S.J. – Jack studied peace at the Mennonite Center. He spent many years with the Jesuit Refugee Services in Uganda, ministering to people who had fled the civil war in Sudan. He served at several parishes in the Pacific Northwest. Jack died in Spokane, Washington in 2012.

Bob Patten – After Bethlehem, Bob served as the Peace and Justice Coordinator for the Presbyterian Church, USA in Western Oregon. In the 1990s, he moved to Washington, D.C. and pursued a career in bicycle and pedestrian planning and consulting, helping develop non-motorized transportation projects and networks. He is married and has two daughters.

Mary Jude Postel Ramirez – Immediately after the walk, Mary Jude and Alice spent four months in silence with the nuns at Grand

Champs in Switzerland. She spent years helping refugees from Central America. She teaches English as a Second Language (ESL) at colleges near Chicago. She's married.

Fr. George Zabelka – In addition to many speaking engagements after Bethlehem, George participated in the annual Tokyo to Hiroshima walk in August 1984. He died in Flint, Michigan in 1993.

Resources

For Further Learning:

Cram, Shannon. Unmaking the Bomb: Environmental Cleanup and the Politics of Impossibility. University of California Press, 2023.

Jacobsen, Annie. Nuclear War: A Scenario. Dutton, 2024.

Most Reverend John C. Wester (Archbishop of Santa Fe). Living in the Light of Christ's Peace: A Conversation Toward Nuclear Disarmament. Printed copies available from Pax Christi USA or online at https://www.archdiosf.org/living-in-the-light-of-christs-peace. 2022.

For Taking Action:

Arms Control Association – Works to eliminate the threats posed by the world's most dangerous weapons. https://www.armscontrol.org/

Back from the Brink – Brings communities together to prevent the growing threat that nuclear weapons pose to our health, environment, and all we hold dear. https://preventnuclearwar.org/

Hanford Challenge – Works to create a future for the Hanford Nuclear

Site that secures human health and safety, advances accountability, and promotes a sustainable environmental legacy. https://www.hanfordchallenge.org/

International Campaign to Abolish Nuclear Weapons (ICAN) – Strives to stigmatize, prohibit & eliminate nuclear weapons. ICAN is a coalition of non-governmental organizations promoting adherence to, and implementation of, the United Nations nuclear weapon ban treaty. https://www.icanw.org/

Physicians for Social Responsibility – Guided by the values and expertise of medicine and public health, they work to protect human life from the gravest threats to health and survival. https://psr.org/

Students for Nuclear Disarmament (SND) – A non-partisan coalition of high school, college, and graduate students from across the United States dedicated to ridding the world of nuclear weapons. They are a motivated group of young, vastly different people united by a common goal: the preservation of the human race. https://www.students4disarmament.org/

Voices for a World Free of Nuclear Weapons – Composed of dynamic voices from across the political, professional, spiritual, and geographical spectra, united in a single purpose—to eliminate nuclear weapons once and for all. https://www.voices-uri.org/

Acknowledgments

Two history professors at Oregon State University, Jake Hamblin and Linda Marie Richards, interviewed me for an oral history project in 2018. This sparked the journey of writing this book by reawakening my sense of responsibility. Indirectly, they reminded me to leave a record of what I learned about the secrets of the Hanford plutonium factory.

When I set out first to write a definitive history of Hanford, the comments I received on the first three chapters made me realize that I had to start with the Bethlehem Peace Pilgrimage. Without that experience, I probably would never have become involved with Hanford. At the very least, I certainly would not have had the confidence or persistence I needed to probe Hanford's deception. So once again, I express my profound gratefulness to my fellow Bethlehem pilgrims.

I must acknowledge my debt to the mentors who helped me: Jack Morris, SJ, Jim and Shelley Douglass, Peter Henriot, SJ, Bill Houff, Bob Alvarez, and Tara O'Toole.

I am grateful for my writing coaches, Susan Meyers and Theo Nestor, and the classes I took through Hugo House. The following people read drafts of either chapters or the whole book: Bill Cox, Anne Galisky, Bookda Gheisar, Cliff Honicker, Carolyn Hostetler, Pam Ingalls, Judith Jurji, Louise Kaplan, Jackie Kittrell, Kevin Lafey, O. Carm., Ann Le Bar, Jody Lisberger, Donna Manders, Steve and Mimi McKindley-Ward, Nick Mele, Fred Mercy, SJ, Michael Monteleone, Steve Olson, Bob Patten, Ben Romano, Louise Roselle, Bill Thorness, Jim Werner,

Lois Wessel, John Williams, and my sister Mary Thomas. I want to thank them for their generosity, insightful comments, and kind help in contributing to this book.

I was also assisted by neighbors Rob and Miyoko for the solitude of their house while they were on vacation and the hospitality of Fr. Gary Lazzeroni.

In researching this book, I received help in accessing archival records and need to thank Debbie Bahn (Washington State Archives), William Fliss, PhD. (Archivist, Marquette University), Ann Knake (Jesuit Archives & Research Center), Fina Martinez-Myers (Nuclear Testing Archive), Janice Scarano (DOE Richland Reading Room), Barabara Underwood Scharff, and Lynne Stembridge.

My sincere appreciation to Jon Gosch, the publisher of Latah Books, and Kevin Breen, my editor. I am deeply grateful for this opportunity to collaborate with you—your creativity and professionalism helped make this book a reality.

Finally, my most profound gratitude is reserved for my daughter Katie and my wife Jan. Thank you for walking this journey with me, for your many kindnesses, and for your love. I am especially glad that I married an English major—as my first reader, you not only corrected my grammar, you called forth my deepest longings for peace.

ABOUT THE AUTHOR

While serving in the Jesuit Volunteer Corps, Jim began advocating for nuclear disarmament as a member of the Bethlehem Peace Pilgrimage. He spent the next quarter-century investigating radioactive pollution from the production and testing of nuclear weapons, mostly focused on the Hanford Site in south-central Washington State.

Jim directed life, justice and peace ministry for the Diocese of Spokane (1984-1987), the Archdiocese of Seattle (2007-2015), and the Washington State Catholic Conference (2015-2020). He has a master's in religious studies from Gonzaga University. He continues to work for peace and nuclear disarmament with local and national organizations. Jim and his wife Jan live in Seattle.

www.ingramcontent.com/pod-product-compliance
Lightning Source LLC
Chambersburg PA
CBHW020438130626
46549CB00001B/193